T0291210

WORK AND SOCIAL JUSTICE

Rethinking Labour in Society and the Economy

Flora Gill

Foreword by
Andrew Charlton

First published in Great Britain in 2023 by

Policy Press, an imprint of
Bristol University Press
University of Bristol
1–9 Old Park Hill
Bristol
BS2 8BB
UK
t: +44 (0)117 374 6645
e: bup-info@bristol.ac.uk

Details of international sales and distribution partners are available at
policy.bristoluniversitypress.co.uk

British Library Cataloguing in Publication Data
A catalogue record for this book is available from the British Library

ISBN 978-1-4473-6993-6 hardcover
ISBN 978-1-4473-6994-3 ePub
ISBN 978-1-4473-6995-0 ePdf

Cover design: Andy Ward
Front cover image: iStock/sesame

Contents

Foreword

Andrew Charlton
Member of Australia's Federal Parliament

Can we create meaning and dignity by reconceptualising work in a post-industrial economy? Will we passively allow new technologies to erode equality? Or do we have the courage to use the dividends of progress to deliver social justice?

Flora Gill tackles these questions and many more in this ground-breaking work which builds upon three decades of research and teaching at the University of Sydney, and brings together three core themes of her scholarship: the economics of work, social justice, and heterodox economic theory.

Through engaging prose and well-researched analysis, this book offers a thought-provoking examination of the role of work in shaping the lives of individuals and communities, and the ways in which social justice can be achieved through meaningful and dignified work.

The fundamental premise of Flora's approach is that economics cannot inform social policy and social justice concerns meaningfully by going it alone. Rather, it should include analysis from multiple fields and move away from solely using financial metrics. By drawing on her extensive knowledge and experience, Flora provides a sound intellectual framework for those who wish to argue for social justice, and it is her hope that this book will have a lasting impact on the field.

As one of Flora's former students, I can attest to her exceptional talent as a teacher and her passion for her subject which inspired me and countless others to pursue our own careers in the field. Flora's thoughtful research and her dedication to her students has made her one of the most respected and influential voices in the field.

This book is a must-read for anyone interested in the future of work, the economy, and social justice. Whether you are a student, policy maker, or concerned citizen, you will come away with a deeper understanding of the challenges and opportunities facing our society as we work to create a more equitable and just world.

I am confident that Flora's innovative and insightful work will inspire a new generation of leaders and thinkers to take up the cause of work and social justice."

Preface

This book, which is a clarion call for social justice, highlights the urgent need for economists to widen their perspective on paid work beyond the limited scope of trading leisure time for financial gain. What is needed is a far deeper and more comprehensive grasp of the actual role that paid work plays in our lives, as both individuals and as a society. By proposing ways for economics to broaden its perspective on paid work, inspired by perspectives borrowed from other academic disciplines, this book fills a conspicuous gap in the existing literature. Written in plain English, it aims to be accessible to a broad readership.

The standard economics textbook dispenses with paid work as a necessary evil that robs us of precious leisure time so that we can access the things that money can buy. In other words, economics asserts that the paycheque is the only positive contribution of paid work, and the loss of leisure time is the only drawback. Meanwhile, other academic disciplines draw our attention to an array of both positive and negative impacts of paid work. This book stresses both the positive impacts and the negative conditions described in the literature, to highlight the importance of full employment and, conversely, the social injustices associated with employment.

Our workplaces lack fundamental health and safety measures that would greatly reduce the loss of life and debilitating work accidents we see today. With better investment in occupational health and safety measures, we could greatly reduce workplace injuries and accidents. There is also a need to regulate more successfully against deliberately negligent behaviour by employers. For example, the suppression of information about the risks of handling toxic materials. In several well-known cases covered in this book, this latter example has resulted in painful and drawn-out illnesses, followed by premature death.

The unfortunate reality of the social and economic discrimination that permeates our societies has been addressed by scholars from a range of academic disciplines, including economics. Race discrimination permeates worker's experiences in the labour market. In the US, for example, slavery no longer renders human beings into traded market goods. But slavery has its modern transfiguration, in the form of forced prison labour performed by an incarcerated population overwhelmingly over-represented by black Americans. The rampant discrimination against black people (and others) in the US, and the brutality with which they are treated, has a direct link to the historical legacy of slavery.

Because it has been such a regular blind spot for many (but not all) economists, the book also looks at how, and to what extent, the actual properties of paid work comply with major tenets of social justice. The vastly unequal bargaining power that exists between employees and their employers in a world without trade unions was recognised as early as 1776 by Adam Smith in his book, *The Inquiry Into the Nature and Causes of the Wealth of Nations* (1776). In his 1759 book, *The Theory of Moral Sentiments*, Smith also noted that the poor are acutely aware of their lower social status which, in turn, saddles them with genuine emotional pain (Smith, 1759). This book draws on intellectual contributions from as far back as the 18th and 19th centuries to interrogate workplace relations within the framework of the 1948 Universal Declaration of Human Rights and the Human Rights Conventions that came in its wake.

The Universal Declaration of Human rights is relevant here because a key concern of this book is the inequality of rights within our workplaces. Currently, employers control the design of jobs assigned to workers and almost all other aspects of paid work. These include the physical conditions and the hierarchical structures under which people work. They have these rights because, effectively, society deems employers to be the sole stakeholders in the workplace by dint of their ownership of the required financial capital and assets.

We have a long way to go. Despite the huge contribution they make in the labour market, workers currently have inadequate say over the conditions under which they work, or the design of their jobs. Society is yet to fully acknowledge their stakeholders' rights, or to grant workers a degree of agency commensurate with their contribution. The rise of neoliberalism has only exacerbated this injustice, weakening the role of trade unions and eroding industrial relations protections.

It is high time to start a social conversation about the implications that social justice tenets have for the nature of paid work. Only then will we fully realise the potential of our collective human labour, which is currently undermined by the primacy of the dollar. Economists must embrace this larger view of work and strive to bolster our discipline's approach to the topic, so that our analysis – and, more importantly, our policy advice – contributes meaningfully to the improvement of working lives everywhere.

1

Introduction

Does paid work as we know it meet basic standards of social justice? This is the main question that drives this book. At stake are both levels of pay and our emotional and physical wellbeing. The owners of capital still make the lion's share of the decisions regarding the technology, design of jobs and the command systems that govern our workplaces. But as history shows, governments also play a major role in deciding when the prerogatives of employers trump their duty of care to employees.

As the challenges of automation and globalisation reshape the nature of work in radical and dramatic ways, it is critical that we also pause to consider the tools with which we chart our course forwards. Economists in particular have a responsibility to ensure that our methodologies are correctly applied and up to the task of providing meaningful analytical insight. Yet the standard economics textbook still describes paid work, by way of a simple equation, as the sacrifice of precious leisure time in return for the ability to acquire things that money can buy.

In contrast to economists, social psychologists, sociologists, political scientists and others have a far richer perspective on the meaning of paid work and its impact on our life. Sociologists, social psychologists and human relations scholars point to the contribution of valued social relationships that develop with workmates, and the individual contribution of jobs that allow scope for autonomy, authenticity, creativity and a truly positive interaction with fellow humans.

For now, a few examples would suffice. In his book *Why We Work*, Barry Schwartz (2015) challenges the idea that work has little meaning beyond money. Schwartz, a psychologist, argues that even the most menial jobs are rewarding when they are well-designed and provide a scope for personal initiative, integrity and meaningful social interaction. But, he laments, far too many jobs are yet to realise this potential. He lays the main blame at the doorsteps of a misguided view that work has little reward beyond money.

In 2014 Rainer Strack, who had led the Boston Consulting Group's (BCG) human resources globally for 10 years, shared with us what he had discovered when he asked 200,000 people across 189 countries to rank a set of 26 specific work conditions from the most to the least valuable. The top four were (1) appreciated for your work (Rainer Strack emphasised that this was true worldwide), (2) having great relationship with colleagues,

(3) good life–work balance and (4) good relationship with superior. Salary was ranked as merely the eighth.[1]

A 2019 Harvard Business Review article by Evan W. Carr et al (2019) argues that 'Social belonging is a fundamental human need that is hard wired into our DNA'. But, the authors lament, too many workplaces seem to fail to provide workplace culture that recognises this human attribute. They note that 40 per cent of their surveyed population reported that they feel isolated at work.

Medical experts, clinical psychologists and social epidemiology scholars draw attention to problems arising from the uneven power relationships in the workplace.[2] Philosophers have long debated the roots and the forms of both the use and abuse of power over others. The philosophical discourse on power and the literature on what transpires at the coal face, are at the centre of Chapter 11. Worse still, is the despicable behaviour of employers who have allowed the profit motive to override their duty of care, with lethal consequences.

There is a fairly widespread belief among economists that although many significant aspects of paid work are removed from the intellectual purview of economics, economic analysis is rarely 'biased'. This book begs to differ. The fact is that an exceedingly narrow intellectual perspective can, and often does, lead to the wrong analytical conclusions. When this happens, economists (primarily those operating outside of the academe) run the risk of presenting policy makers with seriously misguided diagnoses of root causes of social and economic malaise.

For example, when we believe that paid work is sought only for the income it provides, it becomes far easier to blame the 'lifestyle choices' of victims of unemployment and poverty for their circumstances.[3] This narrow purview of paid work also plays into the hands of politicians looking for a justification to further shrink welfare payments, in order to ensure that any so-called 'incentives' to work remain robust.

Examples abound. In 1996 the Australian government of John Howard introduced the 'Work for the Dole' program[4] that obliged the long-term unemployed who receive unemployment benefits to work (without any additional pay) in areas such as tourism, heritage and community projects.[5] Yet, in their 2015 study, T. Philip and Kerry Mallan conclude that policies such as Work for the Dole have had a negative impact on the wellbeing of the unemployed. Specifically, their study identifies a significant incidence of ill-health, including cases of suicide. Among the academic studies of the Work for the Dole program is also a 2004 quantitative analysis by the Australian economists Jeff Borland and Tseng Yi Ping. They conclude that ironically the Work for the Dole program has impeded recipients' job search efforts.

At the time of writing, the Prime Minister of Australia was urging employers to report unemployed individuals who reject their job offers.

To the credit of major business groups, they have publicly voiced their opposition to this request. On 28 February 2021, Australia's ABC television program, The Drum, asked *Guardian Australia* journalist, Amy Remeikis, to comment on the government's dobbing request. Remeikis pointed out the obvious fact that there are many reasons why workers might refuse a specific job offer. She also cited an example of a woman who turned down a job offer from a lawyer because he expected her to work alone with him, at his own house.[6] Adding insult to injury, the level of Australia's unemployment benefit falls well below the poverty line.

The International Labour Office's (ILO) June 2020 report notes that since the 1990s even the richest countries have been reducing their financial support for the unemployed. It cites Austria, Belgium, Denmark, Finland, France, Germany, Iceland, Luxembourg, Netherland, Norway, Portugal, Spain, Sweden and Switzerland as the most generous providers of 'unemployment protection systems' among the ILO member countries. Evidently, no English-speaking country has made it onto this list.[7]

Mary O'Hara's 2020 book, *The Shame Game: Overturning the Toxic Poverty Narrative*, offers a compelling interrogation of our very unfair treatment of the poor and the jobless. Growing up in poverty (in Britain), she experienced first-hand the stinging impact of social stigma. Painfully, she had also witnessed the emotional agony experienced by her own father when he was suddenly rendered jobless after many years of working hard and faithfully paying his taxes.

Likewise, Pete Dorey's 2010 article, 'A poverty of imagination: blaming the poor for inequality', is as eloquent as its title promises. As I see it, times of economic crisis are ripe for scapegoating and class prejudice and xenophobia find fertile ground. The blame for low pay and lack of jobs is placed at the doorsteps of the poor, welfare recipients, people of colour, immigrants and members of non-mainstream religious groups.[8]

But history also shows that, although government policy has been largely tilted in favour of capital owners, there is also a significant historic precedent for governments working to improve the lot of working people. The 19th century was a remarkable era of progressive legislation, as far as work conditions are concerned. The progressive Factory Acts, that were enacted by the British parliament throughout the 19th century, were also accompanied by similar measures in other major European countries and culminated with the welfare state of the early post-Second World War era. Chapter 6 narrates the story of that remarkable era.

By the late 1970s, the pendulum had swung sharply in the opposite direction. This swing is discussed in Chapter 7. As I write these lines, we are 40 years into a broad epoch that begun to gather pace with the ascent of the presidential administration of Ronald Reagan in the US and Margaret Thatcher's government in the UK. In the English-speaking countries, this epoch has been defined by the ascent of neoliberalism, the result of which has been a radical upheaval of work conditions and the loss of many hard-fought gains. But it is also true that practically no Western country has been left unscathed.

Make no mistake. While the decline of the manufacturing sector and the changes in the global structure of production and trade have taken place for quite a few decades now, they are not inherently to blame for the radical rise in the inequality of income and wealth. Proponents of laissez faire regimes cite changes in the global economy as an 'imperative cause' for labour market 'deregulation'. The fact is that societies – whether or not they face the challenges of structural economic change – have at their disposal a whole range of alternative policy options.

They can choose to adopt a neoliberal perspective and let free-market forces take charge, erode the foundations of the welfare state, deplete the public sector revenue by dishing out very large tax cuts at the upper income and wealth echelons and allow rising levels of inequality and poverty. Alternatively, however, they might adopt elements from the socio-economic policies of the Nordic social democracies. For example, by setting aside substantial public funds for manpower re-training programs that equip the workers with the skills that will substantially improve their earnings' prospects.

Unfortunately, research bears out the contention that the vast majority of Western governments have chosen the former approach. This has inevitably resulted in a vast increase in the scale of both income and wealth inequalities, particularly in the US and Britain. In 2014, Oxfam researchers found that the 85 wealthiest individuals had as much wealth as half of the world's poorest (Wearden, 2014). In 2016, this number fell to 62 (Elliot, 2016). In 2017 that number declined to 43 and by 2016 it fell to 26 (Elliot, 2019).

On 18 January 2018, Oxfam wrote that 'Credit Suisse recently revealed that the richest 1 per cent have now accumulated more wealth than the rest of the world put together'. Eloquently, this report bears the title 'An economy for the 1%: how privilege and power in the economy drive extreme inequality and how this can be stopped' (Hardoon et al, 2016).[9]

Lawrence Mishel and Julia Wolfe's 2019 study focuses on the growing gap between the compensation levels that are enjoyed by Chief Executive Officers (CEOs) and the typical worker within the US. Their study reports that in 1965, of the US's 350 top corporations, the typical CEO's compensation was 20 times the size of the average worker's pay. It remained so until the late 1960s. But then, during the 1970s, CEOs' pay began charging ahead of their workers' level of pay. Mishel and Wolfe report that by 2018, CEO compensation was 940.3 per cent higher than it was in 1978, whereas the typical worker's wage grew during the same period by a mere 11.9 per cent.

Worse still, large swathes of the workforce have lost job security. Struggling to make ends meet, many have been left to the vagaries of precarious employment in casual jobs that lack even the most basic sick and annual-leave entitlements. In the US, the purchasing power of low wages has been eroding steadily for six decades. In other Western economies, it has barely risen in recent years.

Unfortunately, 'economics science' has done far too little to advance our understanding of the root causes and dynamics of socio-economic deprivation, and not as a result of a dearth of progressive views among economists – far from it. Indeed, we have leading academic economists, a fair few of them Nobel Laureates, who have been writing assiduously on the inequality of both income and wealth. We also have a large volume of empirical studies that address the vexed problems of gender and racial discrimination in the labour market and beyond. And last, but certainly not least, we also must address the social and the economic plight of the indigenous members of our society.[10]

The truth is that economics itself can expand its theoretical perspective in a manner that would allow it to shed better light on the dynamics of economic inequality. Were it able to address important issues of social justice, economics would have no choice but to draw on the rich volume of scholarship readily available within a wide array of intellectual academic disciplines.

Unfortunately, economics still carries some theoretical baggage that is no longer terribly relevant in our modern capitalist economic system.[11] The standard economics textbook discusses the 'free market' quite extensively while it remains largely silent on the chasm that lies between the battle for freer markets that Adam Smith and others had fought and the battles that are nowadays waged by advocates of 'small governments'. The 18th century liberals fought for far more level economic and political playing fields.[12] Present day neoliberals, in contrast, have been fighting against the welfare state and the safety net provisions that workers had been granted via state legislation since the early 19th century.[13]

The standard textbook also remains largely silent about the fact that, since the early 1950s, many economists (major Nobel Prize Laureate and other leading economists among them) have been painstakingly stressing that real world markets are very far from the 'level playing fields' that economists had hoped for in earlier times.[14] Indeed, chances are that the vast majority of academic economists agree that an unbridled laissez faire system is not tenable in a modern society that claims to be interested, however modestly, in the need for social equity. If we are to pay heed to social justice and the ecological challenges that our planet faces, we certainly cannot escape the need for statutory regulation and a certain degree of direct public sector involvement in the economic domain.[15] This simply means that this time around markets will need to be reined-in, not for the sake of monarchs whose goal is to siphon economic resources into their own coffers (as they still did in Adam Smith's days), but in order to promote a civil society that hews to higher moral standards. As I see it, social justice also demands that we attend not only to the vast and growing economic and social inequality and the risk they pose for our democracies, but also to the large power imbalances that still govern our workplaces.

Even a modest concern for social justice can't be adequately served in the absence of state regulation of the conditions under which paid work is performed. Since the early 1980s, the corporate sector has increasingly been demanding 'self-regulation', and governments have been only too happy to acquiesce. This has had an unfortunate impact on the welfare of workers and their households, including on their physical wellbeing.[16]

Academics and other public intellectuals have also been pointing out that our notions of democracy, social citizenship and human rights have direct implications, both within the workplace and in the labour market at large. The intellectual discourse of this literature is the subject matter of Chapter 12. Finally, Chapter 13 questions whether some kind of Universal Basic Income (UBI) is the best way to address the growing economic inequality and threats to employment security that might follow from changes brought by Artificial Intelligence (AI) technology and climate change.

At its heart, this book argues that we should be striving to understand the positive value that work holds beyond money – the social, psychological benefits felt on the personal level, as well as the broader social and economic benefits of full employment. In this respect there are valuable lessons to be learned from disparate fields such as psychology, sociology and beyond. But it is equally important that we pay a great deal of attention to the web of factors that undermine our emotional and physical wellbeing in many of our workplaces.

PART I

Through the lens of economics

2

The unfortunate legacies of the 18th and 19th centuries

Introduction

Economics has shed light on quite a few important aspects of our market-based capitalist economies. However, it has had very limited capacity to advance our understanding of a large number of major socio-economic issues. As a brainchild of the late 18th and 19th centuries, modern economics has been inevitably shaped by the social culture, intellectual climate and political battles fought at that time. Those have all left an indelible mark on the analytical core of economics.

The 'free market' model that was developed during that era was perfectly satisfactory as an intellectual weapon that was aimed at the royal assertions that the monarchy was essential to the maintenance of the political and economic order. But nowadays, unbridled free market systems do not sit well with the values of any modern society that believes in genuine equality of opportunity for all.

Unfortunately, economics has also been overly affected by 19th century concepts of science. Among other things, this viewpoint justifies a radical simplification of both the motives of human conduct, and the structure of the economic system. Consequently, economists have removed a large array of factors from the purview of economics, even though they play a major role in the economic domain. This was done in pursuit of what Albert Hirschman's 1984 book describes as the 'quest for analytical parsimony'.

In a nutshell, 'analytical parsimony' is an ideal that values the theoretical simplification of what, in reality, is a very complex system, transforming it into a simple analytical model; a model that is underpinned by a very small number of assumptions. However, in doing so, economists have, knowingly or unknowingly, chosen to leave the task of exploring many major aspects of paid work to other academic disciplines, while thoroughly excising them from the purview of economics.

The 'free market' – an idea past its use-by date

In the West, the battle for political democracy during the 18th and early 19th centuries went hand-in-hand with the battle for economic liberalism. These battles were fought on a number of fronts, with the intellectual arena playing a pivotal role. The advocates of political democracy developed a powerful intellectual armoury with which to counteract the royal assertion that a strong monarchy was essential, if humanity were to be spared from social, economic and political chaos. The proponents of political and economic liberalism counterargued that political democracy and free market systems would establish order rather than chaos. Just as the demand for political liberalism was accompanied by an intellectual argument designed to allay anxiety about the anarchic potential of a democratised political system, political economists of that era did their best to argue that freer markets would not wreak havoc on the economy.

At that time, the royal regulation of markets was fundamentally driven by the revenue needs of the profligate lifestyle of the royal courts of Europe. One very lucrative source of revenue was the British sale of royal 'charters' to selected enterprises. Those charters granted exclusive production and trading rights (that is monopoly power) to selected business concerns, for example, the British East India Company.[1]

Clearly, therefore, the concepts of democracy and deregulated markets held significant progressive appeal at that time, since both represented social systems with decisively more diffuse power structures than existed under powerful monarchies. Both systems had the potential to empower individuals against tyranny – democracy replacing the absolute political power of monarchs, and the multi-participant market replacing the absolute monopoly power of firms that enjoyed exclusive production and trading rights. Regrettably, that historical role of the agitation for free markets has bequeathed modern-day economics with an unfortunate legacy.[2]

The reason is obvious – social justice was not on the economic agenda of those monarchs. Their only social concern was for maintenance of order and stability. Consequently, the original crude concept of a free market was aptly suited to its historical task because it succinctly outlined the properties of a market system that is perfectly capable of yielding orderly market transactions with no need for close royal regulation of trade and production. Indeed, it would have been clumsy and outright superfluous to overload that market model with more elaborately descriptive content, even if the resulting theoretical portrait would have become more 'realistic'.

Oddly enough, arguments raised in the 18th and early 19th centuries against the excessive economic power of the royalty are nowadays employed by advocates of pure laissez faire, as a rebuttal of government involvement in the economic domain, regardless of the government's intended purpose. The fact that the historical argument was actually waged against royal governance has slipped into oblivion.

If we have any concern for social justice, it behoves us to limit the scope of the free market system. However, a dearth of taming capacity or trustworthy political institutions does not negate the need to interrogate the impact of a system as central to our individual lives and social culture as the market system. Indeed, strong public support for limiting the prerogatives of markets by setting up appropriate governance structures is more likely to emerge when the public better grasps the systemic failures of free markets. Most striking among these failures are the inability of free markets to secure even minimal standards of social justice, or address the urgently needed repair of our ecological systems.

The long shadow of the Victorian outlook on society

The Victorian notion of 'homo economicus' (or 'economic man') still dwells at the centre of economics' frame of analysis. It refers to the fact that by being focused on money making activities, economics has largely removed the social context and our broader value system from its depiction of human conduct.[3] The term 'homo economicus' was coined by the British philosopher and political economist John Stuart Mill (1806–1873) in his book *Essays on Some Unsettled Questions in Political Economy*. Mill (1844) was actually deriding the exceedingly narrow concept of human agency that had been adopted by writers on matters economic.

History also shows us that the social outlook of the 19th-century upper classes (particularly their views on women and gender divisions in labour, the nature of manual labour, the roots of capital accumulation and the causes of low pay and poverty) were shared by most of the founding fathers of economics. The majority of those in privileged Victorian circles perceived paid work as a necessary evil, involving the dirtying of hands and lacking in intellectual prowess. Those who needed to provide for themselves through manual labour were generally deemed mentally deficient, and incapable of engaging in intellectual endeavours. The possibility that manual activity can be associated with a great deal of mental prowess, particularly when appropriately designed, was beyond that mindset.

As for the poor: '(t)he poor were considered autonomous economic agents responsible for their own condition' (Clément, 2005: 65). For instance, a leading 19th-century British political economist, Nassau William Senior (1790–1864) deemed the poor lacked diligence and the emotional capacity to save for a rainy day. Those were the specific reasons Senior gave for his opposition to the Amended 1834 Poor Law. Instead of housing and feeding the poor in the workhouse, as that amended law decreed, he argued that the poor should join the active labour force. This, he maintained, will inculcate in them higher standards of diligence and possibly also an emotional capacity for saving for future exigencies (Fujimura, 2018). In contrast, the process of the accumulation of capital, Senior opined, was the outcome of the capitalists' frugality and their diligent investment of a portion of their earned profits in their business enterprises.[4]

It is unfortunate that the standard economics textbook is silent about the financial barriers faced by low-income recipients and the poor, or about the inferior quality of education that much too often prevails in poor neighbourhoods. Yet, these two factors often limit future employment opportunities in a highly predictable manner (Gill, 1994a).

Along with limited opportunities that some face in the job market due to underlying factors such as poverty, others find their toils excluded from the economic analysis of work altogether. Family care work, for example, is by definition unpaid. Because of this, it has been historically omitted from the discourse around work and social contribution. The legacy of the Victorian frame of mind is emphasised by feminist economists, who stress that the singular focus placed by economics on the market, and on money transactions, grossly undervalues the economic contribution that women make through the home economy, and their caring services generally.

If we still have any doubt about the Victorian mindset concerning matters such as 'the social place of women', we need go no further than Alfred Marshall (1842–1924), one of the major founders of modern economics. In her 1926 book, *My Apprenticeship*, Beatrice Webb (1858–1943) relates what Marshall told her time and again over dinner and lunch conversations in his own house (she notes that she wrote the following lines in a diary, some 6 months after the conversation with Marshall took place; incidentally, still unmarried, she was Beatrice Potter, not Webb, at that time). She reports as follows:

> The conversation [with Marshall] opened with some chaff about men and women: he holding that woman was a subordinate being, and that, if she ceased to be subordinate, there would be no subject for a man to marry. That marriage was a sacrifice of masculine freedom and would only be tolerated by male creatures so long as it meant the devotion, body and soul, of the female to male. Hence the woman must not develop her faculties in a way unpleasant to the man: that strength, courage and independence were not attractive in women; that rivalry in men's pursuits was positively unpleasant. Hence masculine strength and masculine ability in women must be firmly trampled on and boycotted by men. Contrast was the essence of the matrimonial relation: feminine weakness contrasted with masculine strength: masculine egotism with feminine self-devotion.[5] (Webb, 1979: 350–351)[6]

Marshall doubled down later in the conversation, Webb reports. 'If you compete with us, we shan't marry you, he summed up with a laugh' (Webb, 1979: 351).

Sidney Webb (1859–1947) certainly didn't share Marshall's outlook on the role of women, and neither did John Stuart Mill, who had had already published his pioneering book, *The Subjugation of Women*, in 1869. But, arguably, the latter two remarkable men did not represent the outlook of the majority of their male compatriots in 19th-century Britain, or Europe for that matter. How else to explain the fact that French women gained the right to vote only in 1944, while Swiss women had to wait until 1971.

The legacy of 19th-century perspectives on science

By the end of the 19th century, the desire to mimic the role of logic and formal mathematical language in physics had a strong influence on the founders of economics. Unfortunately, this has had an exceedingly restrictive impact on the evolution of economic analysis. In saying this, I do not intend to deny the invaluable contribution that has been made by the leading theoreticians among economists. Their adroit use of sophisticated mathematical tools has in fact shaken the foundations of the simplistic supply and demand model and its promise that there is such a thing as a 'level-playing-field free market'. Their deconstructing contribution is described in plain English in the following chapter.[7] Nevertheless, the dominance of formal (that is, mathematically articulated) models comes at a price. For example, commenting on the Global Financial Crisis of 2007–2008, Paul Krugman notes this: 'As I see it, the economics profession went astray because economists, as a group, mistook beauty, clad in impressive-looking mathematics, for truth' (Krugman, 2009).

Since many real-world aspects, including causal factors, cannot be properly represented by mathematics, many relevant real-world dimensions end up being disregarded in spite of the actual role they play in the issue that is being analysed. Consequently, we have the unfortunate situation where, far too often, mathematical tractability becomes both the architect and (by default) also the judge regarding decisions about what shall be incorporated in the analytical model, and what shall be presumed non-existent. Preferably, the real-world phenomena we wish to analyse, and the specific questions we wish to explore, should drive our choice of simplifying assumptions.

In addition, as I see it, the disciplinary specialisations that have emerged in academe also explain the limited intellectual perspectives of economics. Academe's intellectual disciplines have evolved in virtual silos, with limited intellectual interaction. Consequently, some aspects of the various phenomena that economics addresses, and some major root causes of those phenomena, remain ignored simply because they 'belong' in the domain of another academic discipline. This is unfortunate because in our complex economic system, purely pecuniary (that is, monetary) and non-pecuniary motives are intricately interwoven with each other.[8] Among the latter, our discipline should pay more attention to ethical and moral concerns, cultural norms of behaviour and, most importantly, the role played by political institutions and corporate wealth in prevailing structures of power.

The logical positivist view of science, popular among philosophers of science until the mid-20th century, has also made an unfortunate contribution. As Daniel Housman observes in his 1989 and 1992 publications, either explicitly or implicitly, economists still tend to share the belief (borrowed from the 'logical positivist' view of science) that wrong theoretical models will be weeded out by empirical (statistical) analysis.

While the logical positivist perspective of science also asks us to embrace the belief that scientific analysis can be entirely divorced from value judgments, most philosophers of science have now abandoned the idea that it is possible to entirely remove value judgements from scientific inquiries.

3

The scope and limits of economics

Introduction

In May 2014, Philip Inman reported that 'Economics students from 19 countries have joined forces to call for an overhaul of the way their subject is taught, saying the dominance of narrow free-market theories at top universities harms the world's ability to confront challenges such as financial stability and climate change' (Inman, 2014).[1] These students certainly have a point. As mentioned earlier, the most crucial aspect of the birth of economics is the fact that it was explicitly conceived by the leading spokesmen of a political movement which was determined to wrest away economic and political power from the monarchy. These activists did their best to argue that democracy would not intrude upon the political peace of the country, nor would it wreak havoc on production and trade. The basic analytical apparatus that those spokesmen erected still occupies centre stage in the analytical core of present-day economics.

That said, it is also true that a quite different portrait of economics emerges from the pages of the most prestigious scholarly journals of economics; likewise from book-length publications of economists, a significant number of whom are Nobel Prize Laureates. The content of this body of literature seems to rarely find its way to the classroom. This might be related to the fact that professional journal articles typically come with an extensive mathematical apparatus that is beyond the reach of the majority of undergraduate students.

The diversity that one would find in that wider range of professional literature is in fact quite remarkable. At one end of the spectrum sit academic economists such as Tony Atkinson and Nobel Prize Laureates George Akerlof, Amartya Sen, Michael Spence and Joseph Stiglitz. All have devoted much of their academic careers to in depth study of wealth and income inequality.[2] At the other end of the spectrum are Nobel Prize Laureate economists who subscribe to the Chicago School of Economic Thought. For instance, Robert Lucas, a 1995 Nobel Prize Laureate and prominent member of the Chicago School of Economic Thought, has noted that he has no interest whatsoever in the study of inequality. Worse still, as Paul Krugman notes in his 2014 publication in the New York Review of Books, Lucas describes the study of inequality of wealth and income as 'poisonous' (Krugman, 2014).[3]

In any event, regardless of whether the scholarly journals literature ever reaches the classroom, the extensive attention that is given to the market system is certainly there. True, economists have identified quite a few flaws that would afflict any market system that is governed by an absolute laissez faire regime and actually describe them as 'market failures'. However, in the absence of a lecturer who adequately emphasises the significance of these 'failures', the extensive discourse on the virtues of the free-market competition can easily overshadow the textbook discourse on market failure.

The fact remains that the individuals that are depicted by the economic textbook are entirely stripped of their social context, cultural environment and their moral and psychic self.[4] They are represented as robot-like actors who keep tabs only on their own personal satisfaction, or 'utility' (as it is known in the economist's jargon) that they derive from the things that money can buy. Those robot-like actors do their best to ensure that the dollar cost of the satisfaction they derive from any given basket of commodities they buy is kept to its bare minimum. The fact that those robot-like economic actors get no satisfaction from anything other than the things that money can buy was almost alright in older days, when students of economics were purported to be learning only about how market prices are determined.

It is no longer satisfactory (if it ever was) that economists regularly pass verdicts on major social issues, such as the roots of poverty, income inequality or unemployment, without reference to the broader contexts within which they exist. Let us take the case of unemployment and the often-debated question of whether unemployment is real or a sham inflicted by 'skivers' or 'dole-bludgers'. The standard economic textbooks assume that, other than securing money, work is an evil that robs us of precious leisure time. An alternative perspective, and one that I believe is more valid, affords paid work a much larger place in our lives. Understood that way, we can no longer simply dismiss unemployment as 'free-riding' on the public purse. In fact, there is a substantial body of published scholarship that concludes that large numbers of unemployed people would rather be in paid work, regardless of the impact of joblessness on their financial resources.

For instance, missing from the picture is the personal relationships that evolve between buyers and sellers of goods and services, or between people who have been working at the same workplace over extended periods of time. These relationships do not tend to conform to conventional notions of market competition, which is perhaps why they tend to be excluded from economic analysis. Their exclusion, however, dilutes the analytical abilities of the discipline, misrepresenting the true meaning of work in our lives and producing policy advice that misidentifies the causes of unemployment and the factors that disrupt the functioning of healthy workplaces.

Unlike economists, psychologists generally seek to define paid work in ways that go beyond financial rewards. Medical scholars, for example, argue that workplace power structures have a significant negative impact on the emotional and physical wellbeing of the workforce.[5] The same applies to factors such as the impact of job design and the pace at which assigned tasks need to be executed, both of which have a measurable impact on the health of employees.

As mentioned earlier, neither has the historic partitioning of knowledge into individual academic disciplines helped matters. Although a more specialised analytical effort has a better chance of reaching intellectual depth, territorial partitioning has undermined the capacity of economic theory to shed light on important socio-economic issues; likewise what, for want of a better word, I describe as 'purely' economic issues.

One final blindspot that has eluded the broader community of academic economists was recently exposed by two Nobel Prize Laureate economists, George Akerlof and Robert Shiller (2015), in their book *Phishing for Phools: The Economics of Manipulation and Deception*. Akerlof and Shiller expose the fact that notwithstanding their virtues, markets also provide deceptive businesses with ample scope to manipulate and deceive their customers.

A sample of major intellectual divides among economists

Economists do not speak in one voice and neither should they. There are quite a few major economic (not only socio-economic) issues that set economists apart. A major fault line runs between the upholders of the Chicago School of Economic Thought who have a strong belief in laissez faire market systems, and other academic economists who hold a quite different intellectual perspective. Here are examples of some of the most prominent disagreements.

Can the free market be the level playing field the founding fathers hoped for?

By now, it should come as little surprise that while some academic economists believe that markets should be absolutely left to their own devices, other academic economists reject this view. The founding fathers of economics were confident that free market competition keeps profit levels at a minimal level across the board. Large monopolies, they surmised, are created practically always by royal rulers who endow a small number of businesses with exclusive production and trading rights. However, as the Second World War ended, mainstream academic economists embarked on a painstaking analytical journey that arrived at the conclusion that market competition has a very limited capacity to eradicate very large profit margins.

John Maynard Keynes's 1936 book, *The General Theory of Employment, Interest and Money*, had already undermined the belief that free markets always have the capacity to generate enough jobs for all who wish to work. Keynes has invalidated the idea that unemployment could never persist in countries that have a well-developed competitive market system. But even more articles of faith about the virtues of entirely unrestrained market systems were put to rest in the wake of Kenneth Arrow and Gerard Debreu's seminal 1954 article, 'Existence of equilibrium for a competitive economy'.

Subsequently, a younger generation of scholars examined the specific belief that having a large number of sellers necessarily results in a 'perfectly competitive' market, with a multitude of dwarfs and no giants among them. They focused on the question of whether there could ever exist a real-world process that would lead markets into that promised land of competitive markets with level playing fields.

To the surprise of many of those scholars themselves, their own logical reasoning and mathematical analyses established that what economists describe as the 'perfectly competitive equilibrium' is a pipedream. As John D. Hey describes it, citing one of those younger generation authors:

> Fisher [a leading MIT Professor of economics] himself remarks after struggling manfully with a most impressive paper designed to tell a story with a perfectly competitive ending that 'Depending on one's predilection, the story may seem rather less than more sensible, and, indeed, one way of looking at the results is as showing how hard it is to tell a sensible competitive disequilibrium story'. (Hey, 1979: 181)

It transpires that firms that command a disproportionally large market power will always exist. Having technology that favours large-scale production is one source of competitive advantage. But during the 1960s and 1970s, major economists have concluded that regardless of the nature of the technology that is employed by firms, the latter will always have substantial market power simply because accurate information about prices and the quality of products and services sold in the market is anything but easy to access.[6]

Could market competition end gender and race discrimination?

Different economists have very different views regarding what markets can do about the vexed issue of gender, race and ethnic discrimination. Gary Becker (1964) placed his faith in the profit motive and market competition. Fierce market competition and single-minded pursuit of the highest volume of profit, he believed, would end discrimination against women and members of other disadvantaged social groups. In contrast, Kenneth

Arrow (1972, 1973), Michael Spence (1973, 1974) and more recently Carla Hoff and Joseph Stiglitz (2010), among others, have strongly disagreed with this perspective.

Specifically, Arrow and Spence conclude that when there is entrenched social prejudice against particular social groups, no amount of market competition can eliminate discrimination in areas such as pay, access to jobs and access to bank credit. Hoff and Stiglitz's 2010 analysis revisits the issue, and ends up drawing precisely the same conclusions as Arrow and Spence.

Is unemployment genuine or a 'lifestyle choice'?

When examining this specific debate, it is worth revisiting Robert Solow's December 1979 Presidential Address to the American Economic Association. In that address, Robert Solow took to task economists who assert that there is no such thing as 'real' (or in the economic jargon, 'involuntary') unemployment, and that we have no economic theory that can explain a lack of jobs for all.

Solow makes two distinct points. One is that, actually, we do have economic theory that foresees the possibility of substantial and prolonged unemployment. The second rebuttal is laced with a witty sense of humour. Solow points out the obvious fact that, in any event, real world facts exist regardless of whether or not science has the capacity to explain those facts satisfactorily. He writes:

> I remember reading once that it is still not understood how the giraffe manages to pump adequate blood supply all the way up to its head; but it is hard to imagine that anyone would therefore conclude that giraffes do not have long necks. At least not anyone who had ever been to a zoo. (Solow, 1980: 7)[7]

Does economics tell us that markets should be left to their own devices?

Suppose for the moment that we happen to have a society that does not care about poverty, discrimination, extreme inequality or ecological deterioration, and has its eyes set only on the size of its national income (or identically, the average standard of living). Does economics say that such a hypothetical society should let free markets take charge of its economy? Some readers might be surprised, but the answer to this question is 'certainly not'.

There are economists who seek to restrict governments to the administration of law and order tasks. They are entitled to their own individual views, but they make a mistake when they invoke economic theory in support of such personally owned beliefs. The fact is that economics provides, not just one, but two distinct sets of reasons that call for government intervention in the economic domain, even in a country that is oblivious to matters such as social injustice or ecological deterioration.[8] One set of reasons is explained by the theory of imperfect competition, where a small number of sellers or buyers dominate the market. The other set of reasons involves the case in which the private sector is incapable of providing vitally needed products or services.

One, economic theory warns us that when just one, or only a few large firms dominate a given product or service market, the value of the national income falls short of its full potential. The detailed argument that lies behind this analytical conclusion is provided by the theoretical analysis of the so-called 'theory of imperfect competition'. In fact, this theory is part and parcel of any standard economic textbook (whether lecturers draw adequate attention to this in the classroom is another matter). The theory of imperfect competition addresses the cases of both the 'monopoly firm', and its complete analogue – the 'monopsony firm'. The term, concept and model of the monopsony firm were all introduced by the prominent Cambridge University economist, Joan Robinson (1933) in her book, *The Economics of Imperfect Competition*. Whereas the first is known as the large seller (in plain English), the second, the monopsony, is known as the large buyer. A monopoly firm has the power to raise the price of its product, and in order to make the higher price sustainable, it restricts the volume of its production and sales. In a similar vein, the large buyer, the monopsony, can force the sellers (of a good or service) to accept a lower price than the price that would have been established had there been a competition between many small buyers. Think, for instance, of the very large supermarket chains and the prices they manage to extract out of small farmers.

Taking the monopoly case first, the neat analytical result that is proposed by economic theory is that a country that has a regulatory body, one that is both astute and well-equipped, could compel the firm that enjoys monopoly power to not only reduce the price it charges its clients, but also to expand the volume of the products (or services) it offers for sale at the lower state-regulated price. Note that if the monopoly fails to respond to the lower regulated maximum price by increasing levels of production, it would end up failing to maximise its own volume of profits. Of course, this is a very counterintuitive proposition. Yet, it is logically impeccable.[9] Indeed, one of the hallmarks of good science is its capacity to establish a case for what is very counterintuitive to the uninitiated.

One of the very important insights that the 'monopsony theory' endows us with is the fact that a truly profit-maximising employer who has monopsony power would expand (not contract) the size of its workforce, once it is subjected to effective and well-monitored state regulation of minimum wage levels. This, of course, is yet another counterintuitive proposition, but nonetheless, it is an impeccable, logically compelling, proposition.

The second set of reasons that call for government action in some economic areas, is very different. This particular set has to do with a number of specific features that are shared by certain goods and services. This particular need for government action is explained by the so-called theory of 'welfare economics' (which is entirely unrelated to its namesake, the 'welfare state'). The key issue here is that in the absence of government initiative, a number of vital goods and services that are essential to any well-run economy, might nevertheless remain unsupplied if left entirely to the discretion of the private sector.[10]

One more incisive analytical insight about the economic role of governments is presented by Bruce Greenwald and Joseph Stiglitz in their 1986 path-breaking publication. Their study categorically establishes that the market system could not possibly generate the highest level of national income in the absence of a direct government intervention in the economy.

Academia's intellectual islands

The notable economist Kenneth Ewart Boulding (1980) famously observed that 'physicists can only talk to other physicists and economists to economists'. This kind of thinking leads to a siloing of disciplines, to our great detriment. There are numerous questions about the claims that are made by scientists about the features that set their own field of study apart from other knowledge discourses. Such claims merit attention in their own right, but here I wish to raise just one particular methodological question: what are some of the analytical consequences of the barriers that have been erected as a consequence of the progressive 'partitioning' of knowledge-generation into individual academic disciplines?

Those boundaries tend to automatically license leaving out of the analysis all that lies across the border in another academic disciplinary domain. Adventurers with a penchant for travel to these 'foreign lands' risk stumbling over language barriers. Not surprisingly, such individuals remain few and far between. The result is that much of academic knowledge is produced largely within the boundaries of single academic disciplines.

Why should we trouble ourselves over this fact? After all, we have already accepted that useful knowledge entails abstraction, keeping in only the bare essentials. My answer is simple. Recognition of the need for simplification does not endow us with a 'carte blanche' to follow it cavalierly. When we leave out of our analysis all the aspects that history has placed within the confines of another academic discipline, we inevitably abdicate the responsibility for deciding which aspects of the real-world case we are dealing with should be explicitly incorporated into our own analysis of the real-world issue(s) we are addressing, and which aspects could be safely left well outside our analysis. If we abdicate this responsibility, then that decision is simply driven by the history of the forces that have dictated where the academic disciplinary boundaries run. This state of affairs has some methodological consequences that might, and quite often do, lead to erroneous conclusions.[11]

Economists do know that analytical assumptions are merely simplifications of complex real-world situations. They also emphasise that, in any event, statistical data, and analytical conclusions in general, can never provide an accurate portrait of a real-world situation. However, at the same time, there tends to be an assertion that the resulting errors are akin to 'white noise', which in a more lay jargon means that although quantitative and analytical conclusions in general are imprecise, they are not biased. The reality is that often enough what superficially looks like white noise is not quite white.

In principle, it is indeed possible that no bias is generated when we stay within the walled city of our own academic discipline. However, when major root causes of a given socio-economic phenomenon are excluded from the analysis, the conclusions of the study are compromised.

Political economists have rightly been stressing that economic analysis would be substantially enriched by a more fundamental understanding of the political forces that shape the economy. For example, large corporations and billionaires hold sway with governments, who make decisions that directly impact the lives of workers. In his publication, 'Economics and inequality', in the *Boston Review*, Kenneth Arrow stresses the sway that the financial sector has held on government policy since the 1980s (Arrow, 2011). And as Joseph Stiglitz notes, in the US, democracy has increasingly become a system in which one dollar equals one vote, rather than one person having one vote.[12]

Methodological pitfalls that await the unwary researcher

The 'economic theory of investment in human capital' offers us a perfect example of the methodological pitfalls that await the unwary social scientist. Economists have made extensive use of the 'investment in human capital theory', in an attempt to explain differences between levels of income across the population. This theory predicts that people with higher levels of education have (or more precisely, tend to have) higher incomes. If that is the whole story, fine; but the story does not end here. That theory also asks 'what might explain the differences between the actual levels of education that have been acquired by different individuals'?

The answer of the investment in human capital theory is that the differences between the acquired levels of education are the consequence of one's personal character. Those who earn a higher income are people who got there, because their personal nature is such that they can deprive themselves of pleasure at the present time, in order to better their future standard of living.[13] They live frugally while investing money, time and effort in acquiring higher levels of education. But logically speaking, unless we recognise that human character alone could not possibly be the only factor that determines the level and the quality of an individual's stock of human capital, we inevitably fall into the trap of placing the cause of economic poverty at the doorstep of the poor.

Economic opportunities, particularly but not only in the US, are anything but equal. In very poor families, the offspring often have to take up paid work in order to supplement the parental income. And when you work for pay while you study, often your academic results suffer. On top of this, primary and secondary schools in low income geographic regions are routinely inferior to those in higher income regions. And unlike the children of the wealthy, children from poor families have no recourse to paid tuition. Frequently, there is also a lack of adequate parental academic tuition for the same reasons that their own educations are compromised.

Rather, this state of affairs calls for having a rigorous theory that adds to the 'theory of investment in human capital' an explicit set of assumptions that recognise the fact that there are systemic forces that entrench both intergenerational privilege and disadvantage.[14] In addition, discrimination against underprivileged socio-demographic groups, whether based on gender, sexuality, ethnicity, race or class, is real. The different circumstances of disadvantage can and should be represented by a comprehensive description of the systemic social and economic barriers that various demographic groups face.[15]

In fact, we do have quite a few quantitative studies that conclude that, on average, the offspring of the disadvantaged have a higher chance of being themselves disadvantaged; and symmetrically, that the offspring of the economically privileged tend to be economically privileged. In just about all countries, intergenerational mobility across either occupation or income is not random but, rather, systemic to a degree. Joseph Stiglitz notes in his 2012 book that, in the US, intergenerational mobility from lower to higher income levels has declined sharply in recent decades (Stiglitz, 2012). It is the worst among advanced economies. Notwithstanding any 'rags to riches' beliefs in the US regarding income, whatever intergenerational mobility does exist in the US has almost always been lower than in Europe (Stiglitz, 2018). In his book *On Life's Lottery*, Glyn Davis (2021) notes a similar pattern in Australia.

Economic theory recognises the impact that different levels of income have on the magnitude of individual and household consumption and savings. But disparities in our levels of income and wealth also tend to affect the employment opportunities that our children have available to them via their social networks. These networks tend to further perpetuate privilege and entrench economic misfortune across generations.

Sociologists and other social scientists draw attention to the function of social networks in the job market; but this is an idea that is altogether absent in the conceptual framework of economics. The Stanford sociologist Mark Granovetter has been widely recognised among sociologists for his analysis of the crucial role that is played by social networks in the labour market. His seminal paper on this subject was published in 1973.

As for economists, the late Princeton professor of economics, Albert Rees, did try to draw the profession's attention to the importance of social networks in the job market. He had already identified their role in his 1966 article, 'Information networks in labor markets'. He also discusses them at some length in his 1973 labour economics text, *The Economics of Work and Pay*.[16] But to no avail. The intellectual framework of the academic discipline of economics is yet to give Rees's seminal observation its due place.

4

Paid work through the lens of economics

Introduction

Paid work affects our wellbeing in more than one way. Meaningful work, which makes use of our capabilities as creative and resourceful human beings who like the opportunity to rise to a challenge, enhances our wellbeing far beyond the contribution of our paycheque. But, as psychologists and medical scholars inform us, at the same time tedious jobs that demand relentless repetition of simple tasks, and oppressive workplace power structures, end up undermining both our emotional and physical wellbeing. The intellectual framework of the sub-discipline of labour economics does not attend to these less tangible yet significant aspects of paid work. Its attention remains largely focused on the attributes that set the labour market apart from other markets.[1] Still, though limited in scope as far as the meaning of paid work is concerned, labour economics has made quite a few salient analytical contributions.

Labour economists have thrown light on many of the factors that inhibit the capacity of employees to move across workplaces, particularly from one occupational market to another.[2] They also shed light on factors that inhibit movement across geographical areas, particularly when this entails relocation of a whole household. The profession has also paid serious attention to gender, race and ethnicity-based discrimination. As well, labour economists have interrogated the uneven bargaining power between workers and employers and highlighted quite positive overall economic impact of trade unions within the market economy. This having been said, it is also true that trade unions shouldn't all be given 'carte blanche', because as the well-known labour economist George E. Johnson noted, in the US the spectrum of various trade unions ranges from 'gangster unions … [to] social uplift unions which pursue policies which promote the general welfare of the working class as opposed to the narrow interest of their members' (Johnson, 1985).[3] This chapter narrates the story of the historical evolution of the intellectual perspective that economics nowadays has on the meaning of, and the role played by, paid work in our lives.

Adam Smith

Adam Smith (1723–1790) who is widely acknowledged as the father of economics, certainly stressed the virtues of free market competition. But he did not lose sight of the downside of a laissez faire market system. In volume 1 of his *An Inquiry into the Nature and Causes of the Wealth of Nations*, Adam Smith writes:

> It is not, however, difficult to foresee which of the two parties [employers and workers] must, upon all ordinary occasions, have the advantage in the dispute, and force the other into compliance with their terms. The masters, being fewer in number, can combine much more easily; and the law, besides, authorises or at least does not prohibit their combinations, while it prohibits those of the workmen. We have no acts of parliament against combining to lower the price of work; but many against combining to raise it. In all such disputes the masters can hold out much longer. A landlord, a farmer, a master manufacturer or a merchant, though they did not employ a single workman, could generally live a year or two upon the stocks which they have already acquired. Many workmen could not subsist a week, few could subsist a month, and scarce any a year without employment. In the long-run the workman may be as necessary to his master as his master is to him; but the necessity is not so immediate. (Smith, 1776: 83–84)

Clearly, Adam Smith is concerned about the uneven bargaining power between the individual worker and their employer. He is drawing attention to two distinct factors that favour the bargaining power of employers over workers. The first is the contemporary legal framework which favoured the employers (masters) over the workers by allowing the first, but not the latter, to collude by forming business associations. The second factor is more universal – it points to a purely economic source of uneven bargaining power between the individual worker and the employer – the very uneven size of the financial reserves that are available to each side. The bargaining process can be described as a tug of war which is resolved in favour of the side with the larger financial reserves which allow them to hold out for longer in a pay dispute. Indeed, most workers do not have the necessary financial resources that would allow them to refuse to work until their conditions are met, unless they act collectively and with a significant strike chest at their disposal.

The emergence of collective bargaining, however, had to await the evolution of trade unions and their attainment of a recognised legal status. This process took place over many decades; and some of the rights that were eventually won by trade unions were fought for over more than a century before they were attained.

Trade unions were preceded by associations of workers that were primarily focused on self-help. These early organisations were often known as 'friendly societies', fulfilled a range of functions, among them the provision of financial help to members in times of sickness. The friendly societies emerged among skilled workers by 1815.

By 1824 campaigns also led to a successful repeal of many of the very oppressive clauses of the Combination Laws that prohibited the formation of workers associations. Still, these associations had a long road to travel before eventually being permitted to represent workers collectively.

In 1851 a new model of unionism emerged with the formation of the larger and better-organised Amalgamated Society of Engineers in the UK. In that same year Britain also granted trade unions a legal status that for the first time allowed them to represent workers in bargaining with employers. To become truly effective, trade unions also had to develop the art of bargaining collectively, substantial solidarity and effective leadership.

Alfred Marshall and John Hicks

Alfred Marshall (1842–1924), who was one of the major founders of modern economics, had a truly comprehensive grasp of the multifaceted nature of paid work. Marshall started his analytical journey with an incisive narrative in plain English language. For instance, he described at some length the inequalities that exist in the labour market, and the social and economic barriers that limit the capacity of certain people to acquire truly well-earning skills. Like Smith, he too emphasised the inequality of bargaining power between individual employees and their employers when he wrote: 'it must be remembered that the man who employs a thousand others, is himself an absolutely rigid combination [meaning having substantial market power] to the extent of one thousand units among buyers in the labour market' (Marshall, 1890: 472).[4]

Marshall also noted that the bargaining power of professional employees greatly exceeds the bargaining power of unskilled workers. As well, he told his readers that the earning capacity of parents has a critical impact on the chance that their children would be able to acquire a financially-rewarding skill-set. (This observation is yet to make an appearance in the set of premises that underpin rigorous modern economic theory.) Marshall also recognised that since paid work entails a 'continuous relationship' with the employer on a daily basis, paid work also has significant emotional and psychological consequences for the worker.

But then, this quite comprehensive account of the essence of paid work leaves little trace in the more formal analytical discourse he bequeathed present-day economics. This omission includes the asymmetry of bargaining power between the single worker and her/his employer and the economic advantages of having well-off parents. It also includes his very perceptive observation that employment relationships are emotionally charged because the worker spends every single working day under the command of the employer or the person who is answerable to the employer.[5] Fundamentally, the more formal conceptual framework consisted of a tale of market supply and demand forces.

The Oxford professor and Nobel Laureate economist, John R. Hicks (1904–1989) followed a similar path. For example, Hicks began his discourse with a fairly comprehensive description of the unique behavioural patterns that tend to seriously limit the impact that changes in the balance between the supply and demand forces are allowed to have over the magnitude of wages. He noted that employers often showed a reluctance to cut pay, fearing a loss of morale, open conflict with workers and consequently a reduced productivity.[6] However, he also concluded that there were no practical means by which he could incorporate these observations into economic analysis. He told us that, instead, he resolved to present us with a description of what he saw as the more preferable state of affairs: an economic system that allows the level of wages to change freely in a manner that follows closely the changes in the balance between the supply and demand for labour.

Thus, like Marshall, many of the issues Hicks raised in his wide-ranging discussion fail to appear in the more formally specified analytical framework that he contributed to economics. Hicks and Marshall have certainly enriched the scope of economic analysis. But they also sidestepped addressing the possibility that by separating the 'purely' economic from the political and social factors that operate in the marketplace, analytical conclusions might be compromised.

The Institutionalists' battle against a narrow market approach

Marshall's analysis did raise a strong reaction among scholars, who maintained that the unique features that Marshall identified in his wider narrative must not be removed from the intellectual perspective of economics. Collectively, these writers are commonly referred to as the 'Institutionalists'.[7]

Their core position was that the analytical framework of 'market supply and demand' is far too narrow, because it does not shed adequate light on the true nature of the relationship between employers and employees. They also argued that the specific economic description of the process by which pay rates and work conditions are determined is unsatisfactory. They supported their position with four distinct lines of reasoning.

First, they argued (correctly, I believe) that the mainstream models depict individuals as self-centred buyers and sellers of labour services who exist entirely outside of any social context. Consequently, they pointed out, the impacts of social organisation, social norms of behaviour and the power structures that govern in the workplace are entirely overlooked.

Second, they argued that an array of social institutions – including the family unit, workplace culture and broader political system – have been unduly removed from the frame of the analysis.

Third, they argued that any analysis that does not attempt to account for the evolution of the economic system over time is inadequate. Instead, they stressed, historical perspective is essential to any attempt to come to grips with major contemporary economic issues.

Fourth, they also argued that they could not possibly accept a frame of analysis that is built on a set of unexamined assumptions about human conduct, as economics is.[8] Instead, their own methodological approach stressed 'inductive reasoning', meaning adoption of basic analytical assumptions that are themselves based on patterns that are identified in large databases of real-world observations.

This description distils the shared core of an otherwise quite diverse group of thinkers. This group includes Thorstein Bunde Veblen (1857–1929), John Roger Commons (1862–1945) and Wesley Clair Mitchell (1874–1948), all of whom worked in the US, John A. Hobson (1858–1940) in the UK and Karl Gunnar Myrdal (1898–1987) in Sweden.[9]

In the end, this group of scholars failed to convince the majority of new academics recruited to bolster university economics departments during the early post-Second World War years. By the late 1960s, the Institutionalists had lost the battle for intellectual influence in economics, including the specific field of labour economics. A couple of decades later, a new institutionalist school emerged under the formal name of 'New Institutionalism'. However, apart from their shared emphasis that real-world institutions, and not simply 'pure' market forces, determine wages, prices and other economic outcomes, the two schools have little else in common. The Old Institutionalists stressed the fact that the single workplace and the whole labour market are governed by various formal institutions, such as trade unions, employer peak organisations and professional associations. But in addition, they stressed that the whole economy is also governed by 'informal' institutions that essentially function as the 'mediators' between claims that are made by market forces and the claims made by social norms of conduct and broad values systems. The New-Institutionalist school of thought made no such claim.[10]

In contrast, the New Institutionalists sought to provide economic rationale for the fact that prices of goods, wages and salaries are often determined within the individual enterprise. They also stressed that, generally speaking, neither do wages and prices necessarily follow closely the 'balance of supply and demand forces'. What the New Institutionalists most importantly stressed is that such intra-firm price fixing systems tend to augment the economic efficiency of the individual firm's operations. In plainer terms, it is often less wasteful to do things in this way.

It was Oliver Williamson's seminal contribution that drew attention to what actually takes place inside the workplace as far as pay rates are concerned. Williamson's seminal 1975 book, *Markets and Hierarchies: Analysis and Anti-Trust Implications – A Study in the Economics of Internal Organization*, abandons the analytical perspective that treats market supply and demand forces as the sole determinants of all prices (wages and salaries included). Effectively speaking, his analysis has seriously undermined the view that employers have no power to determine the actual level of wages.[11] In recognition of this major intellectual contribution of his, Oliver Williamson was awarded the Memorial Nobel Prize in Economic Sciences, in 2009.

Change in the wind

During the late 1960s and the 1970s, a substantial number of economists turned their attention to the yawning gap between the real world and the mythical 'perfectly competitive' market, focussing on the market in general, and in the labour market in particular. This time around, it was the strong dissatisfaction with the assumed ease and frequency with which workers can switch from one employer to another, from one job market to another, or from employment in the 'prestige-lacking' business sector to the high-prestige end of the market. Issue has also been taken with the assumed ease with which individuals and their families can traverse across wide geographical distances.[12]

The actual reality is markedly different. Typically, substantial financial and emotional costs are required when making changes to our working lives. The rewards available elsewhere must be significant for it to be worthwhile for individuals and their households to voluntarily embark on such changes. The decision to change workplace may also be inhibited by uncertainty about the prospective workplace. This deterring factor is conveyed by the adage 'better to stay with the devil you know than the devil you don't know'.

Major among the new intellectual frameworks that have been offered are the 'internal labour market theory' (Doeringer and Piore, 1970) and the 'dual labour' and 'segmented markets theory' (Gordon, 1972; Reich et al, 1973).[13] A recent book edited by Damian Grimshaw et al (2017) stresses that the degree of segmentation that prevails in our modern labour markets is still very high.

More recent perspectives on the economic impact of trade unions

Historically, just about all economists treated trade unions simply as monopolies that push wages up at the expense of both the employing enterprise and non-union members. The Chicago School of Economics still adheres to this view. But nowadays, many economists tend to see them as more complex institutions.

The Harvard economists Richard Freeman and James Medoff have been recognised as leading representatives of this latter group. Their description of the role and the impact of trade unions in their 1979 and 1984 studies is built on the conceptual framework pioneered by Albert Hirschman (1970) in his book-length treatise *Exit, Voice and Loyalty: Responses to Decline in Firms, Organisations and States*.

Hirschman makes an obvious, yet salient, observation that whether they are workers, business partners, or spouses who are dissatisfied with their present state of affairs, they are all free to 'quit' their relationships. Workers can quit their jobs, businesses can quit their business partnerships and personal love relationships can be ended by saying goodbye. But, Hirschman also notes, there is an alternative course of action. Those who are dissatisfied with the status quo, he suggests, can actually 'voice' their dissatisfaction (rather than simply walk out) because this might result in a better outcome.

Studies by Freeman and Medoff (1979, 1984) apply Hirschman's ideas to the realm of work. They point out that in the employment relationship, giving voice to dissatisfaction is a valid strategy. But, they stress, this option is ordinarily effective only if it is exercised collectively. As for employees who wish to voice concerns individually, they are more likely to be dismissed as 'squeaky wheels'. In the employment relationship, Freeman and Medoff remind us, strength is in numbers. A union representation, therefore, becomes vital.

Broadly speaking, only very high-ranking salaried employees and professionals with exceptional skills have a chance of success when they negotiate pay and work conditions with their employer on their own. Hirschman's and Freeman and Medoff's analytical departure from the standard market supply and demand model has influenced the train of thought of quite a few economists who, largely speaking, could be classified as mainstream scholars.

For example, in his book, *Labor Markets under Trade Unionism: Employment, Wages, and Hours*, the Stanford University labour economist, John Pencavel (1991), presents us with an analytical perspective that is significantly at odds with both Marshall's and Hicks's.[14] Implicitly disagreeing with Hicks, Pencavel argues that even if workers did not 'cling' to yesterday's wages (as Hicks maintained they do), and even if they conformed to the textbook description of the 'rational economic man', the labour market could not possibly have the dynamics portrayed by the standard supply and demand model.[15] Neither does Pencavel believe that trade unions can raise wages only at the expense of non-union workers. This verdict certainly represents a major departure from both Marshall's and Hicks's analytical purview.

Pencavel stresses that historically, trade unions were not preceded by a 'competitive level-playing-field labour market'.[16] Rather, he notes, both in the past and nowadays, the typical employer presents the vast majority of individual employees with a 'take it or leave it' pay offer. In his own words, Pencavel notes that:

> [V]iewed in this way, in many markets the union does not supplant a wage-taking competitive labour market with a monopolistic combination of workers, but rather it supersedes a single worker bargaining with a single agent who represents many workers. In most non-union bargaining contexts, a single worker negotiates in isolation from other workers and usually in ignorance of the terms of employment other workers have secured. (Pencavel, 1991: 7–8)[17]

As for the economic impact of collective bargaining and trade unions in general, Pencavel cites approvingly a number of writers who argue that although trade unions do deliver higher pay rates for their own members, they also offer employers with an opportunity to augment the level of productive efficiency.[18] More recent quantitative studies bear out this proposition.[19]

5

Equity, social justice and the 'efficient economy'

Introduction

Economists often assert that if we wish to raise the standard of social equity, we have no choice but to pay for this by compromising (or sacrificing) the country's 'economic efficiency'. They make this assertion when they claim that there is a 'trade-off between equity and efficiency'. Efficiency means avoiding waste, and who would like to waste; but to describe the act of taking social equity seriously as being a waste is bizarre. Indeed, it is not merely bizarre, but as we shall see in this chapter, it is also wrong as far as a rigorous grasp of economic theory is concerned.

A closely related proposition of the 'equity and efficiency trade-off' concept is the problematic idea that reduced levels of equity and social justice could be better redressed via money payments. Accordingly, matters such as health and safety negligence on the part of employers, or government policies that prioritise low inflation over full employment, could be equitably redressed with a grant of money. I beg to differ on this matter.[1]

'Efficiency' and 'equity' in economic theory

So, what is it that economic theory does say about the notion of 'efficiency'? And what is the actual origin of the odd idea that when social justice concerns are addressed by our governments, we end up compromising 'economic efficiency'? First, let us see what economic theory does say about the notion of 'efficiency'.

To begin with, economic theory says that we cannot possibly know the most efficient pattern with which we should use our natural, human and financial resources before having a clear idea about what it is we are trying to achieve. In other words, we must determine our intended purpose before we can know how to best allocate our economic resources among competing claims. This applies to a single person, a household, a large corporation or the nation as a whole. Indeed, common sense itself provides the same advice – know what you are aiming for, and only then you might know the most economical (that is, least wasteful) way to reach your goal. This is precisely what economics describes as the efficient way of doing something, big or small. Note, however, that once our goals change, so does the pattern that describes how our resources should be deployed in a truly efficient manner.

It logically follows that a concern for equity should be reflected in efficient patterns of resource use. This applies both within the family and to the nation as a whole. For instance, a country that at some point becomes concerned about its natural ecology would need to change the way it deploys its human, financial and natural resources, if it were to remain being an efficient resource user in line with these new priorities. In the same vein, a society that takes social justice seriously could be said to be allocating its resources inefficiently if it fails to set aside the resources required to achieve its social justice goals.

I now turn to the historical event that wrongly brought into the economic discourse the idea that there is a conflict between the pursuit of social equity goals and the need to avoid waste (namely, to be 'efficient' users of our country's or the global productive economic resources). The term 'equity-efficiency trade-off' has gained currency since 1975, when the economist, Arthur Melvin Okun (1928–1980) came up with the metaphor of the 'leaky bucket' in order to vividly illustrate his strong personal support for a redistribution of income from the wealthy to the less well off (Okun, 1975).

The 'leaky bucket' metaphor is designed to remind us that, if all a person who carries water from a well to his house has is an old bucket that leaks a fair amount of water, he would still use the leaky bucket because water is essential. Okun was a strong supporter of the idea that the inequality of income that he had been witnessing was far too high (imagine his reaction to the much higher level of economic inequality that prevails today). His view was that even if only 40 cents of every dollar that is taken away from the wealthier taxpayer ultimately reach the low-income person, he would still advocate the redistribution of income in spite of the hefty entailed loss of 60 cents per each dollar. Okun described the loss of the 60 cents as a loss of 'efficiency', and then went ahead to coin the term (and concept) – 'equity-efficiency trade-off'. Of course, Okun was not lamenting this 'loss' of 'efficiency' because clearly, he came up with his metaphorical example precisely in order to emphasise how strongly he felt about social equity.

However, in doing so, Okun had unquestioningly accepted the argument of politically conservative economists who oppose progressive tax systems. Those opponents often claim that progressive tax structures take a toll on the level of the national income, allegedly because of (i) a 'disincentive effect' that induces people to reduce the number of hours they spend in paid work and (ii) allegedly, progressive tax structures that undermine business enterprises' interest in investing in productive activities. The result, they argue, would be a lower level of national income, and therefore a lower average standard of living. This, they maintain, is a loss of 'efficiency'.

However, as the notable Oxford economist Tony Atkinson incisively observed, even if one were to believe that such 'disincentive effects' are likely to occur, economic theory would still not support the proposition that the ensuing cut in average standard of living would necessarily represent a loss of efficiency. Atkinson explains why this is the case in his seminal 1970 article, 'On the measurement of inequality'.

Atkinson stresses that the actual truth is that in strictly rigorous analytical terms, economics tells us that in a society that cares for equity as much as Okun did, the 60 cents would not represent a case of 'loss of efficiency'. On the contrary, a loss of efficiency would have occurred, had that society failed to allocate its economic resources in a manner that takes full account of its concern for social equity.

Okun's intent was noble but, analytically, Tony Atkinson's definition is absolutely more accurate. Indeed, common sense itself should tell us that Tony Atkinson's conceptualisation of 'efficiency' is a far more apt description of how we, as economists, and the society as a whole, should conceptualise exactly what we mean by an efficient allocation of our resources, when we are concerned about matters such as social justice, ecological deterioration, global warming or any other important issue.

The limits of using tax relief to combat social injustice

Well-resourced and high-quality health and education systems are a hallmark of communities that prioritise social justice. In such societies, all students have access to quality education, regardless of their parent's income levels. Likewise, quality health care is available according to need, not measured out according to the depth of one's pocket. Of course, a genuine concern for social justice also demands that we have truly progressive income tax systems that keep income inequality in check.

There seems to be a fairly common belief that, fundamentally, social justice can be secured simply by channelling large enough volumes of tax revenue to the 'right' destinations. This, I propose, is a misguided notion because, as they say, 'money cannot buy everything'. For instance, when we subject workers to risky job tasks and an unhealthy work environment, there seems to be the view that all is well as long as the workers are paid sufficiently high wages. Or in more general terms, all is well if we simply put in place sound financial worker-compensation measures.

Similarly, when the economy goes through phases of substantial structural change and workers are laid off, the common belief seems to be that all is fair, provided they are given redundancy pay to retire on. Implicit in those beliefs is the assumption that the only significant aspect of paid work is the money it fetches. But in fact, as this book argues, this is a far too narrow view of the role that paid work plays in our lives.

Far better for individuals, and for the community as a whole, would be a robust, generously financed vocational retraining program. On this subject, we should take a leaf from the Scandinavian social democracies. Vocational retraining programs are absolutely essential if the laid-off workers are to have a reasonable chance of finding a meaningful job. This would not happen unless we put in place programs that are specifically tailored to the aptitude and age of the laid-off workers. In the absence of such programs, the majority of the laid-off workers would fall into the pool of the long-term unemployed. At best, they would be in precarious employment in low-paid jobs, with significantly extended intermittent periods of joblessness.

Paid work that is meaningful, healthy, safe and well designed, and at a workplace that is governed by management that values its employees and allows them to have a sense of dignity and a measure of autonomy, is of utmost importance well beyond the paycheque. In its absence, both the mental and physical health of the individual workers tends to deteriorate.[2] That is why redundancy payments don't have the genuine capacity to replace the vital aspects of well-designed job tasks in a well-run workplace.

A concern for social justice in the workplace also requires a rethinking of job design itself. Far too many jobs are tedious, and too many tasks are repetitive with little scope for initiative and creativity. Established job patterns are often maintained because of the supposed, but rarely examined, assumption that they are essential to the firm's profits. In any event, if we are at all concerned about equity and social justice, then job design could not possibly be a sheer derivative of the profit motive.

Government policies also matter because they often have a substantial impact on distributive justice. For instance, when the government opts for a rise in the level of unemployment in an attempt to stave off price-inflation, a well-defined segment of the population is likely to foot the bill – they lose their jobs so that the rest of us can keep the purchasing power of our own incomes largely intact. The same happens when, for instance, the government promotes structural economic change, as in response to global change in the pattern of trade and production, or in an attempt to stave off global warming. In more general terms, the fact is that as a society, we tend to turn a blind eye to the unfortunate impact that economywide policies tend to have on a well-defined subset of the workforce, who bear the bulk of the cost. Ironically, instead of acknowledging the sacrifice made by the laid-off workers (as for example, when fighting the spectre of inflation or promoting structural changes that promise to raise the average standard of living), far too many of us refer to them with demeaning terms such as 'bludgers' or 'skivers'.

Social justice concerns also require (i) wide-ranging state-regulation of the standards of health and safety at the workplace, (ii) close monitoring of those standards and (iii) the introduction of effective punitive measures on substandard health and safety conditions. Even when punitive measures do exist, they are often too little and introduced too late. In contrast, a well-equipped monitoring arm that is accompanied by effective enough punitive measures should have a significant preventative impact.

Returning to the subject of income inequality, many economists, perhaps even most of them, do wish to restrict the magnitude of income inequality. And many are also likely to opt for a more modest quantum of national income, rather than allowing the economy to spawn a mass of people living in abject poverty.

In fact, the history of economic thought shows that economists have indeed been seriously concerned about poverty and large inequalities in the distributions of income and wealth. There used to be a strong belief among economists that economic growth (manifested as a continuous growth in a country's average income) will progressively reduce the overall level of income and wealth inequalities. More recently however, the belief 'that a rising tide lifts all boats' seems to have lost its grip. The trickle-down theory has lost its lustre. Some might still adhere to the belief that a rising economic tide lifts all boats, but it appears that many others are convinced that recent history has thoroughly undermined this proposition.[3]

Experience has also shown that the scope for addressing equity solely through redistribution of money income via the tax system is rather limited because private provision is only within the reach of the sufficiently well-off. Clearly, direct public provision of quality health and education services, as well as proper, and not demeaning accommodation, are all essential in any society that values social equity and genuine equality of opportunities.

Minimum wage regulation is yet another major structural measure that serves the goal of any society that keeps social justice concerns in sight. Here again, we might wrongly fear that equity concerns are being served at the expense of productive efficiency. But there are a number of reasons why this is not the case. One, as Tony Atkinson pointed out in his 1970 article, if we value social equity concerns then a loss of productivity is not necessarily a loss of 'efficiency'. Another reason has been highlighted by the Nobel Laureate economist George Akerlof in his 1982 article, 'Labour contracts as partial gift exchange', where he proposes that better pay standards often have a direct positive impact on labour productivity.

PART II

The rise and fall of progressive policies

6

From the 'Dark Satanic Mills' to the welfare state

Introduction

For more than two centuries the regulation of the labour market by government has been met with both intense opposition and a strong support. Despite a strong opposition from employer circles and advocates of free markets, the regulation of the labour market did advance steadily for nearly 200 years, beginning with the very first decade of the 19th century. It was only with the advent of the neoliberal tide in the late 1970s that governments have turned sharply against the welfare state and the protective legislation of pay and other work conditions.

The history of the 19th century offers us a window into the predicament of workers when employers enjoyed a laissez faire regime in their workplace. But it also shows us how a truly effective state-regulation system can transform the workplace into a significantly more humane place. Those early factories had been rightly described as the 'Dark Satanic Mills'.[1]

Although state regulation of the conditions under which work was performed had been resisted, history offers us many examples of widespread changes in work conditions that were at first sought only by a minority of social reformers, but once they were imposed by a government edict, they ultimately became the shared social norm. For instance, child labour is now deemed abhorrent, but that was not the case during much of the 19th century. This tells us that state regulation can also be an agent of cultural change.

From the 'Dark Satanic Mills' to more humane workplaces

The progressive legislation of the 19th century was driven by the 19th-century response to the urban squalor and the harsh working conditions that prevailed in the emerging factories of the 'industrial revolution'.[2] It is thanks to the Enlightenment philosophy of the late 18th century, and persistent agitation by 19th-century social reformers, that we now have in place some limits on the outcomes of unfettered markets. The relentless effort of the social reformers ultimately resulted in a spate of novel legislations that improved both the lot of workers and the urban landscape. They also paved the way for the modern labour market institutions and public sector services that we are familiar with nowadays.

The process of industrialisation in Britain, as in other European countries and in North America, depended on long hours of work that was performed by both adults and young children. It was only after a long and arduous battle by philanthropic individuals and humanitarian movements throughout the 19th century that effective regulation of hours of work for children, youth and women was enacted by the government. The advocates of protective legislation ended up prevailing over the employers' opposition. For a long period, these restrictions applied only to female workers and those under 19 years of age. It had also taken a fair few decades before regulation ceased to be focused solely on cotton and textile mills. In addition, there was a significant time-lag between the passing of the Acts and when they became effective.

Although regulatory Acts were enacted in Britain as early as 1802, those Acts did not have much effect until the last decades of the 19th century, once a large enough number of government-appointed inspectors kept visiting the factories.[3] The factory scene in the 19th century is poignantly illustrated by the following two accounts of working conditions in the early 1840s:

> J. Murray, 12 years of age, says: 'I turn jiggers and run moulds. I come at 6. Sometimes I come at 4. I worked all night last night, till 6 o'clock this morning. I have not been in bed since the night before last. There were eight or nine other boys working last night … I get 3 shillings and sixpence. I do not get any more for working at night. I worked two nights last week'. (Collins, 2003: 16)

> The manufacture of matches dates from 1833, from the discovery of the method of applying phosphorous to the match itself. … The manufacture of matches, on account of its unhealthiness, has such a bad reputation that only the most miserable part of working class, half-starved widows and so forth, deliver their children to it, their 'rugged half starved, untaught children'. Of the witnesses examined by the Commissioner White (1863) 270 were under 18, 50 under 10, 10 of these were only 8 years old, and 5 were only 6 years old. Work in the match factories was very unhealthy and unpleasant, we are told. It was so bad that only the poorest of the poor worked there. With a working day ranging 12 to 14 or 15 hours, night labour, irregular meal-times, and meals mostly taken in the workrooms themselves, pestilent with phosphorous, Dante would have found the worst horrors in his inferno surpassed in this industry. (Collins, 2003: 4)

Collins refers to Karl Marx's *Capital: A Critique of Political Economy*, for his source, informing us that Marx borrowed this citation from the *Report of the Children's Commission*, 1842, First Report, liv.

In 1802 British parliament passed the first of its 'Factory Acts'. That was the Health and Morals of Apprentices Act 1802. This Act was followed by the Cotton Mills and Factories Act 1819. Both Acts were confined to cotton mills, prohibiting the employment of children younger than 9 years of age, and restricting the hours of work of youth between the ages of 9 and 18 to 12 per day. Fourteen years later, the 1802 and 1819 Acts were extended to virtually all textile mills (with the exception of silk factories). This time restricting the hours of work for ages 9 to 13 to 8 per day; those aged between 13 and 18 years of age remained restricted to a maximum of 12 hours a day. Calico printing was added to the list of textile factories in 1845.

The 1833 Act also instituted factory inspectors. Without them, and without a sufficiently large number of them, the regulation would have most likely been a mere paper tiger. By the 1860s the inspectors produced volumes of concrete information that led to the subsequent strengthening of the restricting legislation (Collins, 2003).[4] In 1842, the British Parliament passed the Mines and Collieries Act. This act prohibited the employment of women and girls underground.

In 1864, there were further signs that the regulation net was spreading. The 1864 Act incorporated previous factory acts and extended their coverage of industries. The definition of 'factory' was extended to all the establishments that employ hired labour, including small workshops, though this still applied only within the specifically regulated industries. Then, 3 years later, the 1867 Factory Act applied to all the manufacturing establishment that employ at least 50 people or more. In addition, the act permitted the employment of women and children only during certain hours of the day.

The adult male was brought into the ambit of regulation only in 1851. In that year, the British parliament addressed the so-called Ten-Hour Bill for all adults. It was passed under the compromised version of ten and a half hours. Awareness of safety had also begun to grow – the Factory Act of 1842 ordered the fencing of machinery. In 1860 government legislation introduced protective measures for women and girls in the bleaching and dyeing factories.

Yet, even though the first regulatory step that forbade the employment of young people took place in 1802, inspectors still came across 6-year-olds working long hours in factories in 1863. Moreover, at the end of the 19th century there were still substantial pockets of entirely unregulated working conditions. For instance, farm labour, shop assistants and office workers (this could include messenger children) all remained untouched by state legislation.

Among the very vocal British agitators for reform were Robert Owen, who went on to establish his own model factory – the New Lanark, Lord Shaftsbury, who upon inheriting his father's country estate established a model agricultural farm, and Edwin Chadwick, who along with Robert Owen and Lord Shaftsbury, forcefully campaigned for regulation of the hours of work and other work conditions, including those affecting health and safety.

Robert Owen had granted his workers an 8-hour working day in 1818. But it then took virtually an entire century before any national government set the 8-hour working day as the obligatory standard for all its workers.

By the second half of the 19th century, there had been a growing agitation in the UK, demanding more extensive regulation of market activity, including the demand for better wages. Concurrently, the acceptance of state regulation kept growing. We are informed that in the UK, towards the end of the 19th century, 'It was increasingly realised that far from improvements in working conditions hampering business and trade, production could even be increased, as Robert Owen maintained, when workers were not debilitated by excessive hours of labour and bad conditions' (Bury, 1964: 342).

The battle for the 8-hour working day

One of the most urgent political demands of the 19th century social reformers, and workers associations that preceded the trade unions, was the shortening of the length of the working day. That was the time when even a 12-year-old could have been expected to put in 15 hours of work or more in one shift.

Ironically, one of the first groups of workers (other than Robert Owen's) that won an 8-hour working day was prompted into action by their own employer who in 1889 attempted to increase the length of their work shift from 12 to 18 hours. The employer was Beckton Gas Works in East London, at the time the largest gas company in Europe. Beckton workers went on strike on 31 March 1889. The strike lasted a few weeks. When it ended, three 8-hour shifts had replaced the two 12-hour shifts, despite the company's attempt to introduce new 18-hour shifts.

The intensive campaign for the shorter working day had been in full gear throughout the West during the 19th century. In 1866, the International Workingmen's Association had formally adopted the demand for an 8-hour working day at its Geneva meeting. The following year, on 1 May 1867, Chicago workers began a strike that almost brought the city to a standstill; they were fighting for the 8-hour working day. This strike birthed the May Day movement. In the US, as in Australia and New Zealand, select groups of tradesmen and professionals did win a shorter working day before the end of the 19th century. However, the vast majority of US workers continued to work much longer hours.[5]

Nineteen years after their first strike, on 1 May 1886, the US workers went on yet another strike, battling for the 8-hour working day, with Chicago as its epicentre. The police were determined to disperse the gathering and began beating the people with clubs. When some of the assembled retaliated by hurling rocks at the police, the police responded with gunfire. A larger meeting was called for 4 May 1886. Unfortunately, at that meeting an anarchist threw a bomb at the police, playing into the hands of the irate employers, who found their factories empty of employees. The police responded with gunfire. The outcome was the 1886 Haymarket Affair/Massacre.

The next major landmark in the battle for the 8-hour working day took place the following century, in 1919, in the wake of the First World War. The 8-hour working day became the very first Convention adopted by the newly established International Labour Organisation (ILO).[6] In nearly every country in continental Europe, the 8-hour working day was granted to all workers by the mid-1920s.[7] But Neither the US, nor the UK, got terribly far.

A paradigm shift took place in the US in 1926, when Ford Motor Company introduced the 8-hour working day. It was the first large company to take that step. While Henry Ford eventually reported that the shorter day had increased both productivity and profit margins, the Auto Workers Union (AWU) was instrumental in initially convincing the company of the benefits of such a change.

Two US presidents had previously attempted to legislate a shorter working day, but it was only with Franklin Delano Roosevelt's (FDR) Fair Labor Standards Act of 1938 that large numbers of US workers were granted the 8-hour working day. Still, a significant number of US workers were not covered by this legislation.

The emergence of social insurance and public sector services

The social exigencies that were created by the twin processes of industrialisation and urbanisation had not only fuelled the demands for the regulation of working conditions, but also expedited the calls for social insurance and public sector provision of services and amenities, not just in Britain, but also throughout Europe.[8] By 1914 every European country, with the exception of Russia and the Balkan states, had a code of factory and labour legislation, as well as the beginnings of social insurance systems.[9] Social insurance was vital for the effectiveness of the restrictions that were placed on child labour. Had abject poverty not been kept at bay by the welfare state, young children would have still been forced to work for money, not only in less developed economies where they still do, but also in the economically advanced Western countries.[10]

The country that took the pioneering step towards the introduction of social insurance was not Britain, but Germany. Between 1881 and 1884, under the leadership of Otto von Bismarck, the German government introduced a comprehensive system of sickness, work accident and old age pensions. Austria followed suit during the 1880s, as did Denmark and Belgium. Italy and Switzerland initiated similar insurance schemes in the following decade. Compulsory compensation for workers who were injured at work was also introduced in the UK, France, Norway, Spain and the Netherlands by the late 1890s. This regulation obliged employers to compensate each and every injured worker. In the US, however, compulsory compensation for work injuries was introduced only in 1949. As the following segment reports:

> This country is notoriously lacking in safety nets that are taken for granted in other advanced societies. Medical care is guaranteed by the state, by one method or another, in Canada and all European countries; *in* the United States, upward of 40 million people have no medical insurance. Around 46 per cent of employed Americans get not even one day of sick leave – which is guaranteed by law in 145 other countries. Lawsuits are often a substitute for safety nets. (Lewis, 2009: 58)

Lewis also tells us that prior to 1950, US workers who were injured on the job had to 'bring a tort action against the employer' (Lewis, 2009). Namely, the worker had to prove negligence on the part of the employer. As Lewis notes, some courts developed complicated doctrines to deny the plaintiff any compensation. The situation changed only after a committed battle by a movement that sought to institute the awarding of worker compensation whenever an injury occurred, with no reference whatsoever to whose negligence was implicated. Louis D. Brandeis, who later became a Supreme Court judge, led this movement. Ultimately, his efforts were crowned with success – fairer worker compensation laws were passed by every American state during the second half of the 20th century.

Back in Europe, public utilities (who, among other things, had raised health standards) were becoming more common. By 1914, public utilities were present in virtually all European cities. These utilities included clean water, sanitation, gas, electricity, public hospitals, public schools and public libraries. In addition, by 1914, all European countries had compulsory education for children aged 6 to 13. The UK and France introduced free compulsory primary school education in 1881 and 1882 respectively. In 1870, the UK also passed an act that permitted local school boards to require school attendance by all children; and in 1902 the UK government brought in secondary school grants for able students from poor and low-income families.

Public hospitals, either entirely or partially financed by governments, appeared in a fair number of countries in Europe and the US by the middle of the 19th century. Finally, public housing (called 'council housing' in the UK, and 'social housing' in more recent literature) made its first appearance in the late 19th century in a number of continental European countries. The spread of regulation and public sector provision of services was, in large part, a response to urban squalor. But it was also, crucially, a response to widespread and persistent demands for social justice.[11]

Social and economic reforms can change a great deal, for both the better and the worse. But what sometimes eludes us is the subtle ways in which the past is still with us, and not necessarily in positive terms. Gender, race and ethnic discrimination, as many of us are well aware, are very unfortunate issues that we have inherited from the past. We are far less aware of the manner by which certain pre-industrial era elements still linger in present day employment relationships.

Employment relationships through the ages

The regulation of employment relationships through legislation like the Factory Acts was a slow process, essentially the replacement of a feudal employment relationship system with a (modestly) more modern one. However, when feudal serfs became factory employees, the old 'master and servant' system persevered. In fact, it was legally formalised. The first Master and Servant Act was introduced in the UK in 1845. From there, it spread to the US, Australia, New Zealand and South Africa (all of whom passed Master and Servant Acts between 1847 and 1856).

Master and Servant Acts had taken their inspiration from the feudal customs that regulated employment relationships in the preindustrial era when the duty of loyalty to the master had a dominant legal status. It is little known that in fact the duty to pay a worker for work that had already been done went largely unrecognised. In the US, the UK and the British colonies, the Master and Servant Acts have also placed substantial obstacles on workers' ability to quit a job at will. Workers essentially continued to be deemed servants who owed maximum obedience and loyalty to their 'master'. Odd as this might sound, labour historians argue that some aspects of the Master and Servant Acts have outlasted their formal repeal.

David Montgomery, a major US Labour Historian, notes in his 1993 book, *Citizen Worker: The Experience of Workers in the United States with Democracy and the Free Market During the Nineteenth Century*, that practically speaking, in the US the right to quit a job was virtually non-existent well into the 19th century. Although in the US workers were nominally free to quit jobs, judges nevertheless ruled that workers who quit their job have no right to their pay because 'a payment is only a reward for fidelity' (note that we are talking about payment for work that had already been done). A concrete example is the *Stark v. Park* case that was heard in 1824, in the Massachusetts Supreme Court. In his judgement, the judge described the request for pay for the work that had already been performed as a 'monstrous absurdity' (Montgomery, 1993: 41). That judge's ruling clearly asserted that workers who quit their jobs have 'ipso facto' (meaning in Latin 'thereby') violated the duty of fidelity to their employer; and, furthermore, that by quitting they had thereby forfeited their right to receive payment for work already performed.

This example is particularly telling because, as Montgomery notes, this specific court was very influential; most of the other US courts followed that ruling. Montgomery also notes that in Australia, as late as the 1890s, Australian coal miners and sheep shearers were imprisoned for 'deserting' their masters (Montgomery, 1993: 43).

One of the major functions of Common Law courts is to interpret contracts when parties to any given dispute disagree about their actual obligations under a written contract that they had drawn up jointly. But the typical 18th- and 19th-century work contract was rarely if ever written up, let alone jointly drawn up.

Not only did courts deem employment contracts valid when they were merely verbally stated, but according to Montgomery, judges also agreed with employers that there were unstated 'customary' obligations that are part and parcel of the employment contract. Citing Tomlins (1989), Montgomery reports that while these acts were eventually repealed, many of the rulings made by Common Law court judges prior to the repeal entered employment law in the US. Such is the long shadow of the past.

Legislating minimum wages and improving work conditions

Minimum wage regulation emerged after a protracted campaign for the right of workers to have wages that meet the elementary needs of a working family. This campaign was well underway by the end of the 19th century. The first pioneering legislative step was taken by New Zealand in 1894; Australia followed in 1907. In both countries, the legislation applied nationally across the board. In 1909, the UK enacted the Trade Board Act. That act provided legislation for setting up Trade Boards that have the capacity to set minimum wages in selective trades. The US introduced minimum wage and overtime pay only in 1938 as part of President Franklin Delano Roosevelt's New Deal policy. The minimum wage was a component of the Fair Labour Standards Act of 1938 (FLSA). It allowed the individual states to set their minimum wage rate above the Federal level, but not below it.[12]

The 1938 Act is still in power to this very day. In addition to regulating the level of minimum wage throughout the US, it also empowers the federal government to regulate the minimum level of overtime pay and maximum of total number of hours of work, as well as placing restrictions on the employment of children.[13] According to the Act's administering body, the Act affects almost all private and public sector employees. The obligatory overtime pay rate established by the act is set at one-and-a-half-times the regular rate of pay. This act also restricts the number of hours of work that children under 18 can perform in non-agricultural employment and forbids the employment of those under 18 years of age in jobs that are considered too dangerous. By the end of the 20th century, nearly 100 countries had introduced minimum-wage regulation.

The US had no federal legislation mandating sick leave prior to the enactment of the Family and Medical Leave Act (FMLA) of 1993. This act grants only unpaid leave; it mandates a leave of up to 12 weeks during which the job is protected. The leave is granted for serious illness and for the arrival of a new child. But, it does not cover all workers. To be entitled, employees must be full-time workers and employed by a business with a minimum of 50 employees. A number of individual states have legislated for more generous entitlements – for example, allowing coverage for employees working in much smaller businesses, and also adopting a more generous definition of a family unit than defined in the federal act.

A 2007 estimate by the US Department of Labor says that of the 141.7 million employees in the US, 94.4 million were working in FMLA-covered workplaces; of these, only 76.1 million were eligible for FMLA cover (presumably the remainder were part-time or casual workers). The report also noted that 79 per cent of non-FMLA covered workplaces offer, from their own accord, leave entitlements that are equivalent to the FMLA's legislation. As for minimum standards of conditions such as extra pay for night work, paid sick leave or severance pay (upon losing a job), these still lie beyond the regulatory framework in the US.

Myths regarding the impact of minimum wages

If minimum wage regulation is implemented effectively, it could truly ensure that the lowest paid workers do not progressively fall further and further below average living standards. Regrettably, minimum wage legislation runs the risk of being a mere vacuous formality when the dollar magnitude of the minimum wage remains stagnant over extended periods of time. Under such circumstances, the real purchasing power of the minimum wage erodes steadily over time.

The purchasing power of the US federal minimum wage last peaked in 1968. It has been eroding steadily ever since. By June 2021, its level declined to 58 per cent of its 1968 level.[14] At the time of writing, an American family of four – with only one wage earner who is fully employed year-long (with an average of 40 hours per week) – subsists on about US$15,080. Despite working full time, this income still falls US$11,100 below the official poverty line in the US, which is currently US$26,200.[15]

Nearly 30 of the 50 US states have mandated minimum wages that are higher than the federal level. Still, according to the Economic Policy Institute, if the minimum federal rate was to be raised to US$15 by the end of 2024, almost 40 million workers would see an increase in pay (Cooper, 2019).

Minimum wages have been a surprisingly contentious issue within the US. The main argument put forward by those wary of mandatory minimum wages has been that minimum wage regulations generate higher levels of unemployment. While numerous studies have attempted to establish whether this proposition has merit, to date, the empirical analyses have failed to support this contention. David Card and Alan Krueger (Card,1992a, 1992b; Card and Krueger, 1994, 1995) argue that the empirical data fails to support this proposition. Although a number of subsequent articles begged to differ (for example, Neumark and Wascher, 2007), Card and Kruger's conclusions have recently been upheld by a 2013 publication of the US Centre for Economic and Policy Research (NBER). The author of that specific publication is John Schmitt. He concludes:

> Economists have conducted hundreds of studies of the employment impact of the minimum wage. Summarizing those studies is a daunting task, but two recent meta-studies analyzing the research conducted since the early 1990s conclude that the Minimum wage has little or no discernible effect on the employment prospects of low-wage workers. (Schmitt, 2013: 24)

Schmitt notes that this result is not surprising, since an increase in the value of the minimum wage actually represents a relatively small component of the total cost structure borne by the employer. He adds 'but probably the most important channel of adjustment is through reductions in labour turnover, which yields significant cost savings to employers' (Schmidt, 2013).[16]

Whether the minimum wage is adjusted for cost-of-living changes or not becomes a moot question in the absence of an effective monitoring body that is equipped with a genuine enforcement capacity. In the absence of such a monitoring institution, state regulation becomes a mere window dressing. Wage theft that ignores mandatory minimum wage legislation is widespread – from the US (Hallett, 2018; Lee and Smith, 2019), through the UK (Hodgson, 2017), the European Union (Kall, 2017), Australia (Ferguson et al, 2015; Macdonald et al, 2018; Wright and Clibborn, 2018; Ferguson, 2020) to Asia and Africa (Khambay, 2021).[17]

7

Enter neoliberalism

Introduction

Enlightenment philosophy inspired the progressive legislation of the 19th century that culminated in the welfare state during the mid-20th century. By the late 1970s, neoliberal policy essentially set out to reverse that progressive course. Governments embarked on major labour market 'deregulation' and public sector privatistion policies, primarily – but not only – in English-speaking countries. As David Marquand aptly put it, 'In advanced industrial societies, one of the central themes of the golden age was "embourgeoisement": the spread to the working class of job security, career ladders and lifestyles which had formerly been the prerogatives of the middle class. Now the engines have gone into reverse' (Marquand, 1997: 4).

Many of those who had a secure and quite well-paid job are now abandoned to the vagaries of precarious employment in poorly paid jobs. Deregulation, or more aptly 'reregulation' (as some writers describe it) has also opened the doors to harsh working conditions that echo the emerging factories of the industrial revolution during late 18th and most of the 19th century.[1]

Harsher has been the lot of the vast majority of the US population whose average standard of living has been eroding. The average standard of living of the lower-income earners is stuck where it was six decades ago. And the average standard of living of the middle-income earners is where it was four decades ago. Together, these two groups include 90 per cent of Amcrica's income earners. Yet, the average standard of living of the US population keeps growing. The growth accrues to the very top earners. This is true even at the very top; the percentage increase in the incomes of the wealthiest top 0.1 per cent is larger than the percentage increase in the incomes of the remaining 9.9 per cent of the top 10 per cent group.[2]

This incredible pattern of inequality, and the stagnation in the level of income of the vast majority of Americans, could not possibly be explained away as an 'inevitable economic outcome'. Rather, both phenomena are fundamentally the consequence of the suite of retrograde policies that have been introduced in the US since the 1970s. They are also the result of a serious lack of proactive policies and bold reconstructive agendas in response to shifts in global patterns of production and trade. The extensive tax cuts that have disproportionally favoured the highest income earners and top wealth owners have also played their role.

The 'Dark Satanic Mills' of the industrial revolution were largely spawned by a major technological revolution. The major breakthroughs were: the steam engine that was patented by its inventor Thomas Savery in 1698, John Kay's 1733 flying shuttle, James Hargreaves's 1764 spinning jenny and Richard Arkwright's 1769 spinning wheel. The industrial revolution occurred at a time when employers had virtually complete control over the conditions under which people worked for them, whether adults or very young children. We might think of that era as a long-gone past that is as dead as the middle-ages' feudalism. But this may lull us into a too complacent mindset because any extensive laissez faire employment regime provides a fertile ground for a harsh work environment. This is not a dystopian prophecy – quite a few reports tell that this is the stark reality in e-commerce warehouses. This reality is closely related to the fact that, yet again, we have been going through a period of major technological change (the AI revolution) at a time when the labour market is quite deregulated.

Amazon workers are nowadays equipped with digital monitors that record the speed of work in terms of seconds. A failure to execute a task within the set stringent maximum time limit, adds to the stock of penalty points. Adam Littler, an investigative reporter for the BBC, clandestinely filmed the conditions under which Amazon's warehouse 'pickers' work. The footage, aired on an episode of the BBC's Panorama programme, was filmed at Amazon's warehouse in Swansea, where Littler worked undercover as an employee for a period of time. The promotional material for Panorama reported the following:

> Undercover reporter Adam Littler, 23, got an agency job at Amazon's Swansea warehouse. He took a hidden camera inside for BBC Panorama to record what happened on his shift. He was employed as a 'picker', collecting orders from 800,000 sq. ft of storage. A handset told him what to collect and put on his trolley. It allotted him a set number of seconds to find each product and counted down. If he made a mistake the scanner beeped.[3]

Littler was expected to collect a new order every 33 seconds. He worked 10 and half hours in each of the nightshifts. The 10 and a half hours allowed for two 15-minute breaks, and a half-hour break for one meal. On one night, Adam Littler wore a pedometer. That pedometer recorded the distance he covered during his nightshift; it was 18 km (or 11 miles). Littler had never been so exhausted in his whole life.[4] The *Observer* journalist, Carole Cadwalladr had a similar idea; she too worked as an 'elf' (as she describes it) in Swansea's Amazon warehouse. She describes that experience in her 2013 article. It dovetails Littler's experience.

In his 2015 book, *The Health Gap: The Challenge of an Unequal World*, Sir Michael Marmot describes a day in the life of Alan. Like Adam and Carole,

Alan was a warehouse picker. At the start of the work shift, Marmot tells us, Alan was given a handheld set that recorded all his moves, and measured the number of seconds he spent on each individual task. He was told that if he falls too far behind, he would incur penalty points. He never managed to complete his daily job quota, even though he was absolutely worn out by the end of the day. One day he was off sick, that cost him one whole penalty point. Arriving late just once, by a mere 3 minutes, further increased the number of his penalty points. Marmot notes: 'It took Alan about 8 weeks to accumulate three points, but he did, and [he] was summarily dismissed' (Marmot, 2015: 173).[5] Marmot adds the following words: 'My reaction to Alan's experience was that it was as if his employer had taken everything that we know about damaging aspects of work, concentrated them in a syringe, and injected them into Alan' (Marmot, 2015: 173).[6]

Amazon opened its first warehouse in Australia in 2017, and a second one in 2018. A worker who spoke directly to Fairfax Media described their experience thus: ' "It's a hellscape", but they declined to be identified for fear of losing their current job or damaging future work opportunities with labour hire firms' (Hatch, 2018).

It does not really matter whether Alan worked as a picker in an Amazon warehouse in the UK, US or Australia. What does matter, and greatly so, is the fact that such employment practices are nowadays legal.[7] Amazon's work conditions would have been unfathomable during the early post-Second World War decades, when trade unions were a force to be reckoned with.[8]

Assaults on trade unions in the UK, US and Australia

There are a number of striking similarities between the strategies that were adopted by the governments of these three countries when they waged their battles against their trade union movements. They had all embarked on a major confrontation with one of their stronger trade unions. Ronald Reagan selected the Professional Air Traffic Controllers Organisation (PATCO) in 1981, Margaret Thatcher battled the National Union of Miners (NUM) in 1984 and Australia's John Howard fought the Maritime Union of Australia (MUA) in 1998. All three confrontations had a widespread and lasting impact on their country's industrial relations framework. In the wake of those battles, employers became far more emboldened in their resolve to toughen their stance against organised labour, knowing that the government would very likely back them up. Writing in the New York Times on the 30th anniversary of Reagan's confrontation with PATCO, Joseph McCartin noted the following about the impact of that event, 'Thirty years ago, today, when he threatened to fire nearly 13,000 air traffic controllers unless they called off an illegal strike, Ronald Reagan not only transformed his presidency, but also shaped the world of the modern workplace' (McCartin, 2011).

In the next paragraph, he adds: 'More than any other labor dispute of the past three decades, Reagan's confrontation with the Professional Air Traffic Controllers Organization, or Patco, undermined the bargaining power of American workers and their labor unions' (McCartin, 2011).

On 6 March 1984, the British Prime Minister, Margaret Thatcher, announced the closure of 20 coal pits and the loss of 20,000 jobs. The miners responded with a strike. As the strike progressed with no end in sight, poverty spread and the population of whole communities became quite depleted. At the beginning of the strike, Britain's National Union of Miners (NUM) was highly organised and very cohesive. Incredibly, 93 per cent were still striking at the very end when the strike ended on 3 March 1985. The tragic death of David Wilkie on the 30 November 1984 had already taken a heavy toll on the strong public support the striking miners had hitherto received.[9]

The full extent of the Thatcher government's agenda came to light in 2013, as a result of the 30-year rule that allows cabinet papers to be publicised once three decades have elapsed. It had consequently been revealed that in a 1984 speech to a backbench committee, Thatcher announced: 'We had to fight the enemy without in the Falklands. We always have to be aware of the enemy within, which is much more difficult to fight and more dangerous to liberty' (Travis, 2013).[10]

The 'enemy from within' was clearly the whole trade union movement: 'The Downing Street papers from 1983 show she told Ferdinand Mount, then head of her policy unit, that she agreed that Norman Tebbit's gradualist approach to trade union reform was too timid' and that they should 'neglect no opportunity to erode trade union membership' (Travis, 2013). The 1984 cabinet papers also reveal that Thatcher's war on the National Union of Mineworkers (NUM) was thoroughly prepared in advance:

> the cabinet papers show that Nigel Lawson, who was the energy minister, had already spent two years building up coal stocks told Margaret Thatcher: 'If Scargill [the NUM's leader] succeeds in bringing about such a strike, we must do everything in our power to defeat him, including ensuring that the strike results in widespread closures'. (Travis, 2013)

In May 2015, the leader of Britain's Conservative Party, David Cameron, won the general election outright. Within 2 months of being in office Cameron embarked on what has subsequently been described as 'The biggest crackdown on trade union rights for 30 years ... including new plans to criminalise picketing, permit employers to hire strike-breaking agency staff and choke off the flow of union funds to the Labour party' (Wintour, 2015).

Cameron had selected the public sector unions for special attention. His government's bill sought to subject trade unions to criminal charges and hefty fines if they engaged in certain forms of strikes that, hitherto, had been legal. The bill seems to have been equally aimed at the Labour Party's financial base as it sought to curtail the scope of the financial contributions that it receives from the trade unions.[11]

Much like the Reagan's presidential administration in the US and the Thatcher and Cameron governments in Britain, in 1998 John Howard's government in Australia was similarly determined to embark on a quite major confrontation with the trade union movement. Its choice fell on the Maritime Union of Australia (MUA). A year earlier, Peter Costello, the future Treasurer of John Howard's government, founded the ultra-right think tank, HR Nichols Society that campaigns for 'deregulation' of the workplace. Braham Dabscheck's 1987 *Journal of Industrial Relations* article, 'New right or old wrong? Ideology and industrial relations', presents a fairly comprehensive analysis of that initiative.

The MUA was engaged in a strike against the Patrick Corporation, a major aviation, rail and shipping conglomerate. The Patrick corporation locked out the striking members of the MUA, while doing its best to bring in a whole new strike-breaking workforce that it was clandestinely training in Dubai. There are reports that suggest that members of John Howard's cabinet were in cahoots with the Patrick corporation. In any event, John Howard's government Employment Relations minister, Peter Reith, did announce that the government fully supports the Patrick Corporation's lock out. But this specific attempt was defeated when the Federal Court ruled in favour of the striking union. Although the High Court of Australia upheld the Federal Court's ruling, the cooperation between the Howard government and the Patrick Corporation appears to have had a lasting impact on the industrial relations framework in Australia.[12]

Seven years later, in 2005, John Howard returned to the battlefield, and this time his efforts were crowned with a success. On 14 November 2005 Howard's government enacted the Workplace Relations Amendment (Work Choices) Bill 2005. This bill received a Royal assent, becoming a law on that same date. Coming into effect in March 2006, this legislation sought to openly bypass trade union involvement via 'individual bargaining' between the employee and their employer.[13] But, as the Stanford economics professor, John Pencavel, notes in his 1991 book, the vast majority of individuals have no recourse to 'individual bargaining'. Rather, they are simply given a 'take it or leave it' job offer.

The Howard government's 'Work Choices' legislation also allowed employers with less than 100 employees to dismiss any employee at will, without having to account for unfair dismissal. It turns out that at that time, this legislation deprived half of the private sector workforce of any right to contest unfair dismissal.[14] This legislation had also allowed all employers who could successfully argue that they are either downsizing or restructuring their business, to dismiss workers at will.[15] The in-coming Labor government, led by Kevin Rudd, replaced the Work Choices Act with the Fair Work Act of 2009. However, the impact of the 'Work Choices' legislation on the industrial relations framework is not entirely gone.[16]

The continuous political efforts to undermine the scope of collective bargaining have had inevitable consequences. Andrew Stewart et al's 2018 book, *The Wage Crisis in Australia: And What to Do About It*, addresses the ramifications of the low rate of wage growth which has, for quite some time now, been at levels not seen since the 1930s. In addition, Australia's central bank, the Reserve Bank, has been warning that with wages remaining persistently low, the purchasing power of low- and middle-income recipients has largely stagnated. Consequently, businesses are experiencing low demand for the goods and services they sell in the local market. Speaking to the media, the Governor of Australia's central bank, Dr Philip Lowe, has also gone out of his way to stress that stagnant wages undermine social cohesion.[17]

Unemployment and 'rugged individualism'

> Alan Krueger taught me a lot about pain. That people are in a lot of pain when they are unemployed, and searching for a job was their most painful part of the day. That men w/out work reported a lot of pain and took a lot of pain relievers. (Stevenson, 2019)[18]

In 1961, the Australian unemployment rate rose from 1.1 per cent to 1.8 per cent. The government of the day had swiftly declared it an unacceptable state of affairs. This declaration was made by Australia's Conservative Party Prime Minister, Robert Menzies, who immediately embarked on a full-fledged Keynesian policy aimed at restoring the lower rate of unemployment. He was not alone, throughout the West (perhaps with the exception of the US) macroeconomic policy remained focused on preserving a genuine state of full employment until the late 1970s.

> Keeping unemployment low was seen as a collective responsibility. … In the 1970s and '80s all of this changed. Liberal free-market ideas rose to dominance across most of the world in what is now often referred to as neoliberalism. Instead of viewing unemployment as a collective problem, neoliberalism painted unemployment as an individual responsibility. (Smith, 2017: 1)[19]

In a fair few Western countries, policy makers have also begun to justify the deterioration in the level of financial support given to the jobless as an 'incentive' designed to keep the overall level of unemployment smaller by encouraging workers to take up a job – any job.

Alan Kruger was a renowned Princeton university professor of economics, who made major contributions to our understanding of how the economics of paid work pan out. We should take his words to heart. Alan Kruger is not alone. Numerous statistical surveys and scholarly studies have described the despair of the unemployed who not only bear the stress caused by financial penury, but also the loss of a social identity and social networks that accompanies that loss.

The title of Michelle Turner's 1983 book, *STUCK! Unemployed People talk to Michelle Turner: Living Without Work – The Stories That Statistics Cannot Tell*, underscores the importance of hearing the voice of the unemployed themselves. A similar reality is described by Mick Young in his 1979 book, *I Want to Work*. The book is based on his encounters with unemployed Australians, both young and old, all of them desperately wishing to be employed. But, as he cogently argues, there were scores of applicants for each of the available vacancies. In 2016, the ratio in Australia between the number of unemployed people seeking jobs and the number of job vacancies was 19.[20] In August 2018, this number was only slightly lower – 15.79.[21] Unfortunately, when some people hear about an existence of an unfilled job vacancy, they erroneously conclude that there is no unemployment whatsoever.

It is also very important to note that the number of people who are keen to have a paid job is generally even larger, because of the so called 'discouraged worker effect'. This phrase refers to the fact that there are workers who, having had their job applications rejected over and over again, end up ceasing to look for a job. Unfortunately, these workers don't leave their footprints in the formal unemployment statistics.[22]

In her 1994 article, the medical sociologist Mel Bartley sheds light on the scale of the negative health outcomes that occur among the long-term unemployed.[23] Bartley also draws our attention to the fact that even in a country such as Norway, where the unemployed receive generous financial support, people who had been fit and healthy prior to their extended experience of joblessness often end up becoming emotionally and physically unwell.

The ranks of the very low paid and the unemployed are crowded with displaced workers and young entrants to the job market, who lack the skills that are in demand. Reskilling them would enhance both their individual wellbeing and the economy's level of productivity. But instead of introducing robust training programs for the unemployed, Australia's conservative government had come up with the punitive Work for the Dole programme. As far as I can tell, this program has no complete parallel in any other Western country. It was initiated by Tony Abbott when he was a junior cabinet member in John Howard's government, in 1998. The academic scholars Jeff Borland and Yi-Ping Tseng's 2004 study argues that ironically this program tends to impede job search efforts. The journalists Tom Allard and Anne Patty's 2014 article exposes the punitive nature of this programme, and the substantial emotional toll it takes on its participants. They also lament the fact that this program offers the unemployed little chance to genuinely enrich their earning skills. And the academic scholars T. Philip and Kerry Mallan's 2015 study offers a comprehensive survey of the literature on the emotional wellbeing of the young among the unemployed. The work choice programme was also prone to significantly higher incidence of work accidents, including fatal ones.

Inequality has been growing not only within countries, but also between different countries. By the end of the first decade of the 21st century, the rate of growth in the average income of the top 10 per cent of the OECD countries was nine times the rate of growth in the average income of the poorest 10 per cent.[24]

Languishing in the US 'Rust Belt'

A large number of the people who prior to the 1980s had fairly well paid and secure jobs have subsequently remained stuck in the 'Rust Belt' regions of the US. The term Rust Belt refers to the northern and midwestern states of the US, the regions that until the late 1970s had housed the thriving manufacturing and mining industries of the US.[25] This term came into wide use during the 1980s. It aptly describes the economic blow dealt to those regions when vast numbers of blue-collar jobs were lost to the Emerging Markets Developing Economies (EMDE), a result of the West's eternal search for cheap labour.

Naturally, the large loss of jobs has also had a domino effect on these regional economies.[26] Large cities, among them Detroit Michigan and Gary Indiana, lost more than one fifth of their population. These Rust Belt regions had historically voted for the Democratic Party. But in 2016, possibly as a result of their economic desperation, a number of these states voted for the Republican candidate Donald Trump. In truth, both major political parties had left the Rust Belt workers to their own devices.

What can be done?

Governments can meet economic challenges that are posed by structural changes, whether as a consequence of technological changes or major transformations in the global patterns of production and trade, either with utter passivity or with a bold proactive policy program. The Swedish example of manpower training programs can teach us a lesson or two. What Sweden has is an exemplary standard of commitment to the wellbeing of its workers and their families. As Thomas Grose reports,

Would you feel relatively sanguine if your job was at risk of being automated? You might if you lived in Sweden. This is because most Swedish workers who are replaced by machines fairly quickly land another job as good as their old one, thanks to the network of job-security councils, jointly run by industries and unions that retrain workers in skills that are still in demand and out of reach of robots. Moreover, while they are unemployed workers are buoyed by a safety net that includes generous jobless benefits. (Grose, 2018)

Sweden first embarked on this commitment in the late 1930s when it resolved to rapidly expand its machine-making industry. Yet, it faced a major stumbling block – it had a huge shortage of skilled labour. Sweden took the bull by the proverbial horns and established tailor-made programs that allowed it to fast-track the retraining of its workers, converting them into highly skilled metal workers.[27] Sweden had understood that the displaced adult worker requires a fast-tracked, highly effective retraining program. The required teaching, it resolved, would reach this goal only when it is done in small groups of four or five trainees, in courses that are taught by skilled workers who are truly masters of their own métier. Such programs are indeed far more expensive to run, but they ultimately make a very substantial contribution to the economy's level of productivity. Perhaps more importantly, they also help reduce the size of the economic and social gaps between the fortunate and the less fortunate members of society.

In contrast, the US, Britain and Australia spend meagre amounts on upgrading the skills of their workforce. A number of continental European countries do better, but Sweden's practice remains exemplary. True, both the Reagan and Obama administrations set up retraining programs. But these programs have not been terribly effective. This is not very surprising, because even with the best intentions retraining programs can fall flat on their face when they are not very well conceived and badly implemented; let alone when poorly financed.

For whom do the tax-cut bells toll?

In the US, Britain and Australia, tax structures have been systematically altered by continuous cuts to income taxes for high earners, corporate taxes and capital gains taxes. Yet it had not always been this way. In April 1942, President Franklin Delano Roosevelt proposed to the US Congress to set a marginal tax of 100 per cent on all incomes above US$25,000 (US$350,000 in terms of 2013 US dollars). He settled for 94 per cent.[28] Under the Republican presidency of Dwight Eisenhower, the top marginal income tax rate was 91 per cent. Ironically it was a Democrat president,

John F. Kennedy, who cut Eisenhower's tax rate to 71 per cent. In 1982, the Republican president, Ronald Reagan, reduced the rate to 50 per cent (while seeking Congressional approval for a much lower rate). Presently that rate stands at 37 per cent.[29]

The US corporate tax rate followed a similar trajectory, falling from 50 per cent in the 1950s to 31 per cent in 2019.[30] The world average has also followed a similar trend, falling from 40 per cent to 29 per cent, while its weighted average fell from 46 per cent to 31 per cent.[31]

George H. W. Bush stands out among all the Republican presidents that followed Eisenhower's presidency as far as tax policy is concerned. In an October 1990 speech, Bush announced that 'The time for politics and posturing is over', adding that 'the time to come together [with the Democrats in the Congress] is now'.[32] Bush was genuinely concerned about the growing size of the US's public debt. Therefore, despite his campaign promise to leave tax rates intact, he raised taxes on luxury items such as yachts. In addition, he raised the top marginal income tax from 28 per cent to 31 per cent. The Democrat president, Bill Clinton subsequently raised the latter to 39.6 per cent. But, unlike his father, President George W. Bush embarked on a yet another journey of large tax cuts. President Barak Obama did raise taxes back, but only by a trickle.

The UK's and Australia's income tax policies followed a similar pattern, albeit somewhat more moderately. We should however note that in 1990, while cutting taxes for the well off, Margaret Thatcher had also introduced a universal Poll Tax. Incredible as this might be, a zealous senior cabinet member (the then Welsh Secretary, Peter Walker) beseeched Margaret Thatcher to impose the poll tax even on the homeless, fearing that if the homeless were exempt, the poor might be inclined to become homeless – information that has surfaced only recently. As Cahal Milmo, a chief reporter of the British newspaper, the *Independent* writes: 'A memo from the Welsh Secretary Peter Walker [a member of the British Conservative party] in 1988 complained that plans to exempt the homeless would create an "enormous loophole" and result in people sleeping on the streets as a method of ducking payments' (Milmo, 2016).

It appears that little has changed. On 2 April 2019, the Australian conservative government of Scott Morrison announced new future tax cuts.[33] The Australian Council of Social Service (ACOSS) pointed out that most individuals who earn A$30,000 or less would not benefit at all from the promised tax cuts because their taxable income is too low to pay any income tax. ACOSS pointed out that this meant that 30 per cent of households would not benefit at all from the tax cuts. In contrast, a middle-income earner who gets A$50,000 a year, would gain A$1,205, while a relatively high-income earner on A$200,000 dollar a year would gain a tax cut of A$11,640.

Neoliberal warriors

Milton Friedman, a Nobel Laureate economist, had been a close advisor of both US President Ronald Reagan and UK Prime Minister, Margaret Thatcher. He is also well known as a major opponent of Keynesian economics.[34] Friedman's 1962 book, *Capitalism and Freedom*, urges us to restrict the activities of the government to the realms of (i) defence of the nation against external enemies, (ii) enforcement of contracts made between individuals and (iii) protection of individuals and their properties against crime. Basically, on the home ground, the sole function of the government is the maintenance of law and order.

Friedman opposed regulation of the safety of baby cots, cars and, most incredibly, even medical drugs. For example, a TV compere who interviewed Friedman confronted him with the fact that regulations introduced by the Food and Drug Administration (FDA) had spared the US from the very lethal impact of the Thalidomide poisoning.[35] Friedman simply dismissed that positive contribution as a fluke. The FDA, Friedman opined, should be abolished. Without presenting data to support his position, he simply asserted that for every good regulatory initiative there is always another bad one.[36] But this was a mere off-the-cuff comment; he had no data whatsoever with which to back this assertion.

What is perhaps less well known is the fact that Friedman's opposition to state regulation stems from his own personal belief in the rights of both individuals and corporations to have absolute freedom, whatever the cost might be. His absolute opposition to state regulation of any kind is a consequence of his personal adherence to the philosophy of 'libertarianism'. Indeed, in recognition of Milton Friedman's contribution to the libertarian ideological cause, in 2002, the founders of the libertarian Cato Institute, Charles and David Koch, established the Milton Friedman Prize to be awarded to an individual who has made a significant contribution to advancing the cause of 'human freedom' (the prize includes US$250,000).[37]

Charles Koch, a major founder of the libertarian Cato Institute, and his late brother, David, have been openly committed to the complete repeal of the legacy of FDR's New Deal legislation, lock stock and barrel. This includes FDR's National Labor Relations Act of 1935, that secured workers' rights to form trade unions, and Fair Labor Standards Act of 1938 that introduced the minimum wage, eight-hour standard working day, overtime pay at one and a half times the standard hourly rate and restrictions on the work of minors.[38]

The Koch brothers have set their guns not only at FDR's 1930s legislation, but also at Bill Clinton's paltry unpaid 12 weeks (only for fulltime workers) Medical and Family Leave Act of 1993 and Barak Obama's Patient Protection and Affordable Care Act that was enacted on 23 March 23 2010. As for trade unions, Reuters reporter Andrew Stern published in 2011 an article titled 'Analysis: Koch Brothers are a force against trade unions'. More recently, *The Guardian*'s chief reporter in the US, Ed Pilkington, reported that 'fears grow as right-wing billionaires battle to erode trade union rights'. Specifically, Pilkington reported that a coalition of conservative think tanks, and the billionaire Koch Brothers, are fighting against the public service trade unions, with highly likely far-reaching repercussions for other trade unions (Pilkington, 2018a).

PART III

When profit and prejudice reign

8

Profits vs the duty of care

Introduction

The British factory acts and the equivalent measures that were taken by the vast majority of the European and the Antipodean countries stopped short of introducing a truly rigorous system of state regulation of health and safety conditions at the workplace.

By default, employers have essentially been allowed to enjoy the luxury of what is sometimes described as 'self-regulation'. Workers still die in significant numbers in a significant range of industries. Yet, in all probability better safety measures would have brought down both the death toll, and the incidence of disabling work injuries. Not all firms ignore ethical principles, but we know that a few bad apples can set the rot in the apple cart. Unless practically all competing business enterprises invest in substantial health and safety measures, competitive market pressures may stop more conscientious firms from increasing health and safety standards in their workplaces.

There is no shortage of examples of tragedies occurring at high-risk workplaces. All too often, firms that are singularly focused on profit also keep their employees in the dark about health hazards even when the firm's own managers are well aware of the problem.

Toxic chemicals in the workplace and beyond

Unfortunately, a major yet subtle obstacle to changing this state of affairs is the manner in which public cognition functions when risk is not at the forefront of our human attention. If we would ask ourselves whether as a society we sense the workplace health and safety issue in its full urgency, the answer I believe would have to be that we don't. We could empathise with the workers who are badly injured or killed in workplace accidents, and we do. But since most of us, our own family members and close friends are not subjected to high health and safety risks in their workplaces, this issue ends up being given much less weight than it requires.

This also tends to be the lot of minority groups: the unemployed, for instance. If every citizen had one unemployed person within their immediate family or among their close friends, unemployment would have a better chance of becoming an urgent issue on our social and political agenda. What I'm trying to say is this: unemployment is primarily concentrated in a few suburbs. Additionally, some demographic categories of households are far more heavily affected by it than others. If instead, the same total number of unemployed people was quite evenly distributed across all suburbs and all social circles, chances are that unemployment would have become a more acute political issue.

The same goes for health and safety issues, except that not only do these issues primarily affect only a minority of workers, their presence is very subtle. Also, since health and safety risks are not here-and-now problems, even the potentially affected workers who might be aware of the lurking danger, tend to turn a blind eye to the risk. At times, it is the case of a human delusion – 'it won't happen to me'. Of course, there are people who take up risky jobs in the full knowledge of the inherent potential risks. They might nevertheless be doing it because otherwise it would be near impossible for them to make ends meet. Arguably fewer are the outright risk-taking daredevils.

Case study: James Hardie's negligent assault on their workers

Unfortunately, we also have in our midst employers who had known the presence of risk long before the workers had any inkling of the grave risk they were facing. Let us take the specific case of a large Australian firm, the James Hardie Corporation. The lethal impact of the raw materials used by the James Hardie Corporation offers us a tragic cautionary tale. Matt Peacock's 2009 masterpiece, *Killer Company*, provides a very comprehensive account of the conduct of a corporation that had been aware for quite a few decades of the lethal impact of the raw material it uses, while its workers had little inkling.

The James Hardie Corporation's products were made of blue asbestos, or 'Crocidolite', the most lethal of all asbestos types. This company had known about the ill-health effects of blue asbestos since at least 1935.[1] Crocidolite causes 'mesothelioma' disease that often lurks in the body for decades before it begins to manifest itself.[2] In his 2009 *Sydney Morning Herald* newspaper article, Ian Verrender tells us that the future CEO of the James Hardie Corporation, John Reid, was concerned about this issue when as a young person he had just joined the family business in the 1960s. But his concerns, Verrender tells us,

> were assuaged by the company's then personnel manager E.T. Psyden, who replied: 'The article is not new. It is merely one of many reports of world studies which have been conducted since 1935 when the association between exposure to dust and carcinoma, *mesothelioma* … and other fatal complaints was first recognised'. The answer he got from the company's manager was: 'There was little cause for concern, he added, because only about 100 workers had contracted asbestosis in the previous 15 years'. (Verrender, 2009)

What makes it only 100, one wonders? The Australian company CSR, a past partner of James Hardie Corporation, closed its asbestos mine (in

Wittenoom, Australia) in 1966 after 100 of its own workers contracted lung disease. But the James Hardie Corporation only stopped using asbestos in their products in 1989. Among the victims were not only James Hardie Corporation employees, but also users of the James Hardie Corporation's products: tradesmen and others who bought James Hardie Corporation's products for their own use. Among them there was also a wife who, unsuspectingly, regularly shook the asbestos dust off her husband's and her father's work overalls before washing them.

Yet another victim was Lincoln Hall who led the Australian expedition to the summit of Mount Everest in 1984. On his second attempt to reach this summit, in 2006, he was left for dead on the way down from the summit. At that time, he miraculously defied death. However, in 2012 Lincoln Hall died of mesothelioma. He was 56 years old. In 2006, he had no idea that he had mesothelioma. In all likelihood, it had caught up with him as a result of two asbestos cubby-houses that he had built with his father's help when he was 12 years old.

New cases of mesothelioma keep surfacing. The first wave of victims were the workers who mined the asbestos and those who made the asbestos sheets, the second were the tradesmen and individuals who used asbestos sheets, and a more recent third wave, is the fairly large number of people who have been renovating their own homes. (Christodoulou, 2017).

In his 2009 book, Peacock reports that the James Hardie Corporation had adopted a multi-prong strategy that was focused on downplaying the risk of exposure to asbestos dust. The management, he argues, did everything in their capacity to discredit the individual scientist whose study exposed the presence of significant risk levels. They organised luncheons for the supervisory government body whose task was to control the risk and secured for themselves key positions on the specially formed safety committee.

Having been entrusted with 'self-regulation', the company was left to its own devices. Ironically, the James Hardie Corporation was also given the full responsibility to run the compensation fund that was set up for the people who have suffered from asbestos related diseases. That fund was set up in 2006 under the name of The Asbestos Injuries Compensation Fund (AICF). In that year, the company insisted that 'there were large enough funds for its future asbestos victims and their families'. A funding agreement was drawn up by the managers of James Hardie Corporation's AICF and the NSW government. In order to:

> ensure the long-term viability of the company, that agreement capped James Hardie payments at just 35 per cent of the company's annual cash flow. The fund was made totally dependent on annual transfers from the company's free cash flow, when funds were available.

A mere three years later, in May 2009, James Hardie Corporation reported a negative operating cash flow of $45.2 million for the

2008/09 fiscal year. Consequently, it was not required to make any contribution to the AICF on that year. This left the fund with total assets of just $140 million. (Binsted, 2014)

Tim Binsted's 2014 article reports that the scheme remains short by millions of dollars while the corporation keeps having enough money to pay 'big dividends'.

It has transpired that James Hardie Corporation issued false public declarations about the adequacy of funds to meet all potential compensation claims. The Australian Securities and Investment Commission (ASIC) sued the James Hardie Corporation when it was discovered that the statement the company made about the adequacy of the AICF fund was false. In April 2009, the ASIC's court reached its verdict. The verdict was against the James Hardie Corporation's CEO and its ten directors. The judge found that '[They] have approved misleading and deceptive statements about an asbestos compensation fund'. Verrender (2009) notes: 'sadly, these are civil offences and no one faces jail'.

After a long fight led by Bernie Banton, who died from mesothelioma on 27 November 2007, the government stepped in to regulate some aspects of the AICF fund. His fight earned Bernie Banton the respect and admiration of the Australian community. In 2005, Mr. Banton won an Order of Australia for his fight to get compensation for asbestos victims. On 27 November 2007, Joe Hildebrand and Robert McDonald wrote:

SHAMED multinational James Hardie made one last effort to rob asbestos victim Bernie Banton as he lay dying, using a doctor's report it has hidden for seven years to claim it did not have to pay him compensation. As Mr. Banton lost his battle with *mesothelioma* yesterday, the building company and its former subsidiary used the critical report on a 34-year-old X-ray to again rort the 61-year-old. (Hildebrand and McDonald, 2007)

Verrender sums it up thus: 'The awful legacy of those decisions [made by James Hardie] will be felt by Australians for generations. Death tolls and soaring health costs tell only part of the story. The human tragedy, the agonising pain and suffering of asbestos victims and those caring for them, can never be measured' (Verrender, 2009).

Covering up research: the case of cigarette manufacturers

Cigarette makers offer us another example of what unfortunately can take place under corporate self-regulation.[3] The harmful effects of asbestos had come to public knowledge since at least the 1890s, and compensation claims were successful in a verdict that was given by a US Massachusetts Court in 1926. Yet large corporations still chose to use asbestos filters in their cigarettes during the second half of the 20th century. As William Longo et al report in their 1995 study, the American company Lorillard used asbestos filters in their Kent brand cigarettes between 1952 and 1956, while ironically promoting them as particularly healthy. It turns out that the health hazard was well known to Lorillard and other cigarette makers.

Toxic products: the shocking negligence of 3M and DuPont

Yet another lethal carcinogenic group of chemicals is PFAS (poly- and perfluoroalkyl substances). These chemicals have been the cause of the aggressive bone cancer, 'sarcoma'.[4] Among its victim have been young children and teens who have undergone amputations and premature death. Carrie Fellner reported this in her 2018 *Sydney Morning Herald* article titled 'Toxic secrets: the town that 3M built where kids are dying of cancer'. On the 2 August 2017, Christopher Knaus reported in *The Guardian* that 17 years earlier, the US Environmental Protection Agency (EPA) had actually warned Australia's government that PFAS is highly toxic. Specifically, the EPA warned 'that [PFAS is] a toxic chemical it was using at defence bases, fire stations, and airports, risked severe, long-term consequences to human health and the environment'. Despite this warning, the government didn't act to limit its use.

Reuters reporter Jonathan Stempel (2018), wrote that in the US, 'NY sues 3M, and five others, over [this same] toxic chemical contamination'. Sharon Lerner (2018) wrote in *Intercept*, that 3M has known that PFOA and PFOS are toxic since the 1970s. We also have a report, *Toxicological Profile for Perfluoroalkyls* that has been issued by the US Department of Health and Human Services Agency for Toxic Substances and Disease Registry for public comment issued in 2021.[5]

Concerns have also been raised about DuPont's PFOA chemical since 1970s. But according to the US's North-Western University's Social Science Environmental Health Research Unit, DuPont actually has known that PFOA is toxic since 1961. Furthermore, in 1981 DuPont learned that babies of its female employees had been born with birth defects.[6] A lawsuit had been brought against DuPont's Parkersburg plant in West Virginia for PFOA pollution, in 1998.

More recently, on the 4 June 2021, communities in the Ohio river have filed a lawsuit against DuPont in response to landfill and wastewater dumping of PFAS laden material from the West Virginia Washington Works Plant. Firefighters have also been filing lawsuits saying that the companies they are suing, among them 3M, DuPont and Chemours knew that PFAS causes health problems (Llamas, 2021).

Still waiting – gender, race and ethnicity

Introduction

Article 7 of the 1948 Universal Declaration of Human Rights says that 'All are equal before the law and are entitled without any discrimination to equal protection of the law'. All are entitled to equal protection against any discrimination in violation of this Declaration and against any incitement to such discrimination. But notwithstanding the 1948 Universal Declaration of Human Rights, access to jobs and levels of pay still vary systematically with the race, ethnicity and gender of the individual. This is true throughout our planet, in both developing and developed countries. White heterosexual males receive higher pay and more privileged access to jobs well in excess of what could be explained by their levels of education and vocational qualifications. Non-white men, non-heterosexuals, disabled individuals and women of all colours are still waiting for the day when labour market discrimination is a thing of the past.[1] Most acute has been the experience of First Nations people. Western imperialism has inflicted significant economic, social and cultural harms on the indigenous populations of Australia, the Americas and Africa.[2]

In Australia, racial and gender pay discriminations were enshrined in law for nearly seven decades during the 20th century. Indigenous Australians were given equal statutory *basic wage* (read minimum wage) only in 1969. Other restrictions also applied. For instance, as Thornton and Luker' study notes:

> In New South Wales, under the Aborigines Protection Act 1909 (NSW), which remained in force until 1969, the Aborigines Protection Board (from 1940 the Aborigines Welfare Board) had the power to control and regulate all areas of Aboriginal life, including the power to indenture Aboriginal children as 'apprentices', collect their wages, place them in the Board's combined interest-bearing trust account, and spend the money at its discretion. (Thornton and Luker, 2009: 650)

And all women, white or non-white, had to wait until 1975 before their statutory basic wage was raised to the level of the white male basic wage. With few exceptions (for example, university teaching) this was the case even when men and women had strictly the same job.[3]

Women faced a long battle for pay equality throughout the West. After more than 100 years of focused activism and legislative efforts, equal pay legislation began gathering pace only during the last three decades of the 20th century. For instance, in 1968 British women who worked as machinists at the Dagenham Ford Factory went on strike demanding equal pay. In the US, female employees of Western Union Telegraph Co. went on a strike for equal pay in 1883.

Formally, Equal Pay Acts come in two specifications – 'equal pay for equal work' and 'equal pay for work of equal value'. The reach of the first is much narrower because it effectively leaves lower-paid women who work in highly segregated female jobs entirely unaffected. As we know, generally there is also a significant gap between the 'de jure' (formal legislation) and 'de facto' (the facts on the ground) state of affairs. The European Commission adopted the principle of Equal Pay for Equal Work upon its establishment, in 1957. In the US, the Kennedy administration followed suit in 1963. And the UK and Australia introduced their Equal Pay for Equal Work Act in 1970 and 1975 respectively. According to a 2020 World Bank article by Katrin Schulz and Nour Chamseddine, at the date of publication a total of 88 countries had already mandated equal remuneration for work of equal value.[4] This certainly is a welcome step.

But despite these legislative efforts, substantial pay gaps still remain in almost every country in the world. Here is a British example. On the occasion of the 50th anniversary of Britain's Equal Pay (for equal work) Act of 1970, Sophie Gallagher (2020) published an article in the *Independent* newspaper. Her article details cases of women who are still paid substantially less than men who are doing the same job, even when they work side by side. Worse still, Gallagher reports on a case in which the better paid man actually worked under the supervision of the less well-paid woman. When this woman complained, the employer retorted that she should have negotiated her rate of pay more astutely. Gallagher also writes on a case where a challenge in the court turned out to be regrettable because of high financial as well as emotional costs. Not a one-off case. In 2008, MSNBC host Mika Brzezinski, discovered that her co-host, Joe Scarborough's pay level was 14 times her own. When she complained she too was told that she should have bargained for a higher rate of pay (Mirkinson, 2011).[5]

Economic justice entails more than just equity of pay and access to jobs. Political power is also vital. But women, First Nations people, non-whites, the disabled and members of the LGBTQ+ community are yet to have equal political and social power. A trove of articles in the 2020 special issue of the *Feminist Economics* journal, edited by Sarah Gammage et al, also argue compellingly that women won't have a genuine economic equality until they have a full access to reproductive health and child care services.[6] As well, the literature stresses that women need far more flexibility in the workplace since they tend to be the main carers of their families. (Baird et al, 2017, 2021).

As I see it, we need a radical change in our social culture's assignment of household and family care responsibilities. Simultaneously, we need to have a change in the way employers perceive the men in their employ. What I mean is this: women will not be fully economically empowered until (i) men are deemed equally fit to be the carers of children and other family members and (ii) employers have equal expectations regarding the likelihood that their male and female employees might be called on to attend caring duties.

None of the urgently needed changes will come about through free interplay of market forces. Progressive government legislations and policy measures are of vital importance if we are to make a real progress. An historical lesson can be found in Gavin Wright's 2013 book, *Sharing the Prize: The Economics of the Civil Rights Revolution in the American South*. The US Jim Crow segregation laws were implemented in the late 19th century in its southern states. They effectively lasted until the enactment of the Civil Rights Act of 1964. Gavin Wright concludes that in the absence of that revolutionary act, the racially segregated economies of the southern states would have missed a major opportunity to improve the incomes of their entire communities, African Americans and whites alike. The education and vocational training opportunities that were opened up by the 1964 act, he stresses, had benefited the incomes of both African Americans and Whites. As Sarah Reber (2014) writes in her review of Gavin Wright's 2013 book, '*Sharing the Prize* tells the important story of the progress made on this front, reminding us in the process that government can accomplish a great deal under the right circumstances' (Reber, 2014: 415).

Intersectional discrimination

Workplace discrimination commonly involves the intersection of several factors, such as gender, race, class, religion and age. African American attorney and legal scholar Kimberlé Crenshaw argues that while it is undeniably simpler to address individual factors such as gender or race separately, this approach risks diminishing the analysis of serious cases of social and economic disadvantage. Crenshaw was the first to describe analysis that, for instance, is focused on the distinct labour market experience of black women (or, for example, a white woman who is disabled) as an 'intersectionality analysis'. She also stressed that intersectionality should be recognised by the legal system, while citing the following court case as an example.[7]

In 1976 five African American women took General Motors to court. This is commonly known as the 1976 '*DeGraffenreid v General Motors*' case. The women argued that they were not allowed access to jobs that were currently given exclusively to men, nor to a number of jobs that were allotted to white women but not to black women. Yet, the court ruled against them, maintaining that it has power to rule either on a sex or a race discrimination case, but not on the conjunction of both (Crenshaw, 1989).

In a 2018 article, Queen's University Belfast professor Dagmar Schiek discusses three cases that had recently been heard in the EU's Court of Justice, and which involved intersections of gender, age, race and religion. The arguments brought in those cases relied on the EU's non-discrimination laws. But the court determined against all claimants. Sheik says that actually, intersectional discriminatory cases must and could be readily addressed within the framework of the EU's non-discrimination laws. Like Crenshaw, she too stresses that it is high time that our legal systems recognise that intersectional discrimination exists and needs to be addressed. While Crenshaw's 1989 call to the legal system is yet to be fully answered, within the academe intersectional analysis has been widely embraced.[8]

The plight of indigenous people

The literature on the labour market experience of indigenous workers in countries that had historically been colonies of European empires is scant. Nevertheless, the core elements of the picture are quite clear – members of indigenous populations are often placed at the very end of the job queue. Some progress has occurred, but the majority of indigenous people, across different countries, are still languishing behind the descendants of the colonisers and the Western immigrants that have followed. Addressing the plight of Canada's indigenous population, Daniel Wilson and David Macdonald describe the economic state of Canada's indigenous members thus, 'Not only has the legacy of colonialism left Aboriginal peoples disproportionately ranked among the poorest of Canadians, this study reveals disturbing levels of income inequality persist as well' (Wilson and Macdonald, 2010: 3).

In Australia, the 2016 Census of Population shows that the median income of indigenous Australians was 61 per cent of the median income of the non-indigenous population. In part, this gap reflects the somewhat lower rate of labour force participation among the indigenous population of Australia, as compared to non-indigenous Australians.[9] However, the income gap remains substantial even when we focus only on those who are in paid work – the median income of indigenous Australians who are in paid work is equal to only 72 per cent of the median income of the non-indigenous employees who are in paid work.

In Canada, the equivalent figure is virtually identical, the median income of the gainfully employed Aboriginals in Canada is 73 per cent of the non-Aboriginal median income.[10] In both countries, the fact that the larger proportion of indigenous people live in non-urban areas explains only part of the overall income gap. The reality is that indigenous incomes lie below non-indigenous incomes in all geographical regions, whether urban or non-urban. Yet another factor that underpins the overall income inequality between the indigenous and non-indigenous populations is the substantially higher rate of unemployment among the members of the indigenous populations.

But, remarkably, in Canada the income gap between Aboriginal and non-Aboriginal Canadians who completed a bachelor's degree has declined from Can$3,882 in 1996 to Can$648 in 2006. Still, as Wilson and Macdonald caution, 'While income disparity between Aboriginal peoples and the rest of Canadians narrowed slightly between 1996 and 2006, at this rate it would take 63 years for the gap to be erased' (Wilson and MacDonald, 2010: 3).

Yet another factor that tends to supress income levels of indigenous people in both countries is their lower levels of educational attainment. But neither does this fact explain the full extent of the racial income gap, because within almost every level of education, indigenous people are the recipients of lower incomes.

This pattern, however, does have one important exception. Within both Canada and Australia, the average income of indigenous females, who had completed a tertiary degree, is higher than the average income of non-indigenous females who completed a tertiary degree (Wilson and McDonald, 2010; Biddle, 2013a). As Nicholas Biddle notes regarding Australia:

> Despite this variation [that is, the rise of income with the level of education], for almost every demographic, geographic, education and employment combination, indigenous Australians have lower average income. The only major exception to this is indigenous females with a degree who had a slightly higher income than non-indigenous women with a degree. (Biddle, 2013a: 17)[11]

Poverty too takes its toll on health standards.[12] The average standard of health among indigenous Australians is substantially below the average standard in the remainder of the Australian population. Russell Ross (2006) notes that the life expectancy of indigenous Australians is 20 years below that of the non-indigenous population. And the health reporter of the Sydney Morning Herald, Amy Corderoy reported that 'The Australian Institute of Health and Welfare Report found that two-thirds of indigenous Australians die before 75, compared with only 19 per cent of the rest of the population' (Corderoy, 2014).

Regrettably this indicates a decline, rather than rise, in the life expectancy of indigenous Australians since the previous decade. Citing the same report, Corderoy adds that 'They are dying of preventable diseases linked to poverty and geography and, the life expectancy gap between indigenous and non-indigenous Australians has not improved in more than 10 years and in some areas of health is getting worse, a report has found' (Corderoy, 2014).

Historically, indigenous employees have been grossly underpaid. Until 1968, state regulation legally prohibited white pastoralists to pay the indigenous stockman a wage that is equal to that of the white stockman, regardless of whose skill was superior (indigenous drovers were often far more skilful).

Until the 1920s, all indigenous Australian workers were paid only with meagre amounts of food and clothing. Money wages finally arrived in 1920, and only for some indigenous workers, not for all. A subsequent act (The Native Affairs Act of 1936) obliged pastoralist employers to also provide shelter and medical care. However, having no enforcement machinery attached to it, this act ended up being largely ineffective.

Indigenous Australians have fought valiantly for higher wages, and for the reclamation of the lands that they traditionally inhabited. Two examples now follow.

The Pilbara 1946–1949 strike

The Aboriginal pastoral workers of the Pilbara region lost patience with their meagre levels of pay.[13] And so, in an ingenious strategy, the Pilbara region strike commenced concurrently on all 27 stations strewn across the large Pilbara region of Western Australia. On one day, 1 May 1946, hundreds of Aboriginal pastoral workers walked off the job.[14] The 3-year-long strike, that at its peak had as many as 800 employees who stayed away from their employers' stations, was a brave and powerful statement against the slave-like conditions under which they were employed.

Many of the Aboriginal Pilbara strikers were jailed for varying periods of time, as it was illegal for them to quit their employers. In August 1949, Western Australia's branch of the Seamen's Union of Australia came to their help, and imposed a ban on shipping the wool that was sheared in the Pilbara stations. Within 3 days of this imposition the government told the strikers that the level of pay received by Aboriginal stockmen would be increased. It was a lie. Though they ended their strike in response to that promise, the pay rise had not eventuated. The Pilbara strike had a sequel in Australia's Northern Territory, but not before 1966.

The Wave Hill 1966 strike

The 1966 Wave Hill strike followed a 1965 failed attempt to introduce equal 'basic wage' (essentially, a legislated minimum wage) for the Aboriginal

Australian stockmen. This attempt failed, because it met the strong opposition of the pastoralist station owners who claimed that a 'wage rise would threaten the very viability of their business enterprises'. It took 3 more years for the Gurindji people to win the battle for equal wage. This occurred in 1969. As the Creative Spirits website reports, 'Aboriginal stockmen were housed in corrugated iron humpies, without floors, lighting, sanitation, furniture or cooking facilities. It was illegal for the Aboriginal people to leave their place of employment, and it was even illegal to pay them wages equal to the white people's'.[15]

At that time, Wave Hill was the Northern Territory station of the British company Vestey Ltd. On the 22 August 1966, 200 stockmen and their families walked off that station. The person who led the walk off was Gurindji elder Vincent Lingiari. The Gurindji people were the traditional owners of the land on which Lord Vestey's pastoral station was situated. They had been living there for approximately 60,000 years before Australia was colonised by Great Britain.

One of the Gurindji stockmen was Billy Bunter Jampijinpa. In 2006 the *Sydney Morning Herald* journalist, Lindsay Murdoch, reported a conversation he had with Billy Bunter Jampijinpa as follows:

> 'We were treated like dogs,' he says. 'We were lucky to get paid the 50 quid a month we were due and we lived in humpies. You had to crawl in and out of on your knees, there was no running water, the food was bad – just flour, tea, sugar and bits of beef like the head or feet of a bullock.' (Murdoch, 2006)

We have yet another testimony. This one was documented by the National Museum of Australia:

> Shirley Andrews, who helped establish the Equal Wages for Aborigines committee, pointed out that people who were paid such a small proportion of the [white male's] basic wage were not able to live like white people, as required under the assimilation policy. For example, the Gurindjii pastoral workers were unhappy about their appalling living conditions: a diet of salt beef, damper, sugar and tea, and white stockmen coming back into camp when the Aboriginal stockmen were still out with the cattle, and taking advantage of Aboriginal women. (The National Museum of Australia, 'Collaborating for Indigenous rights')[16]

Initially the strike was about pay and living conditions, but before long it also became a strike about a land claim. Aboriginal people were given equal pay in 1969. Six years later, this was followed by a land right victory. In 1975

Gough Whitlam's Labor government introduced the Land Rights Bill.[17] That bill lapsed when, at the behest of the then opposition leader, Malcolm Fraser, the Australian Governor General, John Kerr, took the very controversial step of dismissing the democratically-elected Whitlam government on 11 November 1975. However, the Liberal-National Coalition government, under Malcolm Fraser as the subsequent Prime Minister of Australia, did enact this legislation in 1976, albeit in an altered form. The Land Rights Act of 1976 recognises Aboriginal Claims on traditional lands. This Act also established their right to compensation.[18]

Unfortunate government policies

We have yet another major chapter in the history of the unjust treatment of the indigenous people of Australia. In 2007, John Howard's government embarked on the so-called the 'Northern Territory Intervention'.[19] Although the government was concerned about a valid issue, high levels of child abuse in some indigenous communities, the strategy that they chose to address this issue has failed basic tenets of human rights and social justice. In its 2007 *Social Justice Report*, the Australian Human Rights Commission castigated that Northern Territory Intervention in very strong terms.[20]

Jon Altman who has closely studied the economic conditions under which indigenous Australians subsist, proposes that there was a broader policy agenda behind the June 2007 events (Altman, 2007).[21] Jon Altman is the Foundation Director of the Centre for Aboriginal Economic Policy Research (CAEPR) at the Australian National University. Altman also argues that Australian governments in general, and perhaps most spectacularly so during the 2007 Northern Territory Intervention, have been striving to bring (i) private ownership of property and (ii) the market economy into communities that have strong traditions of kinship and sharing of the fruit of fishing, hunting and gathering. Incomes earned from the sale of artworks, and paid work are the main form of 'modus vivendi' in the remote indigenous communities. In many of his publications, Altman notes that Western societies fail to respect, or indeed, comprehend, communities that are built on a strong commitment to a sharing of economic resources.

In broader terms, there is a need for a strategy that understands and respects the cultural differences between indigenous economies and Western capitalism. Michael Chandler and Christopher Lalonde's 1998 study, 'Cultural continuity as a hedge against suicide in Canada's First Nations', shows how vital is the need to allow our First Nations communities to retain their cultural continuity, communal cohesiveness and cooperative economic traditions. They found that half of Canada's First Nations communities had no suicide cases for more than two decades. These communities enjoy extensive self-governing and strong cultural continuity. In contrast, they recorded significant levels of depression and suicides in other First Nations communities that have little scope for self-governing.

The high incidence of poverty endured by indigenous communities underpins their lower levels of enrolment in educational institutions. But statistical portraits of income levels are largely silent about the root causes of this situation. Consequently, the underlying barriers that are created by poverty and cultural and political dispossession remain largely obscured. For instance, most indigenous students have to support themselves economically when they take up tertiary level studies. This deprives them from having adequate time for study or even for diligent class attendance. They also experience the predicament of being the only, or just one of a handful of indigenous students within a very large educational institution.

Educational attainment – barriers and solutions

Fortunately, we have first-hand evidence of the outstanding educational outcomes that materialise, once the economic and social obstacles that inhibit the academic success of indigenous students are removed. This is manifested very clearly by the outstanding scholastic outcomes that have been achieved by the group of indigenous Australian students who study at the Muru Marri Indigenous Health Unit at the University of New South Wales (UNSW) in Sydney, Australia. Roughly speaking, the rate of degree completion among the indigenous students of the Muru Marri Indigenous Health Unit has been 90 per cent. This is much higher than the average completion rate among the non-indigenous tertiary student population in Australia.

The positive steps that removed those prohibitive obstacles have been taken by the Shalom Gamarada program that was jointly conceived in 2004 by the founder of the Muru Marri Indigenous Health Unit and the first indigenous recipient of PhD in medicine, Professor Lisa Jackson-Pulver, and Illona Lee who at that time was the Head of the UNSW's Jewish Shalom College. The Shalom Gamarada program commenced in 2005. This program provides economic security and social camaraderie for indigenous students who otherwise would face economic hardship and social isolation. Specifically, the program provides scholarships, accommodation and food on campus, for the indigenous students who study medicine and other health sciences, in the Muru Marri Indigenous Health Unit at UNSW. The Shalom Gamarada program also offers tutoring help.

In 2004, Illona Lee asked Professor Lisa Jackson-Pulver how Shalom College could help the Muru Marri Indigenous Health Unit. Professor Jackson-Pulver proposed that the Shalom College could provide a residential scholarship for indigenous students, who would be offered a place in the Faculty of Medicine at the University of New South Wales (UNSW). In response, Lee offered to raise funds for residential scholarships by establishing an annual exhibition of artworks, with the participation of artists who agree to contribute a portion of the show's revenue to the scholarship fund. By 2013, the program had 25 scholarships on offer.

Similar initiatives have also been undertaken in other major universities across Australia. By October 2014, thanks in great part to these programs, there were a total of 310 indigenous medical students nationwide. This is a modest beginning, but nevertheless it has been a substantial step towards the amelioration of the dire state of indigenous health. Through their success, the Aboriginal and Torres Strait Islander health unit, Muru Marri, and the Shalom Gamarada program of College Shalom have also strongly exposed the inhibiting impact of the economic and social obstacles ordinarily faced by indigenous students at the tertiary level educational institutions.

Lisa Jackson-Pulver is an Aboriginal Australian woman. In a 2013 interview with Australia's ABC radio interviewer, Margaret Throsby, Lisa Jackson-Pulver described the economic obstacles and social isolation she herself had experienced when she first attempted to complete a tertiary degree.[22] Having to earn income for food, accommodation, tuition and all her other needs, and being socially isolated (as the only indigenous student), on her first tertiary studies attempt she ended up dropping out. Fortunately, she gave it a second try. Presently, Professor Lisa Jackson-Pulver is the Deputy Vice-Chancellor of Indigenous Strategy and Services, at the University of Sydney, Australia.

Inequality of pay and access to jobs

In 2018, the average gender pay gap among OECD countries was 13 per cent. It narrowed between 2002 and 2018, albeit at a slower pace between 2010 and 2018. In most OECD countries this gap lies between 10 per cent and 20 per cent. Korea has the largest gap, 32.5 per cent, followed by Japan, 23.5 per cent and Israel with 22.7 per cent. Far narrower are the gaps in the Nordic countries. Denmark had the smallest gap with 4.9 per cent, Norway and Sweden also performed relatively well, with 5.0 per cent and 7.0 per cent respectively. Australia's and France's gaps are below the OECD average, standing at 11.7 per cent and 11.5 per cent respectively. But Germany, the UK and the US all have larger gaps than the OECD average, at 15.3 per cent, 16.6 per cent and 18.5 per cent respectively.[23]

A study published by Francine Blau and Lawrence Kahn in 2000 had similarly found that the gender pay gap in the US was larger than in Australia, Austria, Britain, Italy and West Germany. They also noted that, while US women had made large inroads in historically male-dominated fields, they were yet to catch up with the women in those other countries.[24] Emilio Castilla's 2008 study analysed a database that held information about pay gaps in very large US firm that had formally adopted a 'performance-based' pay system. Even so, Castilla found that the firm's female and minority employees had systematically received lower pay than the white men, in defiance of the performance-based scores that their own employer had given them.

Cross-country comparisons are informative, but only up to a point. To begin with, these rates only represent the differences between the incomes of male and female employees who work full time. We therefore have no clue about the pay gaps experienced by women who have no recourse to full-time paid work, either because they face discriminatory entry barriers into full-time jobs or because they are part-time employees because they are primary carers who have no access to affordable child care. Indeed, affordable child care is yet to become widely available.

Affordable child care can be a major barrier as far as women's earning capacity is concerned. It transpires that a great deal depends on the country we live in. For example, if we live in Austria or Italy, child care would cost us less than 5 per cent of the households' average income.[25] In contrast, among the OECD countries, parents in the following four countries pay significantly more for childcare. New Zealand has the highest level of childcare cost at 37.3 per cent, followed by the UK with 35.7 per cent, the US with 33.2 per cent and Australia with 31.1 per cent. At 14 per cent, the average cost among the 41 OECD countries is much lower, and in 15 of those economies the cost is lower than even 8 per cent of an average couple's income.

Unsurprisingly, women end up retiring on a much lower income than men. For example, in 2009 Australia's average gender pay gap for full-time employees was 16 per cent. That same year, Australia's Human Rights Commission's Sex Discrimination Commissioner, Elisabeth Broderick, pointed out that: 'The most recent assessment of superannuation balances is for 2006. At that time, the average superannuation account balance was $35,520 for women, compared to $69,050 for men' (Broderick, 2009).

Immigrants are also disadvantaged when compared to those born in their country of citizenship. For instance, Australian immigrants are paid less than their equally qualified native-born counterparts (Islam and Parasnis, 2014), while a US study notes that migrants tend to be overqualified for their jobs (Alt and Iverson, 2017). Likewise, in Britain, immigrants are generally paid less than native born workers and, similarly, they tend to be overqualified for their jobs (Brynin and Güveli, 2012; Longhi and Brynin, 2017). This is particularly true for men of Bangladeshi and Pakistani descent. The latter two groups represent some of the most disadvantaged workers in Britain, being paid 26 per cent below white British national men's pay (Longhi and Brynin, 2017). The British experience is largely repeated across the globe. A global study published by the International Labour Office (Amo-Agyei,

2020) reports that it is specifically high-income countries where this pay gap is most distinct, with women faring worse than the men. That same report finds that migrants in less economically-developed countries actually experience positive discrimination when compared to the local working population.

These problems persist, all around the world. Although Denmark has the lowest gender pay gap, as Maddy Savage (2019) tells us, access to the more prestigious jobs is still very uneven in that country. Meanwhile, in the US, Mary Noonan and et al (2003) analysed a comprehensive dataset that follows the career profile of graduated Law students from Michigan University.[26] The authors discovered that the gender earnings gap was present from the moment of their entry into the job market. Worse still, after 15 years this gap had grown much larger, even for women who had no children.

Claudia Goldin and Cecilia Rouse (2000) identified gender discrimination among musicians auditioning for leading symphony orchestras. The authors recommend that musicians opt for a blind audition regarding gender and ethnicity. Their study showed that the proportion of professional female musicians in symphony orchestras grew significantly once auditions became blind to their gender and race.[27]

In a 2011 radio interview, the international classical music and opera conductor Simone Young described the hiring bias she faced, before she eventually broke into the male-dominated world of symphony and opera conducting.[28] She reported that she was summarily rejected by nearly 30 European music agents, who openly told her that they would not represent her, simply 'because she is a woman'. It was the internationally renowned conductor, Daniel Barenboim, who provided her the break she needed. Barenboim hired her to lead his orchestra through all their rehearsal sessions, but the last one.

Women in high corporate positions are still a minority. Ilene Lang, who was the founding CEO of AltaVista Internet Software Inc[29] and subsequently President and CEO of Catalyst, a leading US organisation focused on the advancement of women in business, had the following to say.

> But despite headline-grabbing news like the recent naming of Meg Whitman as chief executive of Hewlett-Packard, a look at the numbers shows that progress at the very top has stalled. Last year, women held about 14 percent of senior positions at Fortune 500 companies, according to the non-profit group Catalyst, which focuses on women in the workplace. That number has barely budged since 2005, after 10 years of slow but steady increases. So, what's the hold-up? Ilene Lang president and chief executive of Catalyst, says one factor can be traced to an 'entrenched sexism' that is not less harmful for being largely unconscious. (Korkki, 2011)

In August 2020, Catalyst reported that women comprised just 30 per cent of those in serious management positions in the European Union and 29 per cent in North America. The proportion was higher in Africa – 38 per cent, Eastern Europe – 35 per cent and Latin America – 33 per cent.[30] In September 2020, Charlotte Grieve reported that 'only one woman was promoted to the role of chief executive, out of 25 appointments at Australia's large companies over last year, in sign that gender equality in the professional world is going backwards' (Grieves, 2020).

The same patterns apply to women working for lower pay rates. A study by Neumark et al (1996) reports that the authors sent a group of female and male students to apply for vacant restaurant waitperson jobs. The pattern displayed by this study's numerical results shows that male applicants were preferred to female applicants; and this was especially true of the high-priced restaurants.

The irony is that the warped prisms through which the Other is visualised are also oblivious to the actual value of diversity and inclusion. This is true socially, politically, economically and also with regard to an individual firm's bottom line. There is ample literature on the virtues of having a truly diverse workforce. Ankita Saxena (2014) surveys an extensive body of literature and concludes that diversity of age, cultural background, ethnicity, race and religion, gender, sexual orientation, intellectual and physical disabilities in the workplace is highly valuable. She acknowledges that such workplaces could be challenging to manage but, when managed properly, such diversity can have significant productivity payoffs. A 2020 report by McKinsey & Company similarly finds that 'the business case for inclusion and diversity (I&D) is stronger than ever'.[31]

So, it's worth asking ourselves what the roots of discriminatory mindsets might be. Arguably, one is our incapacity to see the Other. But as we shall see, this is not the only root cause of discrimination.

In the mind of the beholder

Simone de Beauvoir noted our limited capacity to see the 'Other', a term she coined. As she eloquently put it in her 1949 book *Le Deuxième Sexe*, the Other is essentially defined as a 'Not-'.[32] A Woman is perceived as a Not-Man, while a Black person is perceived as Not-White, and so on. The African-American scholars Rhonda Williams and Carla Petersen (1998) discuss the inferiority inherent in the social construct of the Other – both the Other race and the Other gender.[33] Williams and Peterson argue that white narratives of Blackness often portray Black poverty as a consequence of character faults and 'dysfunctional families', rather than the result of poverty, job market discrimination and a long history of economic and political deprivation.[34] They note:

Building on the tenets of 'romantic racialism' that defined Blacks as childlike, simpleminded, lacking in self-restraint, and incapable of moral and intellectual development, these spokesmen further elaborated a doctrine of dissociation of mind and body: the mind was associated with scientific thought, technological progress, and capital, the body with machinery. Identified as pure body, Black was but a machine. (Williams and Peterson, 1998: 9)

In their ingenious study, David Hekman et al (2010) expose the incredible scale of blindness to the quality of the Others. They produced a series of scripted videos featuring actors who faithfully recreated a number of real-life interactions between a bookstore's employees and customers. The script used each time was identical, but the videos featured different groupings of actors, some men and some women, some black and some white. Hekman and his co-authors reported that the students who watched the videos evaluated the quality of the services that were dispensed by the actors differently. Despite the identically scripted dialogue, women and non-white personnel were consistently perceived as providing an inferior quality of service, compared to that provided by the white males.

A large 2004 study exposed another manifestation of the insidious nature of racial discrimination in employment. Marrianne Bertrand and Sandhil Mullainathan sent 5,000 fictitious resumes in response to 1,300 'help-wanted' ads in the Boston area of Massachusetts, US. The advertised jobs were in the sales, admin, clerical and customer service categories. The resumes were all identical except for the fact that half them bore common Anglo-Saxon names (such as Emily Walsh and Gregg Baker) while the other half bore African-American names (like Lakisha Washington and Jamal Jones). The call-back response in the group of 'applicants' with Anglo-Saxon sounding names was 50 per cent higher than the call-back response to the applicants bearing names such as 'Lakisha' and 'Jamal'.

Our incapacity to see the Other goes beyond gender, race and ethnicity prejudices. It transpires that even having a non-standard accent is enough for a person to be perceived as 'different' in a more comprehensive sense. For example, researchers have found that Scottish accents in native English speakers tend to detract from other people's estimation of their social status (Lev-Ari and Keysar, 2010). Studies have also found that 'voice', as distinct from 'accent', has a similar effect (Bestelmeyer et al, 2010).

Engineering bias against women and non-western people

The scholarly literature also suggests that among the root causes of discriminatory mindsets are purposely manufactured demographic hierarchies that are avidly guarded by the politically, economically and socially powerful (Morgan, 1972; Cowlishaw, 1999; Dirks, 2001).

Edmund Morgan's (1972) seminal study, 'Slavery and freedom: American paradox', describes how in the late 17th and early 18th centuries, African Americans were progressively deprived of citizenship rights. The rights were rescinded when British settlers discovered that owning slaves was more profitable than depending on an indentured workforce, particularly since the latter had to be set free within 4 to 7 years. Morgan describes the rights that the purchased African American had at that time thus:

> It seems clear that most of the Africans, perhaps all of them, came as slaves, a status that had become obsolete in England while it was becoming the expected conditions of Africans outside Africa and of a good many inside. It is equally clear that a substantial number of Virginia Negroes were free or became free. And all of them whether servant, slave or free enjoyed most of the same rights and duties as other Virginians. ... They could sue and be sued in court. ... They earned money of their own. Sometimes they bought their own freedom. (Morgan, 1972: 17)

Morgan traces the construction of the social category of slavery to the prevailing views on class and liberty in 17th century England. He points out that John Locke, who is known as 'apostle of liberty', had essentially argued that liberty is the exclusive right of the landed class, not the poor:

> John Locke, the classic explicator of the right of revolution for the protection of liberty, did not think about extending the right to the landless, instead he concocted a scheme of compulsory labour for them and their children. The children were to begin at the age of three in public institutions called working schools because the only subject taught would be work (spinning and knitting). They would be paid in bread and water and grow up "inured to work". Meanwhile, the mothers [who were] thus relieved of their offspring could go to work beside their fathers and husbands. (Morgan, 1972: 10)

The Thirteenth Amendment formally abolished slavery in the US in 1865. But it was not long before the Jim Crow Laws of 1890 introduced extensive racial segregation. It would then take another 75 years before the civil rights movement brought down the legal scaffoldings of racial segregation.

The anthropologist Gillian Cowlishaw (1999) argues that the colonisers of Australia had to rationalise away the conflict between their appropriation of indigenous land and the liberty principle that decreed that 'all fellow humans are equal'. To this end, Cowlishaw concludes, they manufactured a hierarchy of social categories that established the idea of a *biological disparity* between the white immigrants and First Nations peoples of Australia.[35] Nicholas Dirks (2001) concludes that the British colonisation of India was likewise 'built on fabrication, colonial history imputed barbarism to justify, even ennoble, imperial ambition' (Dirks, 2001: 133).[36]

Dirk's observation resonates with the concept of 'White Man's Burden' to which the Harvard economist, Joseph Schumpeter (1883–1950), drew our attention when he criticised the philosophical outlook of notable economist Alfred Marshall (1842–1924): 'He [Alfred Marshall] complacently carried the flag of justice and did not question the validity of the compromise that had been struck, by means of the White Man's Burden, between a creed of utilitarian righteousness and the inheritance of the Great Mogul' (Schumpeter, 1966: 103).

Celia Ridgeway's presidential address to the American Sociological Association in December 2013 discusses the impact of 'cultural-status beliefs'.[37] Citing Charles Tilly's (1998) proposition that 'inequality based purely on organisational control over resources is inherently unstable', she adds that 'To persist, that is, for inequality to become a durable inequality, control over resources and power has to be consolidated with a categorical difference between people such as race, gender or life style' (Ridgeway, 2013: 3). Explaining why consolidation of difference stabilises inequality she says: 'It does so because it transforms situational control over resources and power into a status difference between "types" of people that are evaluatively ranked in terms of how diffusely "better" they are' (Ridgeway, 2013: 3).

The long shadow of slavery

The racist legacy of slavery still casts its dark shadow over the US. But for American capitalism, it has been something of a 'horn of plenty'. The poorest of the US workers are its prison-inmate population, a disproportional number of whom are African American. While the total population of the US represents a mere 5 per cent of the world's total population, it has as many as 25 per cent of the world's prison population in its jails (Bump, 2015). And while a tiny number of inmates are fortunate enough to work (as very cheap labour) for quality Information Technology (IT) companies, the vast majority of them are rented out for the day, either to factory owners or to farmers (while receiving pittance pay) working in jobs that provide no chance whatsoever to acquire sound vocational skills that could keep them safely out of poverty once they are out of prison.[38]

An article that was published in *The Guardian* on 7 July 2012, is headed thus: 'How US prison labour pads corporate profits at taxpayers' expense'. Its author, Sadhbh Walshe, cites an inmate saying:

> 'Currently, we are forced to work in the blazing sun for eight hours. We run out of water several times a day. We run out of sunscreen several times a day. They don't check medical background or age before they pull women for these jobs. Many of us cannot do it! If we stop working and sit down on the bus or even just take unauthorised break, we get a major ticket which takes away our "good time"'. (Walshe, 2012)[39]

Walshe also tells us that the inmates are woken between 2:30 and 3:00am, fed at 4:00am, but don't start their working day until 4 hours later at 8:00am, when they are taken out of the jail for an 8-hour working day.

In August 2018 America's prisoners did what any effective trade union would have done long ago. In an article titled 'US inmates stage nationwide strike over "modern slavery"', *The Guardian*'s chief reporter in the US, Ed Pilkington, wrote:

> One of the most passionately held demands is an immediate end to imposed labor in return for paltry wages, a widespread practice in US prisons that the strike organisers call a modern form of slavery. More than 800,000 prisoners are daily put to work, in some states compulsorily, in roles such as cleaning, cooking and lawn mowing. (Pilkington, 2018b)

On 19 July 2018, Guardian journalist Edward Helmore reported that over 400,000 people worked in servitude in the US. Among them are victims of sex trafficking. Helmore also reports that according to one of Australia's major business owners, Andrew Forrest, who conscientiously constructed the Global Slavery Index in 2018, the global number of people working in modern slavery conditions was at that time 40.3 million. Andrew Forrest has been urging the world's governments to follow the example of Britain's 2015 Modern Slavery Act.[40] This Act demands that heads of companies safeguard against having forced labour involved in any of their supply chains.

Through the lens of feminist scholarship

Feminist scholarship has shed invaluable light on the methodological limits of Economic Science. I am referring to both feminist economists and to scholars writing from within other social science disciplines. A core element of this scholarship is the concept of 'gender'. The virtue of this concept lies in it alerting us to the fact that men and women are seen as different, not merely in biological terms, but also with reference to their personhood, their perceived capabilities and personal interests. This perception, feminists have cogently argued, is a socially constructed entity, whereas sex is a biological datum.

False beliefs about what sets women apart from men as persons still exist. The crux of the social construction of gender is that females lack some socially valuable 'masculine' traits, while having their own unique array of traits. This however is not the whole story. In addition, dualistic gender notions also involve cultural suppositions around the idea that male traits are endowed with superior status in all matters in the public domain, a fair bit of paid work included.

For instance, Carole Pateman (1990, 1997), Antonella Piccio (1992) and Iris Young (1989, 1997) highlight the crucial impact of the dichotomy that has been wrought between the private, family sphere and the public domain on the scope women have for civic participation. Young analyses the philosophical essence of the concept of 'virtuous citizenship', arguing that the prevailing concept of citizenship is exclusive by its very nature. It excludes not only women, but also all socially marginalised groups. For her, the culprit is the notion of a 'universal-citizenship' that presupposes the existence of a 'general point of view' that adequately represents the citizenry as a whole. In fact, the socially privileged, Young argues, have a disproportionate influence on this point of view because it tends to be dominated by the culture, social outlook and general perspective of the socially privileged themselves.

The feminist-economics scholarship began gathering pace in the early 1990s. In her 1991 article, 'The unproductive housewife: her evolution in nineteenth century economic thought', Nancy Folbre argues that the poor value that is awarded to a woman's work, whether at her home or in the marketplace, is a legacy that the 19th century has bequeathed to economics. Similarly, on page 5 of their 1993 book, *Beyond Economic Man*, Marian Ferber and Julie Nelson observe, 'even today, women and families remain strangely absent from many "general" discussions of economic matters'. Marilyn Waring's 1999 *Counting for Nothing: What Men Value and What Women are Worth*, placed sharp critical focus on the way that economics and our social culture undervalue the economic contribution of women.

Could more be lying beneath this description of the divide between male and female personhood? In reality, the notion of 'manliness' that underpins the gender divide harbours far more than simply an alleged difference between men and women. The manliness concept also excludes a range of non-privileged social groups, including great numbers of heterosexual men who do not conform to the 'manly' stereotype. In reality, of course, manliness is not an actual portrait of a male. Rather, it is an idealised image that contains specific social values that, as Young points out, are held by the culturally dominant group. When this yardstick is applied to real individual people many are rendered deficient in terms of the putative ideal. In the labour market, this phenomenon takes on its own acuteness.

The literature on bullying at the workplace, that I discuss at some length in Chapter 11, notes instances of unfair treatment of individuals who simply do not fit the standard mould. Among them are 'effeminate' (heterosexual) men and 'not-feminine-enough' (heterosexual) women. In more general terms, free spirits 'who choose to do it their own way' are not so readily accepted; non-conformity takes its toll, however subtly.

Feminist economists have brought to our attention some analytical features of the discipline of Economics, in particular the manner in which woman's work is undervalued (whether at her own home or in the job market). The economic welfare of women rarely, if ever, appeared in published academic research prior to the era when there was a quantum shift in the number of female economists. Consequently, the economic conditions under which women usually work have received major academic attention only in the last few decades, mostly in research by female scholars.

For instance, Blau and Ferber (1987), Goldin (1992), Ferber and Nelson (1993), to mention but a few, have all drawn our attention to the disadvantaged position of women in the labour market. Ferber and Nelson (1993) also draw attention to the impact of a pivotal component of Economic Theory – the axiomatic assumption that every single member of a society enjoys absolutely free choice in all matters affecting their economic welfare, and that the only constraint under which they operate is the size of their household's income. This assumption, the authors argue, ignores the fact that women who depend on their spouse's income often don't have absolute freedom of choice. Historically, tight-fisted male breadwinners and cultural predicates have combined to restrict both women's paid-work options and their economic options. A significant change has been occurring in the last few decades, but significant pockets of such dependence remain firmly entrenched in the social order.

The assumption of a universal scope for free choice is only one of a whole range of analytical factors that can render research results biased. Major among those additional factors is the emphasis on an amorphous individual who is stripped of all aspects of social affiliation, and taken out of their concrete historical context.

In addition, historical legacy is always present – no epoch is completely free of elements that are generally believed to belong to a bygone era. The combined effect of history and the features of social affiliation, whether race or gender, tend to systematically endow different individuals with different opportunities and scope for choice.

Folbre (1991) reminds us that both Adam Smith (1776) and Alfred Marshall (1890) explicitly posited that women's labour is 'unproductive'.

The perspectives of Adam Smith and Marshall on the value of women's home production value are still with us – women's contribution to society's economic welfare through home production remains altogether unacknowledged. The Gross National Product (GNP), the conventional measure of society's collective level of economic welfare, counts only things that money can buy. Consequently, the full-time daily task of running the home economy is awarded a value of zero in the national account. But, oddly, as is well known, when the home worker's work is contracted out to a commercial entity, the GNP suddenly gets bigger. Feminists note that this practice underscores the fact that women's work at home is taken entirely for granted.

Discrimination has also been shown to have a negative impact on emotional and physical health of its victims. For instance, Pavalko et al (2003) examined a large US longitudinal data set on women's emotional and physical health.[41] They found that the ultimate negative impact on physical health, that is generated by the negative emotional impact of discrimination, ends up being far greater than the emotional trigger itself. They found that while the emotional impact of discrimination ultimately subsides, its impact on physical health is significantly durable.

PART IV

Beyond the measuring rod of money

10

Looking at paid work outside the lens of economics

Introduction

Work has a major impact on our life. It not only takes up a large part of our wakeful hours, but the literature suggests that it also has a major role in shaping our emotional and physical wellbeing. Since jobs are not all alike, their impact on different individuals varies a great deal. It is a daily grind for the many who find themselves employed in tedious jobs that make limited use of their potential as resourceful, thinking human beings, capable of problem solving and initiative-taking. On the other hand, there is a significant number of other workers for whom work is a source of personal fulfilment and pride. Still, even when the tasks are very tedious, gainful employment can increase one's sense of self-reliance and social belonging. Barry Schwartz's 2015 book, *Why We Work*, opens our eyes to the deeply rewarding aspects of even the lowliest of jobs, provided they allow scope for genuine human interaction. Even Studs Terkel, who documented the tedious nature of many jobs, noted that while the attainment of the means to get the things that money can buy is essential, it is clearly not the only function of paid work. As he observed, workers 'have a meaning to their work well over and beyond the reward of the paycheque' (Terkel, 1974: xi). But, although gainful employment per se makes a positive contribution to one's overall mental wellbeing, this positive potential contribution can be partially or wholly undone in workplaces that generate high levels of stress.

The non-monetary value of paid work is also evident in the plight of the unemployed. Social psychology, sociology and cultural studies scholarship, along with medical studies of mental health, provide evidence of the negative consequences of unemployment on people's emotional and physical health. The literature indicates that this applies equally to all people, regardless of wage levels and across diverse demographics. In addition to the academic research carried out by sociologists, psychologists and industrial relations academics, we also have first-person accounts gathered by writers who had interviewed the unemployed.

Those interviews show that the impact of joblessness is often deeply emotional, going beyond the toll inflicted by material deprivation. This has been seen even in countries where unemployment benefits are set at generous levels, as in Scandinavia.[1] The insights offered by these studies expose the inadequacy of the intellectual perspective modern economics applies to paid work, with its singular focus on the paycheque.[2]

For a long-time, major health problems have been traced back to individual lifestyle and material poverty. As for the stress levels that prevail at the workplace, the common view had been that emotional stress is at its highest at the very top ranks of the business enterprise, where decisions are made under substantial conditions of uncertainty. However, Sir Michael Marmot has turned the tables on this belief.[3]

The social conditions of health

Sir Michael Marmot has played a seminal role in bringing about a radically new perspective on the vexed issue of poor individual health. The role of material factors, such as the contribution of genetic background, lifestyle and dietary habits, cannot be denied. Nonetheless, in numerous empirical studies, social structures at the workplace have emerged as the major contributor to stress and, consequently, to serious physical health problems.

The pioneering work of Marmot and his co-researchers was subsequently followed by a significant amount of research into 'the social determinants of health'.[4] Marmot and his co-researchers uncovered the existence of a systematic relationship between the position of the individual in the social hierarchy at the workplace (or what they refer to as the 'social gradient'), and the incidence of serious diseases such as diabetes and coronary heart illness (Marmot et al, 1984; Marmot and Brunner, 2005).[5] They found that the incidence of serious diseases steadily increases as we go down (not up) the workplace job ladder.

The important role of social and economic status of the individual's state of health, is described by Marmot thus:

> Measures of social and economic status, including occupation, are extremely powerful predictors of premature heart disease. Employment grade proved, on its own, to be more powerful than the combination of classic risk factors including smoking, serum cholesterol, and blood pressure, in a follow up of 17,000 British civil servants. (Marmot and Wilkinson, 2006: 19)

Marmot stresses that this statistical pattern recurs in many countries that are culturally and economically very diverse.[6] For instance, when asked about it, the Swedes were certain that this association could not possibly be found in their country's statistics because of their generous welfare system and overall egalitarian ethos. They were wrong – to their own surprise, research revealed otherwise.

The specific design of the job and the organisational structure at the workplace have emerged as very important determinants of physical wellbeing. Individuals who lack control at the workplace and have little variety in their work tasks, tend to end up with continuous deterioration in their psychological wellbeing; their stress levels rise systematically and ultimately undermine their physical wellbeing as well. In their 2006 publication, Marmot and Wilkinson cite a study that was undertaken by the academic economists Martin Conyon and Richard Freeman in 2001. Conyon and Freeman's study concludes that when the workplace has a workers' participation in management program, the level of productivity of the enterprise rises. Marmot notes that through their increased sense of control at the workplace (that results from participating in management decision-making) the workers are also likely to enjoy positive health effects.

Marmot and his coresearchers also explain to their reader the biological paths that underlie the frequent association between the individual's position in the workplace's social ladder and their state of physical health. Specifically, they explain the biological pathways that link stress with chronic illnesses such diabetes and coronary heart diseases also in the chapter written by Marmot and Brunner, in the Marmot and Wilkinson 2006 publication).[7]

The 1978 British Whitehall studies and the following ones have provided a wealth of occupational detail, pay levels, nature of job tasks, the extent of individual control over job tasks and also a quite detailed set of data on the health profile of the individual employee (including matters such as diet, weight and physical exercise regimes). The health profile includes all the conventionally recognised stress factors; and yet, the conditions of paid work emerged as major influential factors. Specifically, the studies found that lack of control at the workplace and absence of task variety are the most substantial stress generators. In the authors' words:

> In general, having a job is better for health than having no job.[8] But the social organization of work, management styles and social relationships in the workplace all matter for health. Evidence shows that stress at work plays an important role in contributing to the large social status differences in health, sickness absence and premature death. Several European workplace studies show that health suffers when people have little opportunity to use their skills and low decision-making authority. (Marmot and Wilkinson, 2005: 19)

Paid work as a social institution

Historically, the psychological literature on the significance of paid work had been largely driven by the attempt to understand the plight of the unemployed during the economic depression era of the late 1920s and

1930s. A leading example of that intellectual quest is the work that Marie Jahoda, Paul Lazarsfeld and Hans Zeisler (1971) published in German, in 1932.[9] That book described in great detail the predicament of the workers of Austria's industrial district of Marienthal where mass unemployment kept going with no end in sight. That book centres on the psychological impact of joblessness.

Jahoda and her co-authors emphasise that a loss of a sense of self-worth was evident among the unemployed. They argue that the psychological impact of job loss could be explained only in part by the psychological consequences of financial stress alone. They propose that activities and social interaction that nowadays take place within the walls of the workplace serve many of the psychological needs that in the pre-industrial era were satisfied by the communal village and the Church (Mosque, Temple or Synagogue).

Along the same lines, Marie Jahoda writes in her 1982 publication that in the modern advanced industrial societies, paid work must be understood not only as serving a vital economic function, but also as being a major social institution. She identifies two major functions of paid employment: 'manifest' and 'latent'. The manifest function is the provision of financial rewards, while the latent function of paid work is the provision of a social institution (Jahoda, 1982: 59).

As academic discourse would have it, the emphasis on the environmental factors in the work of Jahoda (1932, 1981, 1982) has invited disagreement.[10] What has ensued has parallels in the intellectual conversations in other social science disciplines. Those conversations boil down to the question of 'nature vs nurture'. This question is usually presented thus: should we see the misery of the unemployed primarily as a consequence of a personal failure to seize opportunities, or are the true villains in this case the systemic factors that lie well beyond the control of individuals?

Depending on their personal philosophical outlook, some scholars lean towards 'nature' (personal agency that depends on the individual's personality) as the dominant factor, while others are inclined towards 'nurture' (namely, the systemic factors that operate in economic and social environments). Clearly, Jahoda's perspective places the major blame at the doorstep of systemic factors. D. M. Fryer's 1986 critique of Jahoda's analysis stresses the role of personal agency as the major determinant of the psychological consequences of joblessness. In his 1987 book, Peter Warr describes those who blame the unemployed for their plight as taking a 'person-centred' approach, as opposed to a 'situation-centred' approach. Warr himself sides with the 'situation-centred' approach, identifying the state of the economy and the labour market as the crucial root causes of psychological hardship.

Importantly, however, some writers do not see these personality traits as fixed. They suggest that jobs that allow workers more autonomy strengthen their self-confidence, along with their capacity to weather the unemployment storm (for example, O'Brien, 1986). When workers lose control over the conditions under which they work, they end up feeling that they have little control over their broader life, beyond their paid job.

Some people cope fairly well in stressful work environments and can emerge from job-loss experiences relatively unscathed. But for those with less self-confidence, labour market upheavals can be the start of a destructive feedback loop. Members of the first cohort are presumably more likely to receive positive feedback when interviewed for a job, because it is easier for them to project a positive disposition. They have natural advantages in the job interview environment, which rewards their personality traits. Negative feedback effects, on the other hand, are more likely to keep undermining concept of self in those who lack self-confidence.

Unemployment and individual health

The rise in unemployment levels since the late 1970s has prompted renewed research into the impact of unemployment on the emotional and physical health of the unemployed. Epidemiology and public health scholar Mel Bartley's 1994 study surveys the crop of literature that directly examines the link between unemployment and ill health between 1987 and 1994. Bartley concludes that the loss of purchasing power is not the sole root of ill health. Like other observers, she too notes that despite their very generous level of unemployment benefits, the Nordic countries display the same pattern of ill-health consequences among unemployed people who had been healthy prior to their loss of job.[11]

It turns out that the unemployed face higher risk of not only ill health, but also the risk of premature mortality. Partners and spouses of the unemployed are also affected. Bartley stresses that these patterns are discerned not only in British data, but also in Danish and Finnish data. William Darity Jr (2003) reaches the same conclusions regarding the impact of unemployment on the wellbeing of African Americans.

Mel Bartley draws the following conclusion from the studies she surveyed. She stresses that if we were to more comprehensively understand the nature of the impact of unemployment on the health of individuals, we need to consider the following pathways: (i) the contribution of relative poverty, (ii) the consequences of the social isolation that emerges when the gainful job is gone, including the erosion of positive self-image, (iii) health related behaviour associated with affiliation with certain type of 'subcultures' and (iv) the impact that a given spell unemployment has on subsequent employment patterns.

Jonathan Fan et al (2018) offer us a more recent survey of academic literature that interrogates the impact of paid work and unemployment on emotional and physical wellbeing. They conclude that unemployment increases a persons' risk of having negative health outcomes. And while a return to work attenuates this risk, it does not eliminate it altogether. They also find that the overall state of a nation's macroeconomy tends to affect wellbeing of individuals within the country.

Thus far, we have encountered only studies that essentially posit that any job is better than no job. However, Peter Butterworth et al's 2011 study exposes a more complex relationship between employment and individual health. The analytical results of their study suggest that a person's experience of unemployment will be uniformly bad, with one notable exception. Those in jobs the authors term as 'lousy' are so bad, that for them unemployment presents the lesser threat to their health and wellbeing. In fact, their health, their study concludes, had benefited from being made jobless.

Thomas Barnay's 2016 study reviews European economic literature on the impact that gainful employment has on emotional and physical wellbeing. He concludes that 'Being employed with appropriate working conditions plays a protective role on physical health and psychiatric disorders. By contrast, non-employment and retirement are generally worse for mental health than employment, and overemployment has a negative effect on health' (Barnay, 2016: 693).

Barnay also notes that although economists had been rightly concerned about analytical hurdles that make it hard to separate cause and effect on this matter, they have now become more confident that indeed, overwhelmingly, quantitative analysis does support the proposition that unemployment has negative health consequences.

Power over others

Introduction

Philosophers have long been grappling with the root causes of the inequality of power, the patterns with which power is exercised and its impact on the subordinate. Some writers accept the prevailing exercise of power as an essential state of affairs; they also tend to see it in largely benign terms. Others strongly disagree. This debate is rife in the scholarly literature. But in the community at large there is little questioning of the manner in which power is used, whether within the society at large or at the workplace.

Social structures, the power structure at the workplace included, are largely inherited from bygone eras. Yet, the general public accepts the power structure that governs the standard workplace as if it were a quite modern system that is vital to a well-functioning economy. However, as David Montgomery notes in his 1993 book, substantial vestiges of the pre-industrial era 'Master and Servant' laws remain enshrined within the US legal frameworks that still guide judicial decisions regarding work disputes. Culturally, if not strictly legally, this is likely to be the case in other countries as well.[1]

This is ironic. Particularly so, since many scholars are not at all convinced that the manner in which power structures nowadays operate in most workplaces is paramount to the enterprise's profit bottom line.[2] In the standard workplace, the owners of the capital are those who own the rights over the design of job tasks, selection of technology and the pace of work and much more. In other words, the employing business has the absolute prerogative over the whole gamut of demands that are made on the workers' body and soul throughout their entire working day, day by day and year by year. But, as Michael Marmot points out in his 2015 book, the sheer hierarchical structure of the workplace has an immeasurable impact on the wellbeing of employees.

Philosophical discourse on the inequality of power

The answers regarding the root causes and the impact of the vast inequality of power are far from presenting a consensus. On the one end of the spectrum, are writers who argue that power is essential to the social good, and that normally it is not abused, but rather, it is dutifully placed at the service of both the society at large and the immediate subordinates.

However, other writers argue that though a degree of delegation of power is essential to any well-functioning society, in reality power is frequently bestowed by wealth and privilege, and is often used to advance the aims of the power-holders themselves. The proponents of the latter view argue that at times the compliance of the subordinates is attained by a subtle manipulation of their values, while at other times, it is exacted by either the promise of a reward or by a threat of punishment.

For Thomas Hobbes (1588–1679) the delegation of power to the political ruler is essential because in its absence, social havoc would be wreaked by the unfortunate nature of humans. Jean-Jacques Rousseau (1712–1778) on the other hand, saw humans as fundamentally a cooperating species. Hobbs and Rousseau both justified the very strong state, but with a difference. For Rousseau, living in a different century and in a different country, the very strong state was to be installed by a representative democracy. Not so for Hobbs.

About a century later, Max Weber (1864–1920) described the power that is vested in the range of hierarchical social systems, the state among them, as essential but coming at a price. The price is the progressive spread of bureaucratic systems that are driven by the goal of attaining 'efficiency'. The flip side of such systems is that, increasingly, the individual feels trapped within them. This, in a nutshell, is Max Weber's 'iron cage' concept.

By the 20th century, the highly influential American sociologist Talcott Parsons (1902–1979) put forward a far more benign view of power.[3] For Parsons, power is a collective resource that is ordinarily employed in the service of positive social functions. The assignment of power to particular individuals, Parsons contained, is driven by both the interest of the organisation and the society at large and not by the personal interests of the power holders. Parsons saw 'evolutionary' change as the ideal mode of a country's historical course, and somehow allowed himself to conclude that the US has already reached that promised land. Parsons's notion of 'structural functionalism', and his general socio-political perspective, had dominated the sociological scholarship in the US and beyond till the late 1970s. A more limited residue of Parsons's legacy is still present in mainstream sociological thought and among management scholars, particularly through the writings of the management scholar, Alfred Chandler, who was truly taken by Parsons's analytical perspective. For Chandler, hierarchical management is not only essential, but also overall rational and efficient.

Dissenters, however, have a quite different perspective. They also strongly reject the proposition that the US power structure is either benign or pluralist. Major among Parsons's critics was C. Wright Mills (1916–1962). Mills's 1956 book, *The Power Elite*, sees power primarily as a resource that is owned by one group that uses it against another, an unprivileged subordinate group. For Mills, power is ingrained in privilege. He also argues that it is wielded not only knowingly, but also unknowingly.

Parsons's benign view of power has also been rejected by Steven Lukes (1974, 1996, 2005) who describes himself as a radical, as well as by the highly independent thinker, John Kenneth Galbraith (1908–2006). In his 1983 book, *The Anatomy of Power*, Galbraith shares a number of Mills's observations on the power elite while citing him approvingly. Galbraith's and Lukes's analyses share a number of major ideas (although neither cites the other). The core ideas of all three writers are also shared by many of the other critics of Parsons's concept of power.

In his 1974 book *Power: A Radical View*, Lukes identifies three different approaches to the analysis of the domain of power. Each consecutive approach further widens his proposed concept of power. He labels them as 'one-level', 'two-levels' and 'three-levels' power concepts. As Lukes defines it, the 'first level' power concept represents a view that is most clearly articulated by a leading exponent of Parsons's perspective, Robert Dahl (1961). Dahl's view equates power with the winning of a contest over which of a whole set of proposed decisions ultimately prevails. Lukes argues that a true notion of power must also be wide enough to include, not only all visible incidences where decisions of the powerful prevail as Dahl posits, but also the incidences in which the powerful has the capacity to shape the decision agenda itself. Here, Lukes cites Bachrach and Baratz (1970) approvingly, but also emphasises a need for an even wider concept of power. He argues that the concept of power must also recognise the fact that often, the powerful (groups or individuals) influence the preferences and shape some of the values of the subordinates, so as to benefit the power holder's own goals.

In addition, Lukes notes that subordinates can even be talked into voting or acting against their own interests.[4] He adds, and I tend to agree, that this kind of power exists even when neither the power holder, nor the person on the receiving end, are actually aware of the power's presence. It simply comes about as a natural consequence of the privileged status of the power holder.

Lukes suggests that when the subordinates are not aware that their views and values have been influenced by the actions of, and views expressed by, the power holder, power takes on a 'latent' form. In response to Robert Dahl, who had argued that latency of power should not be discussed because it is not empirically measurable, Lukes first argued that even so, it must be addressed. Subsequently, by the time he published the revised edition of his *Power: A Radical View* book in 2005, he reports that, in any event, he now does have a way of empirically exposing the presence of a latent power.

Lukes's notion of latent power is echoed by John Kenneth Galbraith's notion of 'conditioned' power. In his 1984 book, *The Anatomy of Power*, Galbraith introduces three specific forms by which power is being exercised.

These are: 'condign', 'compensatory' and 'conditioned'. The first attains compliance through a threat and punishment, whereas the second attains the same result by means of promised rewards for compliance. In the third form, the exercise of power succeeds by subtly changing the beliefs of the subordinates. This is achieved through persuasion and education. The subordinates, Galbraith emphasises, remain fundamentally unaware that power had been wielded over them.[5] He also adds that nowadays, this third form of power exercise is very common. Clearly, Galbraith's notion of 'conditioned power' echoes Lukes's concept of 'latent' power. By extension, they both disagree with the essence of Parsons's and Dahl's outlook on power.

Lukes and others contend that neither is power always used to achieve ulterior aims – power is also sought as an end in itself. Those who reject the idea that some power holders seek power as an end in itself, maintain that generally speaking, human beings are rational seekers of goals they attempt to reach.

James A. Caporaso and David P. Levine's 1992 book addresses the question of power within the intellectual framework of political economy. In the same vein as Galbraith's and Lukes's concepts of 'conditioned' and 'latent' powers, Caporaso and Levine note that individuals and groups that are on the receiving end of power-wielding are not necessarily aware that power has been wielded over them. This, they propose, is because power wielders often use inducements and persuasion in a manner that the persuaded remain unaware that the decisions they make are not always in their own personal best interest. And like Lukes and Stephen Waring (1991), Caporaso and Levine emphasise the significant role that is also played by differing social value systems.

Yet another poignant insight into the scope and the nature of the power that can be wielded over a subordinate is provided by the notable prison experiment that professor of psychology Philip G. Zimbardo ran at Stanford University in 1971. Recently, Zimbardo told us what he has learnt from that experiment and the various reports he has subsequently written about the prison system. In 2011 Zimbardo wrote: 'I became more aware of power in our lives. I became more aware of the power I have as teacher. … Indeed, the existence of power takes on so many variegated forms that sometimes it is only through its abrupt impact that we become aware of its presence' (Zimbardo, 2011: 47).

The experience of power at the coalface

Uneven power is pervasive in our society, but for most people the place where the inequality of power is experienced most acutely is the workplace. Reg Theriault grew up in a family of itinerant fruit packers. His mother was determined that her children wouldn't miss a day of schooling, except when they were on the road to the next farm. After serving in the army during the Second World War, Theriault studied at the University of Berkeley in California, majoring in English. And although it was suggested to him to become an academic he preferred to return to his blue-collar roots and became a longshoreman.

Theriault published three books, one of which is his seminal 1997 book, *How to Tell When You Are Tired: A Brief Examination of Work*. In that book he describes a scene at a small seafood packing plant in the San Francisco wharf thus:

> The women were mostly Pacific Islanders, and I had to marvel at how good they were at what they were doing. Their hands flashed back and forth so fast I could barely follow them as they separated the crabmeat from the shell. All the while they worked they burst forth with bits of conversation punctuated with giggles, cries, shrieks and laughter. As I watched, one of the owners of the small plant pushed a four-wheel cart loaded with full boxes through two swinging doors. He dumped more crab on the belt and moved it in front of the women. 'Hey!' he said severely in a loud voice. 'Less talk. Let's see more work around here and less noise'. He waited a while before he left, and the women, their smiles gone, settled into a dull, silent, slow routine. (Theriault, 1997: 169)

Did the owner really act in the best interests of his business? The scene described by Theriault does not seem to portray a result of a rationally calculated tactic to enhance productivity. The owner's motives seem more likely to have been driven by a desire to assert power; possibly, also by deep-seated gender and racial prejudices.

In the following account, Theriault describes what is often expected from people when they are granted oversight responsibilities at the workplace thus:

> When a man is hired as a boss, it is made clear to him by the management, by a superintend usually, what his function is: he is to supervise production, make sure that the work is done and that it gets done right. Along with these orders he is told that there is room for improvement. I have yet to hear of a boss being hired who was not told just that. Maybe the boss he replaced was promoted to a position of greater responsibility, meaning that he was doing his job at least okay. But the new man is invariably told there is room for improvement. (Theriault, 1997: 106)

This observation suggests that there exists a systemic element that propels the use of power from the very top managerial echelon down, through the hierarchical levels, all the way to the shop floor. When a new supervisor arrives, this process is enhanced. The newcomer, having been told that 'there is room for improvement' inevitably embarks on assertion of power, possibly because of feeling pressure to prove himself to his higher-ups. It might even go against the grain of his own personality, yet he might have little scope for manoeuvring, as far as the prospects of his continued employment and future promotion are concerned.

Nonetheless, the axiomatic assumption that the production system is always in slack might at some point rebound or, at the very least, fail to yield the expected result. One wonders, might a more rational decision, that is far more closely tailored to the case at hand, be better placed to yield positive results for the management? This question arises, particularly because within bounds, workers could limit the extent to which the management has its way. But to succeed, they would need to be both essential to their employer and act collectively. Here is another account from Theriault's book:

> In that telephone company in Illinois, where everyone was quitting early, obviously, the foreman knew all about it. There were bosses all over the floor, of course, and when the afternoon came and all the workers started cleaning up their workbenches, those bosses knew what to do. They made themselves scarce. (Theriault, 1997: 106)

This is the kind of power that Anthony Giddens seems to have in mind, when he discusses his concept of 'human agency' in his 1979 book, *Central Problems in Social Theory: Action, Structure and Contradiction in Social Analysis*. The workers who left early had also ensured that the set quota of production was reached well before the end of their working day. This is power that is available to a group of individuals who are very skilled at their job. Consequently, they managed to exact the tacit consent of their immediate overseers.

As for an individual worker, only a very small minority of employees have the bargaining power that might allow them to have their demands met when they confront the employer on their own. Their individual threat to quit their job if their demands are not met, would be credible only when they possess highly valuable skills that happen to be quite scarce. In the absence of these conditions, they are unlikely to succeed.

An exception to this pattern can occur when workers' anger at the workplace builds up and reaches a boiling point. This proposition is clearly supported by the case that is described by Stephen Waring in his 1991 book, *Taylorism Transformed: Scientific Management Theory Since 1945*. The events he describes took place at a US General Motors plant in Lordstown, Ohio between 1970 and 1972. The group of workers at the centre of the events,

Waring tells us, defied their own trade union leaders and went ahead to stage an industrial strike. He writes:

> The plant was new, created to make the compact Vega and to compete with imported small cars. GM engineers had designed very specialised tasks; all line jobs could be learned in half an hour and mastered in half a day. The workers, who averaged less than twenty-five years old, and included many Vietnam veterans, had been specially screened to exclude troublemakers, and both wage and benefits were as high as [those given to] any autoworkers in the world. Yet high pay was not enough, particularly for young workers. They refused to tolerate mindless jobs and militaristic authority and consequently withdrew their efficiency. On some Mondays, the line at Lordstown had to be shut down because too many workers stayed home. And when they showed up, they worked slowly, refused to obey orders, and sabotaged thousands of cars. They also defied their leaders and engaged in wildcat strikes. Management made matters worse by introducing a major speedup that tried to accelerate production from one car a minute to one every thirty-six seconds, a rate at least 40 per cent [higher] than [in] any other auto plant. In response, workers sped up their sabotage, and subsequently 97 per cent of the rank-and-file voted for a strike. (Waring, 1991: 145–146)

What we see here is a delicate balance that can be easily tipped over by switching from a state of obedience to an outright revolt. To maintain a state of obedience, the circumstances must have the right chemistry. With the wrong chemistry, sufficient cohesion and a strong determination on the part of the vast majority of the workers not to put up with their work conditions, the stage is set for a Lordstown type of a showdown.

General Motors management must have been taken by complete surprise, given the great care it took when it selected its workers and the relatively generous pay it had offered to those who were selected for the job. Lordstown's well-noted episode should not be seen as 'sui generis'.[6] Indeed, it can be readily explained in terms of Goffman's (1975) dualism of 'front and back regions' of social conduct. In Gofman's concept the front region is a mere façade that stages social conformity.[7] In terms of this dualism concept, it is not at all surprising that the Lordstown management was at first lulled into false confidence by the visible façade of obedience.

Lordstown and Goffman's conformity façade brought to my mind Tera Hunter's (1997) historical account of the years that immediately followed the abolition of slavery in the US.[8] Hunter tells us that the 'Slave owners voiced both surprise and dismay in recalling the characteristics of runaway slaves. As one of the owners described his two runaway black slaves "the dearest" and "the most petted" slaves were the first to abandon their owners' Hunter (1997: 19). This does not seem to have been an isolated case; Hunter also cites a Savannah politician who said: 'In too many numerous instances those we esteemed most were the first to desert us' (Hunter, 1997: 6).

Yet another factor that comes into play is class prejudice. Class prejudice often affects the views that exist among the higher ranks of the workplace regarding the lower paid, shop floor workers. Some of those in the upper management ranks seem inclined to see shop floor workers as people who have ended up where they are because of a lack of natural aptitudes. The possibility that those workers had been at the mercy of unfavourable economic circumstances tends to be overlooked. Unfortunately, wrong perceptions regarding individuals who work at the shop floor are often accentuated when ethnic or gender prejudices collide with class prejudices.

History offers us poignant examples of such prejudice. For instance, during the First and Second World Wars' labour shortages, the US opened up the workforce to black people and women of all colours, inviting them to take up jobs, including supervisory positions, that generally speaking had hitherto been well out of their reach. Many reports indicate that the management circles were taken by surprise when it transpired that the jobs were performed impeccably. Yet, once the war ended most were sent home.[9]

Steep vs flat power structures

Steep hierarchies are common. Yet we have accounts that suggest that when workers are allowed to participate in important management decisions, both individual health and the business's profits improve. For example, Joel Cutcher-Gershenfeld et al's 2015 book, *Inside the Ford UAW Transformation: Pivotal Events in Valuing Work and Delivering Results*, describes the major transformation that took place at the Ford Motor Company as a result of a partnership between the Ford Company and the United Auto Workers union (UAW) workers. Jobs were enriched, workers gained a genuine sense of dignity and the company's overall performance rose substantially. The same point is stressed by Russell Lansbury in his 2009 memorial lecture for Kingsley Laffer. Lansbury describes the positive consequences that took place in a number of Australian and overseas companies that have allowed their workers to actively participate in major decision-making. Referring to economic inequality and its impact on environmental challenges, Julie Battilana and her co-authors draw a connective thread between democracy in the workplace and meeting the challenges of climate change: 'democratic organizing practices may enable corporations to successfully pursue social and environmental objectives alongside financial ones, which is also important for addressing societal challenges' (Battilana et al, 2022).

Writing in the *Harvard Business Review*, Emma Seppälä and Kim Cameron (2015) observe that 'positive work cultures are more productive. And Steven Billinger and Maciej Workiewicz's 2019 study notes that flat hierarchies are gradually becoming more popular within companies – a welcome development.

Heavy-handed top-down power relationships might exist when the social skills of managers and supervisors are not terribly robust, or when those in charge are simply incapable of trusting their subordinates. In yet other cases, a 'do as I say' culture prevails as an end for itself. For example, Pikulina's quantitative analysis led her to the following conclusion: 'The research shows that nearly 30 per cent of people seek power for its own sake – and not necessarily because they have the best interest of their organization, or the people beneath them, at heart' (Pikulina, 2020). In a joint study with Chloe Tergiman, Pikulina also offers the following observation: 'We further show that valuation of power (i) is higher when individuals directly determine outcomes of others; (ii) depends on how much discretion one has over those outcomes; (iii) is tied to relationships between individuals; and (iv) is likely domain dependent' (Pikulina and Tergiman, 2019). In the obituary for Doug Jukes we read that, when he became the chairman of the professional services of Australia's KPMG, in 2001, 'He started to work on a campaign that would be his most significant legacy to the firm, nationally [in Australia] and globally. He set about changing the corporate culture to acknowledge his strong belief in the importance of people' (*Sydney Morning Herald*, 2009: 18).

The sheer fact that Doug Jukes was thus singled out for high praise seems to suggest that such managers are yet to represent the standard norm of conduct in their cohort. To be able to implement Jukes's perspective, the 'right' personal philosophy would not suffice. As mentioned earlier, managers would also need to have the right social skills as well as a capacity to have a genuine faith in their subordinates.

Having emphasised the crucial role played by personality traits of managers and overseers, I do not wish to create the impression that our natures are alone holding us back. At the root of it all we also have capitalism's class structure and the rights it grants to the bosses.[10] A key player is also the cultural stance of the community at large, particularly with regard to capitalism's inclination to place profit above all else. Our social culture is yet to recognise the stakeholder rights that workers have over the design of their jobs, the pace of work and the health and safety standards of their workplace.

Workplace bullying

Social intolerance of extreme bullying is a relatively new phenomenon. The high incidence of bullying at the workplace tells us that we still have a long way to go, both in Australia and overseas (Nielsen et al, 2018). Employees are bullied not only by overseeing staff, but also by peers; but estimates suggest that the incidence of being bullied by an overseer is twice as large as being bullied by a peer. Men bully more often, but women are also among the perpetrators, bullying primarily other women (Crothers et al, 2009).

Unfortunately, bullying is very insidious. Those who find themselves on the receiving end are often severely affected (Cooper et al, 2004; Tehrani, 2004; Samsone and Samsone, 2015). Tragically, there have also been a number of cases in which employees were driven to the point of taking their own life.

Bullying is not confined to any category of workplaces. In Australia, among the people who were driven to immense despair that led them to suicide are medical students who were bullied by their training medical doctors (Aubusson, 2017a, 2018b), an ambulance driver who was severely bullied by her peers (Wallace, 2008) and a waitress who was tormented by both the boss and her co-workers (Turnbull, 2010).

The death of Chloe Abbott, a 29-year-old Australian medical student in her fourth year, who took her own life on the 9 January 2017, 'was one of several recent suicides by doctors that prompted the Health Minister and the medical profession to act' (Aubusson, 2017a). The scale and the duration of this unfortunate behaviour had reached such a high level in Sydney's Westmead Hospital that the state government stripped its Intensive Care Unit (ICU) of its training accreditation over alleged bullying (Aubusson, 2018a). Barely a week later came the news that 'the prestigious cardiothoracic surgery department of Sydney's Royal Prince Alfred hospital will be barred from training doctors in the following year amid allegations of bullying and dysfunction' (Aubusson, 2018b). Thankfully, these events raised the alarm: the College of Intensive Care and Medicine (CICM) of Australia and New Zealand conducted a survey of its members and of trainee-medical doctors. The survey established that both men and women are bullied, and that doctors from Asian and African countries, whether men or women, are far more likely to be bullied.[11]

Perpetrators routinely justify their aggressive behaviour by saying that they are merely doing their best to 'build-in resilience' in the junior medical doctors (Aubusson, 2017b). By beating them remorselessly into submission? (One is rendered speechless.) Aubusson cites Professor Ian Hickie, Co-Director of Health and Policy at The University of Sydney's Brain and Mind Centre, on that alleged need for 'building resilience' in junior medical doctors. Hickie noted: 'It is this con of individual resilience that is part of the problem. ... We operate on a collegiate system that has been unregulated, but has demonstrably failed to move into the 21st century' (Aubusson, 2017b). Aubusson wrote that 'He drew parallels with the aviation industry that had industrial safeguards in place so that pilots did not fly while fatigued. "Why should doctors treating patients be any different?" he asked' (Aubusson, 2017b).

Medical specialists who misbehave are, after all, only human. They have all grown up within our social culture, a culture abundant with ethnic and gender discrimination. It is also a culture that accepts the hierarchies of power holders with little, if any, questioning. This is not to condone the behaviour of the bullying doctors but, rather, to point out that we, as a society, need to strongly rethink our power structures and the manner in which power is exerted over others in the workplace and beyond.

Drawing on existing academic literature on workplace bullying, Carlo Caponecchia (2008) describes bullying at the workplace as harassment and violence that often has a serious negative impact on the wellbeing of the victims.[12] He nominates organisational structure, specifically the culture of the workplace, as one of the major root causes.

> Solving workplace bullying is not just about weeding out the 'bullies'. Anyone is capable of using bullying behaviour, and unfortunately some workplace cultures promote it. … The person displaying bullying behaviour needs to be seen in the context of their organisation and the demands placed on them: competitiveness and increasing pressures on workers concerning working hours, deadlines and performance all have an impact. (Caponecchia, 2008)

Bullying is also far from being a scarce event in our schools. It takes place even among very young kids. But the truth is that kids can be taught to be either considerate and kind to other kids, or unkind. Parents, of course, have a role to play, but so do our schools. Instead of meting out punishments and scolding the bullying students in their charge, teachers might try to engage the whole class in an open conversation about how it feels to be on the receiving end of bullying. This could be discussed even with 4-year-olds at kindergarten. No teaching strategy guarantees success, but there certainly is no harm in trying (Menesini and Salmivalli, 2017).

The academic research on bullying at the workplace is still in its infancy. Bullying, of course, is anything but new. Rather, it is our social awareness that has thankfully caught up with the ugly face of this global phenomenon.[13] In 1993, Norway and Sweden were the first countries to introduce legislation that targets workplace bullies. A fairly large number of Western countries have since followed suit in one form or another. But of course, a great deal depends on the effectiveness of the legal framework, the attitudes of the courts, general education of the public and the concrete administrative support that is provided by the government of the day (Hoel and Einarsen, 2010).

We also have statistics that allow us to compare the incidence of bullying across countries. But these need to be taken with a grain of salt, because such comparisons are fraught with comparability problems. To begin with, survey questions could be framed in many different ways, and framing can affect the answers.[14] Comparisons across countries are also imperfect because of cultural differences about what is perceived as an inordinate, or full-fledged bullying, behaviour.[15]

Studies investigating the circumstances that are more likely to give rise to bullying behaviour suggest that this disturbing behaviour has a higher chance of flourishing in uncertain and stressful work environments. They note that where the chance of extended job tenure is low, the expected pace of work is very high, the working day is long and the overall organisational climate is not positive. A US study by Cooligan and Higgins (2005), notes that lack of autonomy, role ambiguity, isolation (as distinct from lack of adequate level of autonomy, which also matters), managerial bullying and poor general work climate, are all stressors that lead to bullying and harassment among peers. When the bullying is persistent, the authors note, the risk of psychological and physical disorders is enhanced. Another, a Norwegian study, that covers a number of countries, by Hauge et al (2007), also cites role conflictual and destructive leadership style as stressors that give rise to bullying that affects negatively not only the bully's target, but also bystanders.[16]

In addition, studies that have delved deeply into the bullying that takes place within the workplace have found that where the management turns a blind eye, or simply follows a hands-off policy, the incidence of bullying tends to rise (for example, Cooper et al, 2004). In the same vein, a 2004 study by Patricia Ferris finds that the specific manner in which the firm responds when it is alerted to a bullying case, has a significant impact on the mental wellbeing of the victim. Ferris divides the prevailing organisational responses into three groups: (i) the bully's behaviour is accepted, (ii) the bully's behaviour is, inappropriately, equally attributed to both parties and (iii) the bully's behaviour is deemed harmful and inappropriate. She recommends that prior to lodging a complaint about bullying, the counsellor should discuss with the employee the possible different responses of the employer. Studies have also emphasised the need for employers, trade unions and the labour inspectorates (where they exist as in Sweden) to take a proactive approach to dealing with this vexed issue (Cooper et al, 2004).

In more general terms, workplace culture can have a positive or a negative impact on the incidence on bullying, depending on its quality. But Cooper et al (2004) also stress the positive role that effective state regulation plays in endowing this grave issue with credibility. Indeed, it is often overlooked that history actually shows that valuable government regulation often acts as an agent of positive cultural change.

Unsurprisingly, the race and the ethnic affiliation of targeted employees is also among the factors that tends to enhance the chance of being bullied. In her 2004 study, the psychologist Aileen Alleyne addresses the experience of African American employees. Alleyne cites bullying and scapegoating among the stressors that have a particularly damaging impact on self-esteem, health and also quality of work performance.

Bullying also takes the form of sexual harassment, but often ends up with the predicament of adding insult to injury. For instance, in October 2017, *Vox* published an article written by Tara Golshan headed thus: 'Study finds 75 percent of workplace harassment victims experienced retaliation when they spoke up: what we know about sexual harassment in America' (Golshan, 2017). Golshan notes that this finding was made by the US Equal Employment Commission, the government agency that processes workplace sexual harassment complaints.

Sexual harassment, itself, takes a number of different forms. Some are standard, others are far subtler, but equally unpleasant. The latter form of sexual harassment is a more common predicament among lesbian women (Biaggio, 1997) and also gay men.

The conjunction of workplace stress, the effectiveness of anti-bullying legislation (where it exists), the effectiveness of the method by which the legislation is implemented and the disposition of the general social culture towards bullying, probably explain why studies find a particularly high level of bullying in the US. In contrast, in the Scandinavian countries, the incidence of bullying is much lower. As mentioned earlier, comparisons between countries need to be taken with a grain of salt. However, given what we know about the US and Scandinavia, the observed differences are worth exploring.

Human rights and democracy in the workplace

Article No. 23 of the 1948 Universal Declaration of Human Rights states that 'Everyone has the right to work, to free choice of employment, to just and favourable conditions of work and to protection against unemployment' and that 'Everyone, without any discrimination, has the right to equal pay for equal work'. It adds that 'Everyone who works has the right to just and favourable remuneration ensuring for himself and his family an existence worthy of human dignity, and supplemented, if necessary, by other means of social protection'. The last clause of Article 23 stresses the 'right to form and join trade unions for the protection of his interests'.

Introduction

The concept of human rights has its origins in the centuries-old concepts of 'Natural Law' and 'Natural Rights'. The concept of Natural Law defines inalienable rights that we have independently of any country's laws, beliefs, culture or custom. We have Natural Rights by dint of our own individual humanity. The concept of Natural Law was originally articulated by Aristotle, further developed in Roman times and enriched during the Renaissance and the Enlightenment eras.[1]

The concept of 'Natural Justice' has also contributed to the current concept of 'human rights'. Briefly, it says that we all have the right to be treated fairly and equitably. We are also all equal before the law. According to Thomas Aquinas (1225–1274), the notion of Natural Justice first appeared in the writings of Socrates and Plato. Like the concept of Natural Law, the concept of Natural Justice too was further developed during the Renaissance and the Enlightenment eras.

The 1948 Universal Declaration of Human Rights is itself a legal instrument, with the status of a 'soft' international law. We should note that the 1948 declaration remains a work in progress, and its goals are yet to be fully realised.

As for the concept of democracy, at its core it embodies the principle that, as individuals, we are owed the right to a say on decisions that have a major impact on our wellbeing. The principle of democracy has also been linked to the rights that working people are entitled to, more than a century ago. In the late 19th century it underpinned the demand to have the right to bargain collectively via trade unions. More recently, it is at the heart of the demand that workers should have a far more extensive voice within their workplace. This voice is at its strongest in workplaces in which all the major decisions are determined by the votes of all the employees, one person, one vote. Worker cooperatives have the best chance of reaching this higher standard of democracy.

The application of human rights in the workplace

Under the stewardship of the United Nations, human rights have been formally harnessed to the advocacy of social and economic rights. The United Nations' Universal Declaration of Human Rights (1948) and Human Rights Conventions that followed the 1948 declaration say a great deal about the rights that workers are duly owed. This bold step was subsequently followed by The International Covenant on Economic Social and Cultural Rights (1973), both coming from the office of the UN High Commissioner for Human rights.

The 1948 declaration came in the wake of the devastating experience of the Second World War. Interestingly, the formation of The International Labour Organization (ILO), a major advocate for workers' rights, also followed the end of yet another devastating war, the First World War.

Admittedly, not all countries have ratified the full range of the United Nations' Conventions on Human Rights. It is also true that a great deal depends on the effectiveness of the implementations of these Conventions by the signatory countries. Nonetheless, the declaration of a principle per se provides a basis for both political and cultural change. The 1948 declaration emphasises workers' rights to equality. It targets discrimination against women and minorities, and stresses the importance of equal access to employment opportunities, fair pay and safe and healthy working conditions. It also emphasises the right to form trade unions and bargain collectively, the right to access social security, housing, health care and education, and also the ability to enjoy an adequate standard of living, such as sufficient food and clothing. Evidently, these rights are in even more urgent need of implementation, in the wake of four decades of neoliberal policy.

These rights have been incorporated into international law by treaties such as The International Covenant on Economic, Social and Cultural rights (1966), The European Social Charter (adopted in 1961 and revised in 1996), The African Charter on Human and Peoples' Rights (1979), and The American Convention on Human Rights (signed in 1969; and came into effect in 1979). The 1988 protocol of El Salvador amended The American Convention on Human Rights in an attempt to grant a firm position to the so-called 'second-generation rights'; the latter includes the right to employment, housing, health care, social security and unemployment benefits.[2] A second protocol added to the American Convention on Human Rights is the Protocol to the American Convention on Human Rights to Abolish the Death Penalty (of which the US is not a signatory) which was adopted in 1990, in Asunción, Paraguay.

Following is a thumbnail description of one of these human rights initiatives. The African Charter on Human and Peoples' Rights, also known as the Banjul Charter, was formalised in 1979 and came into effect in 1986. The African Commission on Human and Peoples' Rights is in charge of overseeing and interpreting this charter. This commission was established in 1987, in Banjul, Gambia, where it resides. The charter recognises the right to work (article 15), right to health (article 16) and the right to education (article 17). In 2001, SERAC V Nigeria (2001) declared that the African Charter on Human and Peoples' right also includes the right to housing and food. In addition, it emphasises pay and other work conditions, declaring that 'Every individual shall have the right to work under equitable and satisfactory conditions, and shall receive equal pay for equal work'. This list of human rights declarations, conventions and charters, is not exhaustive, but it nonetheless gives us an effective picture of the impact of the 1948 Universal Declaration of Human Rights.

In 2011, the Office of the United Nations High Commissioner for Human Rights published a report titled Guiding Principles on Business and Human Rights: Implementing the United Nations 'Protect, Respect and Remedy' Framework.

Industrial democracy

In their 1897 book-length contribution, *Industrial Democracy*, Beatrice and Sidney Webb present the idea that a democratic society means much more than just having the universal right of political franchise. The principles of democracy, they argued, do not sit well with the command systems that operate within the walls of the workplace. Democracy, they noted, is founded on the principle that individuals must have a say on policies and institutions that have a major impact on their own and their households' wellbeing.[3] The workplace is clearly one of these institutions because both the level of pay and conditions under which people work have a major impact on their wellbeing. The Webbs maintained that, given the asymmetry of bargaining power between the individual worker and their employer, democratic rights could be secured only through collective bargaining that is carried out by workers' trade unions. Indeed, it was Beatrice Webb who coined the term 'collective-bargaining', and it has remained in use ever since.

Sidney and Beatrice Webb also noted that were citizens to become genuine participants in the democratic political process, they would need to have affordable accommodation and adequate access to sustenance, health care and quality education. They also stressed that wage levels would need to be high enough to meet these needs, and the length of the working day would need to be capped at a maximum of 8 hours. These work conditions are essential, they stressed, if workers were to have the energy and time needed to become genuinely informed citizens of the democratic polity. Clearly, these propositions define a whole array of economic rights.[4]

Beatrice and Sidney Webb were also active and committed social reformers. They founded the London School of Economics in 1895 and the *New Statesman* magazine in 1913. They were also among the early members of the British Fabian Society.

Democracy at the workplace – the rise of the worker cooperative movement

In the early years of the 21st century, we might want to take the notion of workplace democracy a step further. Evidently, we are facing two polar options. We either recover the pre-1980 endeavour to have a far more equal society, or we passively go down the path of late day capitalism. Better still, we might do all the good we can to allow worker cooperatives to flourish.

Worker cooperatives that are owned and managed by the workers themselves have emerged in responses to the excesses of capitalism, and have been in existence since at least 1830 (Pérotin, 2012). In Italy alone, there are more than 25,000 worker cooperatives; there are also roughly 2,000 in Spain, and a similar number in France. Cooperatives have also been growing steadily in South America and Asia.

The cooperatives not only provide support to their owner-operators, they also lend support to each other. Often, a portion of the profits that cooperatives earn goes into a fund that is made available to other cooperatives when they run into economic hardship. Coops also have their own credit unions which provide financial services to members at affordable rates. The web of mutual support also extends to the upkeep of members' skills and knowledge. Umbrella training institutions are often employed by coops to ensure that the professional skills and knowledge of their workforce stays current.[5]

Bologna University professor Vera Negri Zamagni notes that the flourishing cooperative economy of the Emilia Romagna region of Northern Italy dates back to at least the 1850s.[6] Emilia Romagna, with a population of nearly 4.6 million, draws about one third its Gross Domestic Product (GDP) from cooperatives. Those cooperatives range from advanced agricultural production to very advanced high-tech manufacturing.[7]

The Spanish cooperative, Mondragon, was founded in 1956 in Spain's Basque region by the Catholic priest José María Arizmendiarrieta. Mondragon now employs 85,000 people worldwide, all of whom are cooperative members (Pérotin, 2012). Employee members are required to invest about €14,000. That amount is usually deducted gradually from their salary, over 3 to 5 years (Bibby, 2012).[8]

Pierre Laliberté writes that there has been a renewal of interest in cooperatives in the wake of the GFC. He also attributes this renewed interest to the negative impact of neoliberalism on job security and levels of pay (Laliberté, 2013). Identifying growing interest in the idea of introducing democratic practices to the workplace, Laliberté notes that hundreds of worker cooperatives have emerged in the Mercosur common market (Argentina, Brazil, Paraguay and Venezuela) in the wake of the financial crisis that Latin America had experienced in the 1990s.

The right to work

As unemployment levels rose during the early decades of the 20th century, there emerged an emphasis on the right to work; and with it, the demand to implement universal public unemployment benefits. At that time, unemployment benefits were available only to selected segments of the workforce. Harold Laski, the British political theorist, economist and Professor at the London School of Economics and an active politician, voiced these demands clearly and loudly in his academic lectures, public addresses and in his 1925 book, *A Grammar of Politics*. He also reaffirmed the link between the vital prerequisites for having a genuine democratic polity and the right to employment, decent wages and a capped number of hours of work, as well as emphasising our right to have sound occupational health and safety measures at the workplace.

William Beveridge took a major step towards the implementation of Laski's principles in practice. His seminal 1942 Beveridge Report laid down much of the foundations of Britain's post-Second World War social and economic policy.[9] Beveridge placed a major emphasis on full employment, with 3 per cent being the maximal acceptable level. He stressed that full employment plays a critical role in the social welfare program that he outlined in his report. That report also contains a detailed blueprint for a universal public unemployment insurance system.

Social citizenship and the welfare state

Sidney and Beatrice Webb's notion of industrial democracy enlisted the ideal of democracy in the support of the workers' right to engage in collective bargaining on wage and other work conditions. Half a century later, T. H. Marshall enlisted the ideal of democracy in support of the welfare state.[10] The case for the welfare state is at the core of his 'social citizenship' concept. Essentially, this concept argues that citizenship is not merely a right of residence and voting for government, but also a right to be a full-fledged non-marginalised membership in the civic society.[11] Meaningful political and social participation, he stresses, could not possibly be realised when people need to work for long hours while endeavouring to earn income that barely makes ends meet. Marshall argues that when we consider demands that are made by political-, civil- and social rights, the combined claim is to a much wider range of rights; and importantly, those rights include adequate command of economic resources.

Probing the notion of citizenship rights

Most writers, including Marshall, implicitly if not explicitly, treat the notion of citizenship itself as unproblematic. But, as the feminist scholarship stresses, the concept of citizenship is not flawless. For at least three decades now, feminist scholars have been questioning the prevailing concept of citizenship. They have exposed subtle, yet poignant issues which had eluded many depictions of citizenship rights. The common thread that runs through this literature is the role of what (for want of a better term) I would describe as 'indirect discrimination'.

This literature has drawn attention to the far-reaching consequences of a type of discrimination that is experienced by all socially underprivileged groups. Individuals falling into this category are rendered partially invisible and barely audible by the dominant social culture, its value system and its social prism. The result, feminist scholars stress, is a lack of awareness of the specific needs and therefore rights of underprivileged social groups. Anne Phillips's 1999 book, *Which Equalities Matter?* provides a very comprehensive treatment of the implications that political equality has for the distributions of wealth and income.

In a study originally published in 1980, Carole Pateman challenges the very core of the notion of citizenship itself.[12] She sees it as inherently biased in favour of men. Specifically, she argues that the notional separation between the 'private' and the 'public' spheres has a very close link with the 'femininity/masculinity' dichotomy. That is the idea being that masculinity alone (and not femininity) is associated with the notion of citizenship. She stresses that the virtues of the 'good citizen' in the public sphere are fundamentally a replica of the ideal-type of the 'masculine'. Femininity, on the other hand, harnesses the ideal type of a woman to the private home-sphere, both by dint of her caring duties, and because of her putative lack of the personality traits that define the 'virtuous public citizen'. This, she stresses, limits the scope for the full inclusion of women as individual citizens.

Iris Marion Young's 1989 publication adopts a similar starting point. The concept of citizenship itself, Young points out, excludes women from the public sphere.[13] But in Young's analysis the root causes lie beyond the two dichotomies addressed by Pateman, and importantly, these root causes affect not only women, but also all marginalised groups. The culprit, she argues, is a notion of a 'universal citizenship' that presupposes the existence of a 'general point of view' that adequately represents the citizenry as a whole. In reality, Young points out, the socially privileged have a disproportional influence on that 'general' point of view, because it tends to be dominated by the culture, social outlook and general perspective of the socially privileged. Worse still, she says, the very term 'general point of view' further enhances the influence of the privileged group.[14] In her own words:

> In a society where some groups are privileged while others are oppressed, insisting that as citizens persons should leave behind their peculiar affiliation and experiences to adopt a general point of view serves only to reinforce that privilege; for the perspective and the interests of the privileged will tend to dominate this unified public, marginalising or silencing those of other groups. (Young, in Goodin and Petit 1997: 260)

Young's core observation, that the perspective of the socially privileged inherently dominates the general point of view, merits attention in its own right. It merits attention, regardless of whether or not one agrees with her specific views on either participatory democracy or the mechanism by which the socially marginalised could be politically empowered. Young's analysis also suggests that thinking about rights in strictly individual terms is quite problematic.

In a similar vein, Lena Dominelli (1999) argues that existing legal frameworks assign privileges that can mask the social exclusion that is inherent in the manner in which privileges are assigned. A major concern of hers centres on the social consequences of the limited scope for portability of entitlements across national borders, because of the prevailing definitions of citizenship. Dominelli raises an issue that becomes even more acute in the more globalised labour market.

Human rights: critical voices

The concept of human rights has its opponents. Interestingly, those who object to the concept form a motley collection of thinkers – from Edmund Burke to Karl Marx. More precisely, while some scholars note that Marx sees 'le droits de l'homme' (human rights) as addressing only the sectarian interests of the 'bourgeoisie', others have formed a more nuanced perspective (Lacroix and Pranchere, 2012).

Present-day critiques of the existing human rights framework have provided further examples of omissions that render human rights less than universal. For instance, Jacqueline Bhabha (2009) comments on the absence of human rights that specifically address the rights of children. Indeed, this issue becomes poignant when refugee children are concerned. Others raise concerns about the limited reach of human rights when we turn attention to specific local cultural and historical features that require certain adaptations of the literal perspective of the general human rights rule. New historical developments create their own dilemmas. For example, what might be the implications of human rights when we might have to pay heed to political constraints that may backfire badly if overlooked, as in the case to be discussed next.

In the 1980s, countries such as Argentina and Chile were returning to democracy after extended periods under military regimes. Human rights had to be applied to the specific reality at hand, because those countries had to be careful not to create political conditions that could bring back a military rule (Arthur, 2009). The process adopted in both cases was based on the concept of 'Transitional Justice'.

More generally speaking, a critique could be advanced in either one of two different spirits: one negative and the other positive. The negative critique tends to undermine the qualitative impact of human rights. The positive, however, could be read in a more constructive spirit. The 1948 Universal Declaration of Human Rights and the Conventions that have been following it are works in progress. Naturally, notwithstanding the rhetoric, the terrain covered by them at any one point in time is less than strictly universal because such a monumental journey cannot be taken in one step. In addition, to become effective, all human rights conventions require signatories and national governments that are willing to take them onboard beyond mere rhetoric. In addition, government will is a necessary, but not a sufficient condition. A major obstacle is the economic and political muscle of the business sector.

As Scott Jerbi (2009) demonstrates, historically, business has been wary about supporting principles of human rights, especially in developing countries. And the UN has been concerned about the failure of Western business enterprises to honour human rights in developing countries.

In 2005, the UN created an expert mandate on the question of business and human rights. Professor John Gerard Ruggie was given the mandate to bring the business sector onboard.[15] Ruggie, a scholar who was previously a United Nations official, has been known for his capacity to both raise the level of debates and to successfully bring about concrete changes. Community concerns about the conduct of corporations in the developing world (for example, Royal Dutch Oil in the Congo) have led to a major contribution to the implementation of human rights in the first decade of the 21st century.

John Gerard Ruggie strongly believes that the formulation of human rights has a major cultural impact – their formulation, he notes, raise the threshold of what is acceptable as far as the treatment of workers and all individuals in general are concerned (Ruggie, 2007). But they have also done, and will continue to do, much more – they actually make a concrete contribution to human welfare. Yes, the process is not as fast as many of us would have liked it to be. But what still matters is that progress, however modest, is being made. And if nothing else, the actual formulation of human rights, and the constructive intellectual debate that surrounds them, are the best candle holders we have.

Confronting climate change and the AI revolution

Introduction

Extreme weather events have already shown us the kind of world we will bequeath our grandchildren and the later generations to come, if we continue business as usual. A rapid reduction of our carbon dioxide emissions requires a rapid shift away from fossil fuels to green energy generators. This raises the real possibility that many workers will be forced into long term unemployment or, at best, trapped in precarious employment. The Green New Deal (GND) is essentially an initiative designed to address these two major concerns.

The idea of introducing a safety net, in the form of a UBI that grants everyone, from the wealthiest to the poorest, the same amount of money, is supported by a very diverse group of people across the political spectrum. The proposition is attractive to many because this 'free money' avoids the stigma commonly associated with welfare payments, while in principle providing burnt-out workers with an exit strategy from the increasingly oppressive experience of paid work. But what if the reason that Silicon Valley magnates like Elon Musk and Mark Zuckerberg vocally support the introduction of a UBI is that it offers the perfect cover for a retrograde attack on the quality of our working lives? And rather than paving the way to a utopian era of leisure and creativity, what if the introduction of a UBI becomes the basis for an entrenched two-tier economy of haves and have-nots?

In this chapter, I argue that a UBI could avoid this trap by ensuring that gainful jobs are available for all who want them, alongside a welfare state that is significantly invigorated. The UBI could thus serve a positive function as a safety net for people transitioning between jobs. Having a robust welfare state in place is absolutely essential, whether or not it accompanies a UBI regime. In its absence, we can have neither genuine equality of opportunity nor a satisfactory standard of social fairness.

Support for the UBI has been driven, in part, by the possibility of having significant job losses resulting from the AI revolution and climate change. But the challenges we face are neither technological nor economic. Rather, they are political challenges, requiring political solutions. The threats of incessant growth in global warming, and of the negative employment impact of the digital revolution, can both be averted, but only if we boldly adopt a set of well-designed and adequately resourced proactive policies. Looked at this way, these challenges actually grant us a welcome opportunity to radically re-shape our employment sectors in ways that significantly improve our economic and social wellbeing.

Environmental awareness, climate denial and the GND

Appreciation of the environment and a taste for outdoor leisure were some of the more positive legacies of the 19th century. Along with a love for romantic classical music and poetry, the 19th century romantics went to great lengths to praise the beauty of the natural world. Indeed, we owe the beginnings of environmental awareness to that generation. It is perhaps hard to fathom, given how little progress we have made, but they were actually the first to raise the alarm about rising carbon dioxide emissions.

A 2016 article published by Akshat Rathi in *Quartz* includes a photo of a 1912 newspaper that forewarned its readers about the links between carbon dioxide emissions and global warming. The article cites an historian who discovered that those scientific reports didn't remain hidden deeply in the professional journals. As early as 1883, these warnings were widely reported in major newspaper articles, as well as in regional publications. This has recently been reconfirmed by leading world scientists.[1] But, as the *New York Times* columnist, Thomas L. Friedman writes, public awareness is yet to catch up with reality.

> 'Most people have no clue – no clue – how huge an industrial project is required to blunt climate change.' Here are two people who do: Robert Socolow, an engineering professor, and Stephen Pacala, an ecology professor, who together lead the Carbon Mitigation Initiative at Princeton, a consortium designing scalable solutions for the climate issue. (Friedman, 2007)

Citing Jeffrey Immelt, who at that time, was chairman of General Electric, Friedman relates:

> Summing up the problem, Immelt of G.E. said the big energy players are being asked 'to take a 15-minute market signal and make a 40-year decision and that just doesn't work. … The U.S. government should decide: What do we want to have happen? How much clean coal, how much nuclear and what is the most efficient way to incentivize people to get there? (Friedman, 2007)

Immelt tells Friedman that countries such as Denmark, Germany and Spain have been paying wind turbine operators subsidies since the 1980s. In contrast, the US (along with many other countries) still pays hefty subsidies to fuel fossil companies.

It was Friedman himself who came up with the idea of conjoining curbing of carbon dioxide emissions with a progressive economic legislation modelled on Franklin Delano Roosevelt's New Deal. He first presented it in his January 2007, *New York Times Magazine* article. Friedman specifically calls for the introduction of a Green New Deal (GND) that, like Franklin Delano Roosevelt's (FDR) 1930s New Deal, will involve extensive but very fruitful government expenditure.[2]

Friedman also draws parallels between the concerns that underpin the need for a publicly funded GND program and the geopolitical concerns that played a crucial role in President Dwight Eisenhower's decision to invest large amounts of public funds in the construction of a superfast national roads network during the 1950s. The decision to invest that huge amount of money, he points out, was taken as a precaution against a possible future Soviet attack on the US. The ecological threats we are facing, Friedman stresses, are no less grave. He also cites cases of salutary restrictive regulation initiatives that have been taken by a number of state governors. Those initiatives, he reports, have yielded substantial reductions in carbon dioxide emissions.

Friedman's article was published in January 2007. Six months later, on 21 July 2008, a British group of environmentally concerned individuals published a collective report, signing themselves the Green New Deal Group.[3] In 2019, US Congress representative Alexandria Ocasio-Cortez and senator Ed Markey co-sponsored a GND Bill.[4] The proposed bill they argue, could reduce greenhouse emissions to zero by 2045; but only if the US developed the capacity to meet all of its energy demands with 100 per cent green energy. This goal would require other initiatives, such as the drive to insulate homes and clean air and waterways. Their proposed GND bill also includes a shift to sustainable farming practices, improvement of the infrastructure of the whole country, and having higher standards of equity and social justice. They foresee millions of newly created jobs. Detractors have been quick to react to the dollar cost of the GND, and to what they see as an imminent 'crush of liberal values' (Edwards, 2019; Selgin 2019).[5]

The political clout of the fossil fuel lobby is abundantly evident in the US and in Australia. Edwards's and Selgin's articles were published by the US Cato Institute. A major founder of the libertarian Cato Institute think tank was the fossil fuel magnate Charles Koch. In Australia, Prime Ministers and opposition leaders have won and lost their jobs based on their support or opposition for environmental policy measures. The penultimate case in this chain of changes took place in August 2018, when Malcolm Turnbull was deposed as Prime Minister by his own party, for adopting a relatively moderate environmental legislative agenda. In his place they installed Scott Morrison, a man who in February 2017 proudly displayed a lump of coal in the lower house of the Australian Parliament.

In the US, fossil fuel giants have also been actively footing election bills of individual politicians, hoping they could be counted on to promote their business interests. They have also set up institutional machinery to muster wider political support for their cause, in the hope of swaying public opinion behind them. An example is given by the array of activities of the Cato institute.[6]

The global fossil fuel industry enjoys lucrative financial support from many governments, despite the dangers of catastrophic climate change. A recent International Monetary Fund (IMF) research team led by David Coady (2017) found that in 2013, the world's fossil fuel businesses received government subsidies to the tune of US$4.9 trillion. By 2015, this number grew to US$5.3 trillion. This amount of money is beyond the comprehensive capacity of most minds, but not so once we see it expressed in percentage terms. Incredibly, in 2013, the value of those fossil-fuel subsidies represented a staggering 5.8 per cent of the world's 191 countries' incomes. Namely, the total value of those subsidies was 5.8 per cent of the global GDP (Global Domestic Product) of that year. By 2015, that figure rose to 6.5 per cent of the world GDP.[7] Yet another way to get a handle on the global volume of these subsidies is to compare it to the size of the global expenditure on education. It turns out that in 2015, the global expenditure on education was lower than the total amount of those subsidies. While the fossil fuel businesses received 6.5 per cent of the world GDP, the level of global expenditure on education was only 4.8 per cent of global GDP.[8] The main donors of fossil fuel subsidies are the US, Russia and China. The EU's fossil fuel subsidies add up to one half of the amount handed out by the US.

Guardian journalist John Abraham asked David Coady (the lead researcher on the IMF team) what drove them to investigate the scale of the subsidies that support the global fossil fuel industry, Coady answered that 'A key motivation for the paper was to increase awareness among policy makers and the public of the large subsidies that arise from pricing fossil-fuels below their true social costs – this broader definition of subsidies accounts for the many negative side effects associated with the consumption of these fuels' (Abraham, 2017).

David Coady and his co-authors note that 'Efficient fossil fuel pricing in 2015 would have lowered global carbon emissions by 28 percent and fossil fuel air pollution deaths by 46 percent, and increased government revenue by 3.8 percent of GDP' (Coady et al, 2019).[9]

Will our governments ever learn? At an August 2018 rally in Charleston, Virginia, then-President Donald Trump told his audience that coal is "back".[10] Subsequently, in June 2022, the US Supreme Court curbed the federal government's power to reduce carbon emissions (Hurley and Volcovici, 2022). And in Australia, in October 2014, the then Prime Minister, Tony Abbott, declared that 'coal is good for humanity'.[11] He made this declaration at the opening ceremony of a new coal mine. That coal mine is jointly owned by the two very large corporations, BHP Billiton and Mitsubishi.

Recently, Australia has been in the midst of yet another attempt to open a new coal mine. This attempt is being made by the multinational conglomerate, the Adani Group.[12] The Labor government of the Australian state of Queensland had already made its own dollar investment in Adani's planned mine, while also exempting Adani from paying taxes for the first 5 years of its operation. As it happens, the Adani Group is the world's largest exporter of coal.

In the meantime, there has been widespread public objection to any attempt to open new coal mines. People, of all ages and walks of life, have been staging protests. Some of the protestors have already spent a few days in jail, and the Australian government was threatening even longer jail terms. Notwithstanding the wide protests, the Adani Group had continued to have the backing of Australia's government (Denniss, 2018). These efforts have recently borne fruit. The then prime minister, Scott Morrison, had such disregard for climate change mitigation that he led his government to a huge loss at the polls. His party was ousted, in part, by ten independents who campaigned on an agenda of addressing climate change and reducing government corruption. The Australian Greens party has also increased the number of its federally elected representatives in parliament in this recent election.

Universal Basic Income and the future of work

The threat of massive job losses resulting from the AI revolution can be averted, but only if we adopt a robust program of manpower retraining. The programs Sweden has had in place since the late 1930s serve as an excellent example of what can be done. The surplus of person power that it is proposed will follow the AI revolution could thus be turned into an asset. Our education, health and age care systems, for example, are all crying out for a larger and better qualified workforce.[13]

The concept of a UBI is not new. The idea was mooted in the 16th century by Thomas Moore, in his book Utopia, and again in the 18th century by Nicolas de Condorcet and Thomas Paine. A number of 20th-century left-wing intellectuals, including the Marxists Antonio Negri and Mario Tonti, and the Marxist-leaning thinker Andre Gorz, have also supported the introduction of a basic income.[14] They saw the UBI as a bulwark against capitalism's injustices, an antidote to the materialistic culture it inculcates, and a means for allowing the option of opting out of paid work. They framed their advocacy for the UBI as support for the 'refusal of work'. Materialistic cultures, they argued, serve the vested interests of capital owners in two interrelated ways: by securing demand for their products, and thereby also ensuring a steady supply of willing workers. Basic income, they proposed, would grant working people the freedom to refuse to work for bosses. The 'refusal to work' concept presents a valid critique of the capitalist system.[15] And as Kathi Weeks and David Frayne have both noted, utopian visions are essential because they draw attention to the inadequacies of existing systems thereby agitating for a change.[16]

The Basic Income European Network (BIEN) was founded in Louvain-la-Neuve, France in 1986. BIEN is a broad coalition of individuals and organisations who support the introduction of a UBI, though on the basis of different rationales. Guy Standing, a founding member of BIEN, calls for the introduction of a UBI in response to the ongoing loss of job security and the steady rise in the precarity of paid work.[17]

Coming from a very different philosophical perspective, Milton Friedman also proposed the introduction of a basic income for all in his 1962 book, Capitalism and Freedom. Friedman was motivated by the prototypical libertarian quest for small government. Like Friedman, Guy Standing also notes that a UBI will replace an administratively cumbersome welfare system with a simple, unconditional grant given to every citizen. But for advocates of UBI like Guy Standing, the UBI is primarily sought as a bulwark against the poverty and general insecurity that have become endemic in the modern capitalist world.

Proponents aside, the idea of a UBI has also met with strong opposition in progressive circles. A significant number of progressive commentators, academic economists among them, argue that we would be better off investing the inevitably large amount of money required for a UBI into social programs that can genuinely reduce the vast economic and social inequalities we currently face.

Sonia Sodha, *The Guardian* journalist and chief leader writer of *The Guardian*'s sister newspaper, *The Observer*, offers the following sobering advice to the supporters of UBI from the left end of the political spectrum:

> The left will have to pick its battles. It must focus on the right to a decently paid job for all, not sell out by extolling a basic income as a panacea for the ills of the modern labour market. It must choose the fight for power, not the fight for a dribble of cash. (Sodha, 2017)

Emma Dawson, the Executive Director of the progressive Australian think tank, Per Capita, writes:

> The UBI is perhaps the most widely supported idea in fashion on the progressive side of the political debate, so it's no surprise to see the

Greens jump onboard. But it is no solution to inequality, and far from a progressive answer to the problems in our current tax and transfer system. (Dawson, 2018)[18]

The MIT professor, Darren Acemoglu writes: 'As such, UBI proposals have all the hallmarks of the "bread and circuses" used by the Roman and Byzantine Empires – handouts to defuse discontent and mollify the masses, rather than providing them with economic opportunities and political agency' (Acemoglu, 2019: 24).

In 2019, Anna Coote, a Principal Fellow of the British think tank the New Economics Foundation (NEF), published in *The Guardian* an article headed thus: 'Universal basic income doesn't work. Let's boost the public realm instead'. In the same year, UK's Centre for Social Justice (CSJ) issued a report, 'Universal Basic Income: A trade union perspective'. Very poignantly, in its preface, the CSJ's report explains why progressives should not support the UBI, as follows: 'At the heart of the critique of UBIs contained in this brief is the failure of the most basic principle of progressive tax and expenditure, which can be summarised as 'from each according to their ability, to each according to their need' (Coote and Yazici, 2019: 3).

And writing in *Quartz*, Helen Razor has this to say about the plutocrats' support for the UBI: 'UBI is a hack that may well benefit its Silicon Valley advocates in the short-term, but it'll compound income and social inequality for the rest of us for decades (especially if it's applied in the gloriously "simple" spirit in which it is largely understood)' (Razor, 2017).[19]

While the philosophical justification for the UBI as a safety net *per se* might be virtuous, ultimately the virtue of the proposal depends on the scope of its economic, ethical and political consequences.

The AI revolution

As with the automation scare of the 1950s, there is increasing concern that the AI revolution will radically diminish employment prospects. Drivers would be losing their jobs as soon as driverless cars begin to roll off the assembly lines; the assembly line workers themselves would be replaced by more efficient, and cost-effective, robots. Even teachers, journalists, accountants and translators, some suggest, would find themselves facing redundancy 'because their roles would be overtaken by artificial intelligence machines'.

However, given that currently a large number of people have to put up with working for 12 hours a day or even more, a sheer return to the 8-hour standard might just allow for having enough jobs for all who seek them. In fact, why not have a six- or even five-hour working day?[20] Almost a century ago, John Maynard Keynes foresaw us working only three hours a day. Discussing the prospect of not knowing what to do with so much leisure time, he argued 'Three-hour shifts or a fifteen-hour week may put off the problem for a great while. For three hours a day is quite enough to satisfy the old Adam in most of us!' (Keynes, 1930: 342).

The current woeful state in which low-paid workers and middle-income earners find themselves is, of course, not a consequence of automation. Let's take a moment to consider the impact of government policy, which by any reasonable measure has played a substantial role in undermining job security and wage parity. In the US, for example, income inequality has been rising steadily since at least 1979, reversing an earlier course of continuous decline in both income and wealth inequality that began in the early 20th century.[21] The main cause of this trend is to be found in the suite of policies that have been adopted by successive governments that actively 'deregulated' the labour market, and effectively undermined the collective bargaining power of workers; thereby driving profits up and pushing wages down. They have also been introducing tax cuts that disproportionally favour the wealthiest and highest income earners, while privatising public sector services and selling them at essentially subsidised prices. The unequal consequences of these policies are patently clear. The world's richest 1 per cent now hold more wealth than the rest of the world combined.[22] And as the Panama Papers reveal, the cavalier use of tax havens has been making its own contribution to this state of affairs.[23] We should also recall that CEOs of the largest 25 hedge funds in the US, taken together, are paid as much as all of the country's kindergarten teachers combined (Bump 2016). These are not economic inevitabilities. These are the direct results of successive government policies. As mentioned earlier, the lack of robust manpower retraining has also exacerbated the scale of economic inequalities.

Proponents of UBI have painstakingly identified the ways in which automation is already disrupting the nature of work, but the solutions to the challenges faced by this disruption are abundantly obvious. Unsurprisingly perhaps, the solutions have little to do with UBI.

Consider this: Australia's health system is woefully underfunded and short-staffed. Many aged care facilities struggle to meet minimum standards of care; our school teachers struggle with large class sizes, substandard training and poor administrative support; universities could also do with much smaller classes. Our public transport system lacks the required investment to compete effectively with private cars, a development that would help us address the host of pressing environmental challenges we face.

What if we emulated the 'active manpower-retraining' policies of Nordic countries like Sweden, Norway and Denmark? In those countries, adults who find themselves jobless as a result of various structural changes in the economy are retrained swiftly and efficiently in courses that are tailored to their age and aptitude. The challenges presented by automation could actually propel us towards a better future where workers are gainfully employed in more meaningful, highly skilled jobs that contribute to the communal good. Are people re-trainable? Of course they are.

In Wyoming, coal miners are being retrained to become future wind farmers; and they are being trained for free. The training is provided by the American arm of Goldwind, a Chinese company that produces wind turbines.[24] In Pennsylvania's Greene county, where automation has sharply reduced the number of permanent jobs, coal miners who have already lost their jobs are being trained for free by a team of volunteers led by world-class computer programmers Amanda Laucher and Jonathan Graham. Laucher and Graham run a program that is aptly named Mined Minds.[25] The course is open to coal miners, and anyone else who is interested.

A not-for-profit Appalachian Beekeeping Collective, in West Virginia, is retraining coal miners made jobless by the sweeping mine closures across the state. They are being retrained as bee-keepers, which is both a win for the coal miners and a win for America's dwindling bee colonies.[26] In Australia, Smart Steel Solutions has introduced a highly automated production processes, and retrained its own shop floor metal workers to operate the computers that are required to keep the automated equipment running.[27]

The Automation Advantage, a 2017 report issued by AlphaBeta Advisors, offers an exciting glimpse of the opportunities that are presented by the widespread adoption of digital production technology and its impact on the labour market. Paid jobs, the report concludes, have the potential to be richer in content and satisfaction, while also far safer and, certainly, better compensated than any of the UBI payments currently being mooted. They also foresee a reduction in the hours of the standard working day, freeing up time for other activities. For any society that cares about social justice and the natural environment – and, really, why shouldn't we – technological change that eliminates the need for human operators is a considerable blessing, provided we do not end up allowing the UBI scheme to cast a spell over our policy makers.

Melbourne University economists, Jeff Borland and Michael Coheli, reject doomsday forecasts in their 2017 article for the *Australian Economic Review*. They also argue in favour of robust manpower retraining programs.[28] In 2015, the MIT economist, David H. Auter, published an article on the long history of workplace automation. His conclusions align with Borland and Coheli's conclusion.

The social dividend of technological change

Technological advances that allow us to continue to produce the same amount of goods and services while reducing manpower requirements are an exciting prospect. But the many opportunities presented by technological progress require us to address underlying issues of inequality, which are only exacerbated by declining employment levels. The benefits of technological progress are, by their nature, the result of the work of generations of scientists, mathematicians, engineers and teachers. As such, they are generated by the people, for the people and should not be appropriated by the wealthy for their exclusive benefit.

Overhauling our tax systems

The large tax cuts that have been continuously made during the last four decades have greatly impoverished the public purse. But, if we are to rebuild the welfare state, arrest ecological deterioration and equip the swathes of low and middle-income workers with new earning skills, then we need to reclaim that lost ground.

There is only one fair solution, but it won't be universally popular. Tax rates for corporations and the wealthy must be substantially increased, and tax havens should be eliminated. This is the only way we will be able to fund retraining programs that equip the unemployed with meaningful skills that translate to future employment. The benefits of this approach are universal, and improve the standards of our education, health and age care sectors; and of course, allow us to reclaim the quality standard of our ecological environment. Once these unemployed workers begin to earn income again, their income taxes will help replenish the tax revenue spent on retraining them.

The reality of living on a Universal Basic Income

As a thought experiment, let's have a look at the repercussions of a UBI that is set at the level of Australia's unemployment benefit. For those merely transitioning between jobs, a UBI presents several improvements over the current regime. It offers a source of income support that is free of the stigma associated with welfare payments and is immediately available, unlike unemployment benefits, which usually take many weeks to access. For the long term unemployed, the UBI is a different proposition. In Australia, the current level of the weekly unemployment benefit is A\$250. But Australia's poverty line is A\$426.30. So, for those who must subsist permanently on an amount equivalent to today's unemployment benefits, the UBI would plunge them permanently well below the poverty line.

Other, more generous proposals set the UBI at the level of the minimum wage. But are our nationally mandated minimum wages really liveable? Let's take a look at what the minimum wage buys you in Australia, in terms of accommodation cost. We'll base the analysis on the internationally agreed standard that says that accommodation costs should take no more than 30 per cent of a person's income. In Sydney Australia, 30 per cent of your minimum wage would allow you to rent only a 1-bedroom apartment; and you also would be obliged to live 40km away from Sydney's central business district (CBD). But what are the chances of finding such accommodation, when your income is set at that legislated minimum level? On 9 June 2015, Inga Ting wrote in the *Sydney Morning Herald*:

> Minimum wage workers will receive a 2.5 per cent pay increase to $17.29 an hour ($656.90 a week) from July 1, which means a full-time worker on this wage can afford to spend up to $197 a week on housing, according to the 30 per cent test. This still prices them out of 99.9 per cent of the 440 Sydney suburbs with available data. (About 100 suburbs had insufficient data, possibly because there aren't many one-bedroom units in those suburbs.) (Ting, 2015)

For a Sydneysider, the problem is that the CBD is the place where most of the lowest-paid service jobs are available. Put differently, minimum wage earners living in the CBD (in a one-bedroom apartment) would need to work no less than 22 hours a day, seven days a week, in order to limit their accommodation expenditure to just 30 per cent of their income.

The state of minimum wage recipients in the US is very similar. If workers who receive just the federal minimum wage were to be able to pay no more than 30 per cent of their income for accommodation that consists of a 2-bedroom apartment, in Hawaii, they would need to work 174 hours per week. In California, that would be working 130 hours a week, 120 hours in Massachusetts, in New York – 124 hours, Philadelphia is somewhat more kind, but even there, workers who receive just the minimum wage would need to work for 96 hours a week to be able to rent a 2-bedroom apartment with 30 per cent of their minimum wage income. The lowest number of hours they would need to work in the US is in Arkansas, where they would still need to work 69 hours a week.[29]

Others have proposed setting the UBI at the level of the age-pension. The short answer is that, for instance, in Australia you will still end up below the poverty line on a UBI set at the age-pension rate. If you own your accommodation outright, you will sit only a small way below the poverty line; if you don't, your income will place you well below the poverty line. Here are the relevant figures for Australia. The weekly poverty line is A$433.90. The age pension for an adult living on their own is A$834.4 a fortnight. With an outright owned accommodation, the age pension provides only A$417.2 a week, or 3.9 per cent below the poverty line. But if you need to rent or pay for a mortgage, without a paid job that supplements the UBI, living on a UBI that is set at the age pension rate means life in abject poverty.

Equality of opportunity is an empty principle when the right to a well-paid and meaningful job is not universal. With a UBI in place, we would, in all probability, be in the unfortunate state where governments are also more likely to feel far less obliged to embark on economic management that is closely designed to generate more employment, let alone employment for all. Instead, they might be far more likely to advise all those who fail to find gainful employment that they should simply move away from the large urban centres, where accommodation is prohibitively expensive, to sufficiently remote rural areas on the periphery, where 30 per cent of the basic income grants stand better chance of covering accommodation costs.

In other words, they would be shifted to the regions where jobs are generally even scarcer than in the major cities; where the standard of health care services is likely to be far poorer, and where often the school system is substandard. Thus, ending up entrenched in endemic poverty and inequality on a much larger scale than they already are today.

Whether it is the rural periphery of the US, Australia or the UK, all three countries already contain significant numbers of disenfranchised, angry (often) men, who no longer have the economic opportunities that their parents once had. They are victims of the laissez faire capitalist system that has taken shape during the neoliberal epoch of the last four decades, but unfortunately their economic predicament often saddles them with a bitter sense of personal failure. Seeking scapegoats, they, unfortunately, tend to end up blaming their own economic predicament on immigrants and members of the various ethnic and religious minority groups.

If we choose to respond very passively to a technological challenge that threatens a very large-scale job loss, by merely adopting a UBI system, the size of that bitterly disaffected population would grow quite rapidly. This would most likely have quite ominous social and political consequences.

The actual truth is that technological breakthroughs do not impoverish a country, they enrich it. But, technological revolutions can also redistribute the national income away from the low-paid and middle-income classes, to the very wealthy and radically so. If the dire predictions of collapsing industries and large-scale job losses do eventuate, today's laid-off workers could indeed become the beggars of tomorrow.

The fact, however, is that the challenge we face is neither technological nor economic. Rather, it is a political one. If we fail to retrain our workforce in the face of a technological disruption, and we choose to leave the jobless at the mercy of a UBI regime, we might indeed be catapulted straight back to the times of Medieval Europe – with the vast majority of our future children destined to become either servants to the lords of the land, or left to roam in what will remains of our forests, in search of food and shelter.

Epilogue

Humanity stands at a crossroads, faced with a set of extremely important decisions. We can allow income inequality to grow and wealth to become ever more concentrated, or we can ensure that our shared resources are distributed far more equally. The price of failure is immeasurable. Climate change and the rise of AI present significant challenges that threaten to further increase and entrench inequality, and to negatively impact our quality of life across the board. But, with the right legislative approach, they also provide significant opportunities to improve the wellbeing of individuals and their households.

History has shown us that we do indeed have a say over the socio-economic conditions that prevail within our countries. Democratic systems provide their citizens with an avenue to address these conditions via the ballot box. A large portion of our adult lives are spent working, which makes the workplace an obvious point of focus. Depending on how governments legislate, work conditions can be either harsh or more humane. As voters, we should prioritise electing governments that put the welfare and wellbeing of workers first.

As workers, we should also be demanding a greater stake in the design and implementation of the jobs we do, including such things as the pace and length of the working day. Work is a heavy burden, but only when jobs are tedious and poorly designed. When employees have agency over all aspects of their jobs, work becomes far more rewarding than its paycheque. The shortest route to bolstering the rights of workers is to strengthen the trade union movement. The war waged against the trade union movement during the 1980s has decimated the average standard of living for low and middle-income workers.

Rising inequality is not the only threat to the wellbeing of workers. The twin challenges of climate change and AI both threaten to negatively impact worker's lives, without appropriate government intervention. Without such action, job insecurity and income inequality are only set to increase. Alternatively, we could implement worker-friendly measures aimed at addressing these challenges and simultaneously improving the lives of workers. These would include extensive manpower retraining programs, a shorter standard working day and the provision of secure jobs for all who want them.

The needs of workers extend beyond the workplace, and addressing their rights requires a broad political and social agenda. Key to this is the provision of a generous welfare state that actively supports and enhances the health and wellbeing of all citizens, particularly those on low incomes. In addition to the material needs of workers – health, financial security and so on – are the psychological, social and emotional needs of workers. Well-designed work provides us with a sense of who we are in relation to our families, our communities and society at large. More importantly, it gives us an opportunity to learn, to achieve and to experience self-actualisation.

Our individual fates rest upon the success of our collective efforts. We must move beyond the discriminatory mindset that still shapes so much of public life and allow progress to carry all of us along with it. Until we see each other as equals, no amount of government policy can eliminate the inequalities that permeate our social and economic lives. Without such progress, we are doomed to an endless cycle of unrest and upheaval. It is time to share far more widely the fruit of the earth within and between countries. There is no substitute for acting together, and for all of us. Because only together can we truly stand.

Notes

Chapter 1

[1] See the TED talk on http://www.ted.com/search?q=Rainer+Strack. The address was given in 2014. Rainer Strack has been with BCG since 1998.

[2] Chapter 10 presents a broader discussion of these matters.

[3] For instance, the British Labour MP, John McDonell had this to say in his speech to the British Parliament during a hearing on the Welfare Bill in the House, in 2015: "I make this clear: I would swim through vomit to vote against the Bill, and listening to some of the nauseating speeches tonight, I think we might have to. Poverty in my constituency is not a lifestyle choice; it is imposed on people". Source: http://leapeconomics.blogspot.com/2015/07/poverty-is-not-lifestyle-choice-it-is.html

[4] 'Dole' being the vernacular term for unemployment benefit.

[5] For the details see: https://www.aph.gov.au/About_Parliament/Parliamentary_Departments/Parliamentary_Library/Publications_Archive/archive/dole

[6] See Amy Remeikis on ABC TV's programme, The Drum: https://www.facebook.com/abcthedrum/videos/1853825811453536/

[7] An eloquent voice of the fellow humans who are subjected to this treatment is offered by Mark Goodrick and Jennifer Searson's article 12 September 2022 article in *The Guardian*.

[8] The terms 'dole bludgers', 'skivers' and 'cheats' and Ronald Reagan's demeaning reference to African American single mothers as 'welfare queens', all speak volumes about class and colour prejudice. (The term 'welfare queen' was coined by George Bliss in a 1974 *Chicago Tribune* article about an infamous fraudster Linda Taylor.)

[9] See Hardoon et al (2016). Also see the Alvaredo et al (2013) study and Saez and Zucman (2014).

[10] Chapter 9 is focused on the social and economic discrimination endured by the First Nations people, African Americans and other people of colour, women and members of the LGBTQ+ community.

[11] For a very comprehensive treatment of this old baggage see John Quiggin's 2012 book.

[12] Chapter 2 discusses this issue in more detail.

[13] Chapter 7 discusses this matter at some length.

[14] Chapter 3 presents this literature in non-technical, reader-friendly language.

[15] Some readers may be surprised, but as I explain in Chapter 5, there is nothing radical about this proposition. As the notable Oxford economist, Tony Atkinson explained to us in his 1970 journal article, a truly sound grasp of mainstream economic theory unequivocally supports this proposition.

[16] Chapter 8 describes at some length an example of the dire health consequences workers could experience when corporations are allowed to enjoy the privileged position of 'self-regulation'.

Chapter 2

[1] On the 31 December 1600, Britain's Queen Elizabeth I sold the charter that granted the monopoly rights to the East India Company for quite a large sum of money (Plumb, 1953). As John H. Plumb notes, neither was there a general tendency towards free trade during much of the 18th century.

[2] John Quiggin's (2012) description of 'how dead ideas can still walk among us' perfectly applies to my description of the legacy of the 18th and 19th centuries in economics.

3 The Behavioural Economics school of thought has taken a step towards rectifying the matter, but the road to a better intellectual perspective is much longer.

4 Senior referred to this frugality as capacity for 'abstinence', namely refraining from temptation to spend the whole of earned income. Instead, they diligently save a portion of that income. Present day economics uses a different term for the same concept. The modern substitute for 'abstinence' is the term 'low rate of time preference'. In contrast, by definition those who have 'high rate of time preference' save very little or none whatsoever. This concept is sometimes used to blame low income people for their misfortune.

5 For instance, on the place and the social roles that befit women, we also have the German adage of the triple K, relegating women to the 'Kinder, Küche, Kirche' or 'the 3 Ks', meaning Children, Kitchen and Church.

6 I cite from the 1979 edition. Beatrice Webb's book was first published in 1926.

7 For economists alone: here one must pay homage to Kenneth Arrow and Gerard Debreu's path-breaking contributions. There are quite a few other people such as George Ackerlof's 'lemons' model, Michael Spence's 'market signalling' model, Joseph Stiglitz's 'asymmetric information' and also the contributors to the evolution of game theory. Naturally, this list commits many sins of omission.

8 In addition to Hausman (1989, 1992), see also Hausman and McPherson (1993) and Gill (1996, 1999). All five studies address the analytical and policy advice consequences of the intricately interwoven relationship between pecuniary and non-pecuniary motives.

Chapter 3

1 As Philip Inman tells us, the signatories include countries such as Britain and the US. Verbatim:

> The students, who have formed 41 protest groups in universities from Britain and the US to Brazil and Russia, say research and teaching in economics departments is too narrowly focused and more effort should be made to broaden the curriculum. They want courses to include analysis of the financial crash that so many economists failed to see coming, and say the discipline has become divorced from the real world. Inman (2014)

2 George Akerlof and Amartya Sen received the Nobel Prize in economics in 1998, Michael Spence and Joseph Stiglitz received the Nobel Prize in 2001.

3 See Robert E. Lucas Jr (2004).

4 In academic jargon, this is a description of 'solipsistic' individuals. The Harvard philosophy professor, Michael Sandel, explains this point very eloquently in his 2012 publication *What Money Cannot Buy: The Moral Limits of Markets*. Sandel also stresses that the rise of neoliberalism has unfortunately affected our social culture. For instance, he notes that many mutual help norms that had been common in earlier decades, are now commodified. I wonder to what extend the much longer hours that the majority of people nowadays spend in paid work have also contributed to the crowding-out of mutual free-of-charge help.

5 See Chapter 10.

6 This analytical conclusion dovetails with the conclusion reached by Akerlof and Shiller (2015) regarding the available scope for deception and manipulation.

7 Robert M. Solow received the Nobel Prize in 1987.

8 I would also like to draw attention to the fact that in his 1963 article, 'Uncertainty and the welfare economics of medical care', the Nobel Prize Laureate economist Kenneth Arrow argued for introduction of a national health care system (along the lines of the

systems that at the time had already prevailed in Britain, Scandinavia, France and a number of other countries). Arrow made his argument in terms of 'economic efficiency'.

[9] The standard economics textbook explains why this is the case.

[10] Clearly, this is an important analytical insight. However, although the 'theories of imperfect competition and welfare economics' strictly address the failure of markets to exhaust the full economic potential of a country's economic resources, members of the Chicago School of Economic Thought dismiss both theories. They do this simply because of their own philosophical view that governments should stay well out of the economic system.

[11] I have addressed this issue in more detail in my 1993 publication, 'Statistics in the social sciences – a mixed blessing?'

[12] See Stiglitz (2012: 119).

[13] The reader might note that this explanation is synonymous with Nassau William Senior's 'abstinence theory of capital accumulation'. That theory is addressed in Chapter 2 of this book.

[14] For economists alone. This needs to be done within a dynamic model that focuses on change through time. Among other things, such a model would need to embrace the fact that technically speaking, the 'conditional expectations of both employment and earnings vary significantly across different socio-economic classes of people.

[15] For an example, see my 1979 publication. A summary version of this book-length thesis is available in Gill (1980).

[16] The role of such a network is encapsulated, if in a somewhat overstated manner, in the adage 'it's not what you know, but who you know'.

Chapter 4

[1] The term labour economics is synonymous with the economics of labour markets. One of the most comprehensive textbooks of labour economics is Kaufman (1986).

[2] Among other things, those attempts have spawned the so called 'internal market analysis 'and 'segmented markets analysis'.

[3] Johnson made this comment in his capacity as the conference-discussant of a paper by Andrew Oswald. Johnson was rejecting Oswald's attempt to formulate a one uniform model for all trade unions (Johnson, 1985).

[4] In the 18th and 19th centuries, 'combination' was a term used to describe either a labour trade union or employers' association.

[5] In his 1933 book, John Maynard Keynes notes that the matters that Marshall addresses in his broad discursive narrative are comments made only in passing (Keynes actually used the Latin term, noting that they were mere 'obiter dicta'). Those comments, Keynes stresses, end up playing no analytical role in Marshall's actual analysis of the economic system. Keynes's specific example was Marshall's reference to the 'biological' features of the economic system. The same also applies to the perceptive observations that Marshall made about paid work.

[6] See Hicks (1963: 136–139).

[7] In the UK, the members of this group were seen as belonging to the Historical School. In the US, they have since been referred to as the American Institutionalists. See also (i) Kaufman (2003: 33–35) for a more comprehensive account and (ii) Landreth (1976: 317–364).

[8] For economists alone. The Institutionalists argued that a 'static' and 'hypothetico-deductive' frame of the analysis could not possibly provide an adequate insight into the workings of an economic system that changes constantly over time. Instead, they emphasised the need to move from a purely hypothetico-deductive to an 'inductive' frame of analysis.

[9] Wesley Clare Mitchell produced a very large trove of statistical data and other detailed descriptions of a range of institutions along with their impact on the economy.

[10] Perhaps except for George Akerlof, in his 1982 article 'Labour contracts as partial gift exchange'.

[11] Douglass North's 1990 book, *Institutions and Economic Growth: An Historical Introduction*, is also recognised as a major contribution to the emergence of the New Institutionalist school of thought. Douglas North was awarded the Memorial Noble Prize in Economics Science in 1993.

[12] These issues are also addressed in more detail in Gill (1979, 1984).

[13] The dual labour market theory argues that even an attempt to move from employment in a lowly business sector to a more prestigious business sector is fraught with difficulties.

[14] John Pencavel was also the Chief Editor of the *Journal of Economic Literature* between 1982 and 1988.

[15] Pencavel also stresses that, barring a few exceptions, the economic features of the labour market severely limit the scope for having a truly 'competitive' labour market.

[16] Note that when economics describes an employer as facing a 'competitive labour market' it describes an employer who is absolutely powerless. In this hypothetical state of affairs, employers have no power whatsoever over wage levels – they must pay the 'market wage', or else they will fail to find even a single employee.

[17] 'Wage taking' is a specific, well-defined term that is borrowed from economic theory. For economists, it also operates as a shortcut term for 'perfect competition'. Analytically, wage takers are agents who cannot negotiate prices and conditions; according to economic theory, both employers and employees are wage takers in a perfectly competitive market. In other words, in a 'perfectly competitive market equilibrium', no bargaining can take place.

[18] John Pencavel also cites approvingly the work of the Harvard economists, Richard Freeman and James Medoff (1979, 1984).

[19] See for instance Joel Cutcher-Gershenfeld et al's 2015 book where the authors describe the productive outcomes of a recent collaboration between the United Auto Workers union (UAW) and the Ford Motor Company.

Chapter 5

[1] A very eloquent argument about the disturbing moral failures of markets and the disturbing moral import of the idea that money can buy all is also presented by the Harvard political philosopher Michael Sandel in his 2012 book, *What Money Cannot Buy: The Moral Limits of Markets*.

[2] Chapter 10 revisits these issues in more detail.

[3] See, for instance, Joseph Stiglitz (2016), regarding the elusive 'trickle-down effect'.

Chapter 6

[1] The phrase 'Dark Satanic Mills' refers to the emerging factories of the industrial revolution and the very harsh conditions under which adults and children alike worked in those factories. The phrase entered the English language after William Blake published his poem, 'Jerusalem'. The probable publication date is 1804.

[2] In his seminal 1944 book, *The Great Transformation*, Karl Polanyi wrote at some length about the traumatic impact of the transition from working in the rural economy to factory work. These significant social and economic changes, he cogently argues, propelled the 19th-century legislation of the Factory Acts.

[3] Unless otherwise stated, all the information about the Factory Acts and the reform movement comes from The New Cambridge Modern History (Bury, 1964; Mowat, 1964).

[4] The legislation, especially during the first 60 years of the 19th century, was flagrantly violated. But the inspectors' reports did ultimately lead to a subsequent strengthening of the legislation (Collins, 2003).

[5] In 1867, the state of Illinois granted a 40-hour week, but only to certain sections of its own workforce. In that same year, President Ulysses Grant proclaimed his support for the 8-hour working day for government employees. Even so, only selected sections of federal employees were granted the 40-hour working week.

[6] For more detail, see: https://www.ilo.org/empent/areas/business-helpdesk/WCMS_DOC_ENT_HLP_TIM_EN/lang--en/index.htm

[7] Earlier runners were Finland that legislated the universal eight-hour working day in 1907, Uruguay in 1915, and also France, Germany, Hungary, Poland, Portugal, Russia and Spain, all of which introduced an eight-hour working day in 1919.

[8] Social insurance includes programs such as sickness, unemployment benefits and age pension.

[9] Note that the Balkan countries were colonies of the Ottoman Empire. They won their independence only in the second decade of the 20th century.

[10] A research conducted jointly by the International Labour Organisation (ILO), the Walk Free Foundation and also in partnership with the International Organisation for Migration (IOM) reported to the United Nations, in 2019, that '152 million children are subject to child labour'. They include 64 million girls and 88 million boys. The largest number is in Africa with 72.1 million children aged 5 to 17, 62 million in Asia and the Pacific, 10.7 million in the Americas, 5.5 million in Europe and Central Asia and 1.2 million in Arab states. See ILO (2017).

[11] Thompson (1964) is the source of the information on public sector provision in this section.

[12] Oddly enough, in September 2013 there were still a few US states that have a minimum wage rate below the level of the federal rate.

[13] This Act is administered by the US's Employment Standards Administration's Wage and Hours Division within the US Department of Labor. The source of this information is the website of the US Department of Labor (September 2013): https://www.dol.gov/agencies/whd/flsa#:~:text=The%20Fair%20Labor%20Standards%20Act%20(FLSA)%20establishes%20minimum%20wage%2C,%2C%20State%2C%20and%20local%20governments

[14] See Kurtz and Yellin (2015).

[15] Source of statistics: https://www.investopedia.com/articles/personal-finance/022615/can-family-survive-us-minimum-wage.asp

[16] Schmitt does refer to David Neumark and William Wascher's 2007 publication, but his conclusion is that their study 'is considerably more subjective and arguably less relevant to the US' (Schmitt, 2013: 8).

[17] Kall blames weak enforcement and penalties that are not punitive (Kall, 2017: 5).

Chapter 7

[1] See for example, Callus (2005) and Isaac and Lansbury (2005).

[2] Joseph E. Stiglitz stated this in his September 2018 address to the British Royal Society. Among other things, Stiglitz also noted the fact that in the US, monopoly incomes have been growing as a result of the government's relaxed implementation of anti-trust regulatory measures. See: https://www.youtube.com/watch?v=aemkMMrZWgM. The address took place on 11 September, 2018.

[3] See: https://www.bbc.com/news/business-25034598.

[4] Nicole Gracely was hired by Amazon (in the US) because of her exceptional ability to swiftly locate books. On the 29 November 2014, *The Guardian* published her article 'Being homeless is better than working for Amazon'. I was so disturbed when I read Nicole's article that it has stayed with me ever since. See: https://www.theguardian.com/money/2014/nov/28/being-homeless-is-better-than-working-for-amazon

[5] You can also listen to Sir Michael Marmot's own address to the 2016 Melbourne Writers Festival, where he is reading from chapter 6, pp. 171–173, of his book. See: https://www.youtube.com/watch?v=R6WjmJPOeRE

[6] Sir Michael Marmot is a medical doctor. He also served as a president of the British Medical Association (BMA) in 2010–2011.

[7] As it happens, Jeff Bezos, Amazon's owner, tops *Forbes*'s 2021 billionaires list.

[8] As the heading of Michael Sainato's 8 July 2018 *Guardian* article proposes, 'Exploited Amazon workers need a union', and I concur.

[9] At the time of his death, David Wilkie was driving his taxi. His passenger was a non-striking miner. Wilkie was killed by two striking miners who threw a block of concrete on his taxi from a footbridge that runs above that road.

[10] Britain's Falkland War ended with a victory in June 1982.

[11] See Keith Ewing and John Hendy QC (2015) for a detailed analysis of the potential consequences of this Bill. This bill became the Trade Union Act in 2016, implemented as of 1 March 2017.

[12] Professor Braham Dabscheck provides a comprehensive account of this confrontation in his 1998 publication 'The waterfront dispute: vendetta and the Australian Way'.

[13] See Kristin van Barneveld (2006) for a quite comprehensive account of the Work Choices legislation.

[14] For more information, see: http://www.abs.gov.au/ausstats/abs@.nsf/mf/1321.0

[15] The retrograde nature of Howard's Work Choice legislation is eloquently explained by the law professor, Ron McCallum in his 2006 article and by Sally Cowling et al's 2006 study, titled 'Work Choices: the low productivity road to underclass'. Anna Chapman's 2006 study offers yet another powerful expose this same legislation.

[16] See, for instance, Gregg Jericho's 2016 article '10 years on, the spirit of WorkChoices still lives' and Andrew Stewart et al's (2018) analysis on the stagnation of low and middle level wages.

[17] For more information, see: https://www.abc.net.au/news/2018-11-20/reserve-bank-phi lip-lowe-warns-of-low-wage-growth-impact/10515756

[18] Betsey Stevenson wrote this on the day Allan Kruger tragically took his own his life. See: Stevenson, B. (@BetseyStevenson), *Twitter*, 18 March 2019. https://twitter.com/betseystevenson/status/1107759930377945088?lang=en

[19] Warwick Smith works in Per Capita's Centre for Applied Policy for Positive Ageing (CAPPA) and in its Progressive Economics program. Before joining the Per Capita think tank, he worked as a research economist, consultant and freelance journalist.

[20] For more information, see: http://unemployedworkersunion.com/job-seekers-v-job-vaca ncy-data/

[21] For more information, see: http://unemployedworkersunion.com/job-seekers-v-job-vaca ncy-data/

[22] Many economists reckon that the number of the discouraged unemployed is as large as those who reported that they actively looked for a job on the week of the Australia's Bureau of Statistics survey. See, for instance, Ross (1985).

[23] Bartley's article is discussed more comprehensively in Chapter 10.

[24] This was reported by the OECD in a 2011 publication 'Divided we stand: inequalities in OECD countries'.

[25] For the etymology of the term 'Rust Belt' see the explanation that is provided by the Meriam-Webster dictionary. Source: https://www.merriam-webster.com/dictionary/rust%20belt

[26] Economists might describe this as a 'negative Keynesian-multiplier effect'.

[27] For a comprehensive account of Sweden's active manpower policy, see Winton Higgins's 1985 article, and his 2013 book jointly written with Geoff Dow.

[28] For more information, see: https://www.dailykos.com/stories/2013/2/24/1189512/
-FDR-s-Proposed-Marginal-Tax-Rate-Was-100. Being altogether unaware of FDR's
marginal tax rate (I know this to be a fact) Louis Haddad proposed an income cap in his
2005 book, *Towards a Well-Functioning Economy: The Evolution of Economic Systems and
Decision-Making*. In 2013 the Swiss voted against capping bosses pay to 12 times their
lowest paid workers. See BBC News, 24 November 2013. https://www.bbc.com/news/
business-25076879

[29] See Christian E. Weller's 2017 article for a critique of 'the supply-side' rationale for
tax cuts.

[30] See The Tax Foundation website: https://taxfoundation.org/country/united-states/
?gclid=CjwKCAiAnvj9BRA4EiwAuUMDf8CAGul5q2ADyp-rz5_ntH9QGsMhlEh
K8X4BRJXrGe0QRtGBI8z_uRoCrj0QAvD_BwE

[31] See The Tax Policy Center website: https://www.taxpolicycenter.org/statistics/histori
cal-highest-marginal-income-tax-rates

[32] See the Reuters article at: https://www.reuters.com/article/us-usa-kennedy-bush/geo
rge-h-w-bush-honored-for-courage-with-1990-tax-hikes-idUSBREA4308G20140504

[33] Ian Verrender (2021) wrote an article headed: 'Expecting a fair tax cut in 2024? Don't
count on it, Fair is fair but not when it comes to tax'.

[34] For non-economists: fundamentally, Keynesian economics maintains that governments
must step in and reduce troubling levels of unemployment because the modern market
system would not do it on its own.

[35] Frances Oldham Kelsey (PhD, MD) had to pass the verdict on the Thalidomide drug
upon her appointment as the head of the US's Food and Drug Administration (FDA) in
1960. She categorically prohibited its entry into the US. According to James Meikle's
article in *The Guardian* on 7 March 2016, worldwide the Thalidomide drug caused the
death of 80,000 babies, maimed 20,000 and caused an unknown number of miscarriages.
See: https://www.theguardian.com/society/2016/mar/06/thalidomide-caused-up-to-
10000-miscarriages-infant-deaths-uk

[36] A YouTube webcast of that interview has Professor Milton Friedman (2009) himself
expressing these views. See: https://www.youtube.com/watch?v=dZL25NSLhEA

[37] In July 2019 Forbes identified the Koch brothers as the equally ranked eleventh wealthiest
individuals in the world, with a wealth of US$50.5 billion each (they were even closer
to the top in some earlier years).

[38] See the Cato Institute's website: https://www.cato.org/cato-handbook-policymakers/
cato-handbook-policymakers-9th-edition-2022. The Cato Institute is a libertarian think
tank that owes its existence to Charles Koch.

Chapter 8

[1] There is even a high likelihood that they knew of the Massachusetts court case of 1926,
as well as of the introduction of regulation of asbestos particle density in the UK in
1930. The 1926 Massachusetts court delivered the first successful compensation claim
for the victims of an asbestos inflicted disease. The number of successful claims then ran
in the hundreds.

[2] Mesothelioma was first identified by Dr Christopher Wagner in 1960 when treating
South African workers who mined 'blue asbestos'.

[3] All the information on the use of asbestos in cigarettes comes from an article posted on
24 May 2009. See: http://www.asbestos.com/products/general/cigarette-filters.php

[4] PFAS represents a group of manmade chemicals (such as PFOA, PFOS, GenX and many
others). See the US EPA website: https://www.epa.gov/pfas/basic-information-pfas

[5] See ATSDR (2021) https://www.atsdr.cdc.gov/toxprofiles/tp200.pdf

6   North-Western University, Social Science Environmental Health Research Unit: https://pfasproject.com/parkersburg-west-virginia/

Chapter 9

1   Arthur Goldsmith, Darrick Hamilton and William Darity Jr's 2007 study exposes the fact that racial discrimination in the US is also modulated according to an entire spectrum of shades of blackness. Those with a lighter black skin are better paid than their darker brethren. And Daniel Hammermesh (2011) found that beauty also pays – handsomer white males receive a handsome wage premium.

2   Similar is the case of the 'subaltern', the ethnic and racial social groups in post-colonial societies. The US scholars, William Darity Jr. and Jessica Membhard (2000) found that the subaltern group represents the lowest paid, even in countries in which they are actually the largest group in the population.

3   For a detailed description of the discriminatory mindset of the Australian judges who decreed that women should be paid just over half (54 per cent) of the male wage even when their jobs are the same as those of the men, see Gill (1994b) 'Low pay and gender under wage regulation: the Australian experience'.

4   Note that they also rightly lament that only 88 out of 195 countries have introduced protective legislation.

5   Many readers would know that, as it happens, presently Joe Scarborough is Mika Brzezinski's spouse.

6   The *Feminist Economics* journal raised this same issue in 2000, in another special issue that likewise was devoted to the urgent need to have well defined policies that recognise the care duties that fall on women's shoulders. The 2000 issue was edited by Nancy Folbre and Susan Himmelweit who also wrote the Introduction to that issue.

7   Kimberlé Crenshaw is a lawyer and full-time professor in the University of California in Los Angeles. She is also the founder of Colombia University's Center for Intersectionality and Social Policy (CISPS) and the president of the Centre for Intersectional Justice (CIJ) in Berlin.

8   See, for example, Irene Greenman and Yu Xie (2008). See also Yu Xie and Kimberly Goyette (2003).

9   In 2016 the labour force participation among indigenous people was 52 per cent as compared with 77 per cent for the non-indigenous population. Nicholas Biddle (2013b) finds that the disposable income (that is, post-tax income) of the indigenous population in Australia is somewhat higher than their earned income, reflecting the fact that a significant number of indigenous Australians are very poor, and therefore depend on income-transfers from the federal government.

10   Calculated from data given in Wilson and Macdonald (2010: 10).

11   Note that 'degree' indicates a tertiary level qualification.

12   Morgan Liota (2018) writes on the impact of poverty on their living conditions. The inevitable result is also living in very crowded dwellings where the level of contagion is inevitably higher.

13   See the Creative Spirits website: http://www.creativespirits.info/aboriginalculture/polit ics/1946-pilbara-strike-australias-longest-strike#ixzz3pukaZZeI

14   For more detail on the ingenious organisation of this strike see the Creative Spirits website: http://www.creativespirits.info/aboriginalculture/politics/1946-pilbara-strike-australias-longest-strike#toc2

15   For more information, see: http://indigenousrights.net.au/civil_rights/equal_wa ges,_1963-66

16   For more information, see: http://indigenousrights.net.au/civil_rights/equal_wa ges,_1963-66

[17] It was Gouth Whitlam who negotiated the land claim between the traditional owners and the British Pastoral Company Ltd. As such, credit also goes to the Gurindji Elder, Vincent Lingiari, who led that strike.

[18] On land rights and native title legislation see the Creative Spirits website: http://www.creativespirits.info/aboriginalculture/land/aboriginal-land-rights#axzz3pTH9bxSv

[19] Or as the government of the day preferred to name it, The Northern Territory Emergency Response.

[20] Specifically, the Commission took the federal government to task in Chapter 3 of that report.

[21] He was also its Director from 1990 to 2010.

[22] Professor Jackson-Pulver described her own personal experience during her early tertiary studies in her interview with the Australian ABC radio interviewer Margaret Throsby. Her full journey to professorial chair is described in that program. See: http://www.abc.net.au/classic/content/2013/01/30/3678839.htm

[23] For more information, see: https://data.oecd.org/earnwage/gender-wage-gap.htm

[24] They propose that the larger gender pay gap in the US is a consequence of: (i) the US's significantly higher rate of overall wage inequality and (ii) that although job segregation between men and women has declined in the US, the level of gender segregation in the US is still higher than it is in the other five OECD countries.

[25] The figures are all based on the childcare expenditure borne by a couple with two young children and where each is earning the country's average wage. Data source: https://www.weforum.org/agenda/2019/04/these-countries-have-the-most-expensive-childcare/

[26] Technically speaking, the dataset is 'longitudinal'. This simply means that the data show differences (say between men and women's earning) both at a given point of time and how those differences have evolved over time.

[27] Initially, the admissions were blind to a certain degree, but not at the point of the final selection. See also Rebecca Blank's 1991 study. Claudia Goldin's seminal 1992 book has been one of the major path breakers of the feminist economists' critique of economic science.

[28] Simone Young related this information to Margaret Throsby on the ABC FM interview program on 24 August 2011.

[29] Many veteran computer users will recall the Alta Vista search engine. AltaVista Internet Software Inc. had a meteoric success shortly after being founded in 1995.

[30] For more information, see: https://www.catalyst.org/research/women-in-management/

[31] Similarly, the CISION public relations company reports that 70 per cent of job seekers value a company's commitment to diversity. See: https://www.prnewswire.com/news-releases/70-of-job-seekers-value-a-companys-commitment-to-diversity-when-evaluating-potential-employers-301079330.html

[32] The translators of the 2009 English language version of *The Second Sex* are Constance Borde and Sheila Maluvany Chevalier.

[33] Feminists have similarly stressed that 'gender', as distinct from sex, is a social construct.

[34] Williams and Peterson (1998) cite the Daniel Moynihan Report of 1965 as being a classic example of this genre.

[35] Karla Hoff and Joseph Stiglitz (2010) discuss purposely manufactured racial prejudices, citing Colishaw's and Dirk's studies.

[36] Cited in Hoff and Stiglitz (2010: 142). Professor Nicholas Dirk is a former Chancellor of the University of California at Berkeley.

[37] Celia Ridgeway is the Lucie Stern Professor of Sociology at the School of Humanities and Sciences at Stanford University. She was the president of the American Sociology Association in 2012–2013. In the very first page of the published address, Ridgeway

states that *status* is essentially inequality that is based on differences in awarded esteem and respect.

38 A 2022 article by Andrew Moran lists the names of ten major American corporations who in his words 'rake in profits' from prison inmates.

39 Sadhbh Walshe is a film maker and former staff writer for the CBS drama series The District. Whitney Benns (2015) offers a similarly bleak picture, in *The Atlantic* Magazine.

40 Andrew Forrest is an Australian mining magnate. In 2008, he was the wealthiest person in Australia.

41 As Noted earlier, the word longitudinal, is a technical term for statistical data that allows comparison both over time and across different groups at any given point of time.

Chapter 10

1 Feather (1990) offers a comprehensive survey of the academic literature on the psychological impact of unemployment and, by extension, also on the psychological significance of paid work.

2 For economists alone, technically speaking, I am referring to the economist's 'labour supply' analysis.

3 Sir Michael Marmot is a fully qualified medical doctor. He was the president of the British Medical Association (BMA) in 2010–2011; and he gave his acceptance address, Fighting the Alligators of Health Inequality, on 29 June 2010. See: https://www.bmj.com/content/341/bmj.c3617

4 In the introductory chapter of Marmot and Wilkinson (2006), Marmot notes that he became aware of the impact of the hierarchical power structure at the workplace on individual wellbeing when he began to analyse data from the first 1978 Whitehall study of British civil servants (see Marmot et al, 1978).

5 In Whitehall II study, 1985–1988, Marmot and Brunner (2005) discerned a clear association between the occupational status and the incidence of a number of specific manifestations of stress. Here again, stress is lowest at the top, and progressively increases as we go down the job hierarchy.

6 This is based on research results that are reported in Marmot (2004).

7 That chapter has an excellent diagram that summarises the essence of these biological pathways. See Marmot and Wilkinson (2006: 17).

8 As we shall see shortly, Butterworth et al (2011) found that yes, it is true that having a job is better than not having a job, as far as one's health consequences are concerned, but this rule has one glaring exception – it is not true when the alternative to joblessness is a truly 'lousy' job.

9 It was first published in English, in 1971.

10 Jahoda's approach, critics have argued, is functionalist and therefore leaves no room for personal agency. Yet it is important to note that she does acknowledge differences between individual and group responses to given circumstances. It should also be noted that, at the same time, her critics have nevertheless acknowledged her intellectual contribution to the analysis of the psychological function of paid work.

11 See Bartley (1994: 333).

Chapter 11

1 Montgomery's account is presented in more detail in Chapter 6.

2 For instance, see Conyon and Freeman (2001).

3 His perspective on the essence of power over others is expressed in his 1951 and 1969 books.

4 For instance, some of us would contend that the objection of a significant number of low income and poor American citizens to President Obama's national health program is a consequence of such a capacity.

5 This resonates with Antonio Gramsci's description of capitalism's cultural hegemony.

6 The media, both in print and on screen, has covered the Lordstown revolt extensively. Managers became attracted to job enrichment programs, Taylorism was under attack, and the subject of alienation at work attracted a substantial amount of Academic attention.

7 I have been alerted to Ervin Goffman's work by Anthony Giddens's discourse in his 1979 book.

8 The Thirteenth Amendment abolished slavery in the US. It was passed by Congress on 31 January 1865, ratified by the required number of states in the Senate on 5 December 1865, and proclaimed on 18 December 1865.

9 See Karen Tucker Anderson's 1982 study, 'Last hired, first fired: black women during World War II'.

10 Steven Marglin offers an eloquent argument in support of this proposition in his 1974 study.

11 See Zhang and Yu (2022) for a recent article on abusive supervision of students.

12 Dr Carlo Caponecchia is a member of the Department of Psychology at the University of New South Wales, Sydney, Australia. At the time of writing this book he is the president of the International Association on Workplace Bullying and Harassment (IAWBH).

13

> The Drake International survey of more than 800 employees also revealed 25 per cent had experienced bullying themselves. Silence, isolation, verbal insults and sarcasm were the most common cases, with public humiliation ranking in second place. Bullying from managers or supervisors represented about 50 per cent of cases, while 25 per cent of respondents reported being targeted by other employees. (www.BullyFree.com.au)

14 As Amos Tversky and Daniel Kahneman's seminal 1974 and 1981 publications have shown us, the framing of survey (or any other) questions, can substantially shape the answers.

15 For instance, a 2004 UK study of care professionals by Tehrani found that within a two-year period, 40 per cent of subjects in the sample had been bullied. In contrast, a 2001 Danish study by Hogh and Dofradottir that recorded the experience of 'repeated exposure to a slander and/or nasty teasing' found that (only) two per cent of the subjects in their study had that experience.

16 This study emphasises that its database is large and representative of the countries' workplaces.

Chapter 12

1 Thomas Hobbs (1588–1679) based his social contract theory on 'natural law', perceiving the contract as being in the interest of people who understand that in the state of nature, without a commonwealth, 'a man is wolf to man'.

2 The terminology of first-, second- and third-generation rights follows the proposal made by Czech jurist, Karl Vasak in 1979 at the International Institute of Human Rights in Strasburg. He adopted the French Revolution's principle of 'liberty, equality and fraternity', as an apt description of three phases in the determination of human rights. These phases have, in turn, been given to names of first-, second- and third-generation rights. The second emerged during the period between the First and Second World Wars.

3 In the same vein, Isabelle Ferreras and her co-authors identify a conflictual relationship between capitalism and the core tenets of democracy. Specifically, the authors note that this conflict has been highly visible during the COVID-19 pandemic, when large numbers

of those we rightly call 'essential workers' are still among our the lowest paid and most powerless members of our workforce (Ferreras et al, 2022).

4   Clementina Black's 1907 book, *Sweated Industries and the Minimum Wage* was a major companion to the Webbs' Industrial Democracy. Note that 'sweater' was a pejorative description for an employer who pays very low wages that fail to meet minimum living needs.

5   For an example of mutual help organisations that are created by the cooperative movement, see Mohit Dave's 2021 article.

6   Professor Vera Negri Zamagni is an economist who has been studying the cooperative movement very closely for some time now.

7   The transcript of John Duda's 2016a interview with professor Vera Negri Zamagni provides a quite comprehensive description of the Emilia Romagna cooperative sector and its history. John Duda's 2016b article offers further descriptive detail.

8   Alfonso Rodrigues et al. also note that the 65-year-old Mondragon cooperative remains competitive, while its worker-members attest to enjoying an emotionally rewarding working experience (Rodrigues et al, 2022).

9   The full title of this report is 'The Beveridge Report 1942: Social Insurance and Allied Services'. In 1940, Ernest Bevin as the Minister of Labour in the UK, asked William Beveridge to look into the system of social security that lacked in coherence because it was a collection of disparate pieces of legislation that were enacted at different times. A year later the British government commissioned Beveridge to in addition write a report on how to rebuild the country once the Second World War was over.

10   See his 1950 book, *Citizenship and Social Class: and Other Essays.*

11   Specifically, his case for social rights rests on the proposition that citizenship entails 'a claim to be admitted to a share in the social heritage; which in turn means a claim to be accepted as full members of society, namely, as citizens' (Goodin and Petit, 1997: 293).

12   Also republished in Goodin and Petit (1997).

13   See Young (1989).

14   The actual target of her critique is the advocacy of participatory democracy. The latter, she argues, cannot remedy the 'privatisation of the political process', that is, 'consigning of policy making to back room dealing between regulatory agencies and powerful interests' (Young, in Goodin and Petit, 1997: 257).

15   John Gerard Ruggie is a Professor of Human Rights and International Affairs at Harvard's Kennedy School of Government.

Chapter 13

1   In 2016, a world scientists research team led by Nerille Abram, a professor at the Australian National University (ANU), published an article describing the research team's scientific findings. They discovered that global warming has left very clear traces of its impact on our planet as early as 180 years ago. See: https://www.anu.edu.au/news/all-news/humans-have-caused-climate-change-for-180-years

2   It was Friedman himself who came up with the term 'Green New Deal'.

3   Among other things, their manifesto stresses the need for a very effective insulation of all buildings against heat, well maintained and highly effective public transport systems, shared electric vehicles and affordable accommodation for all.

4   Specifically, H. Res. 109 – 116th Congress (2019-2020) and S. Res. 59 – 116 Congress (2019-2020), sponsored by representative Alexandria Ocasio-Cortez (D-NY) and senator Ed Markey (D-MA). The proposal was passed by the House, on 7 February 2019, but rejected by the Senate on 20 April 2019.

5   Both articles were published on the same day.

6   Reacting to Congress representative Alexandria Ocasio Cortez and senator Ed Markey's 2019 GND proposal, the Cato Institute asserted that global warming has been a negative contributor only since 1975, the next paragraph then begins with the following statement: 'Fortunately, and contrary to much of the rhetoric surrounding climate change, there is ample time to develop such technologies, which will require substantial capital investment by individuals'. See: https://www.cato.org/research/global-warming. Australia's environment minister (who was in office from 28 August 2018 to 21 May 2022), Angus Taylor, is similarly arguing that we should adopt a hands-off climate policy and simply wait patiently for alternative technologies to take charge (Greber, 2021).

7   See: Abraham (2017), who cites the research report written by David Coady et al (2017). See: https://data.worldbank.org/indicator/SE.XPD.TOTL.GD.ZS

8   The source of these data is https://data.worldbank.org/indicator/SE.XPD.TOTL.GD.ZS

9   The global magnitude of fossil fuel subsidies reported in this 2019 publication are identical to those reported in the Coady et al (2017) publication.

10 See 23 August 2018, CNBC: https://www.cnbc.com/2018/08/23/trump-says-the-coal-industry-is-back-the-data-say-otherwise.html

11 See Chan (2014).

12 The Adani Group is a multinational conglomerate with a whole array of different businesses. Its headquarters are in Gujarat, India.

13 The COVID-19 pandemic has also exposed the vital role that is played by face-to-face teaching.

14 Antonio Negri and Mario Tonti are academic scholars. The late Andre Gortz was a writer and journalist (and also the founder of the French weekly, *El Nouvel Observateur*).

15 Isabelle Ferreras et al's 2022 book draws attention to the conflict between the nature of capitalism and the core principles of democracy. Ferreras et al. also note that COVID-19 has exposed the fact that 'society's lowest paid and least empowered continue to work risky jobs that keep our capitalism humming'. This, they stress, fails to abide by the fundamental rights that are embedded in the concept of democracy.

16 See David Frayne's (2015) book, *The Refusal of Work: The Theory and the Practical Refusal of Work*, and Kathi Weeks's (2011) book, *The Problem with Work: Feminism, Marxism, Antiwork Politics, and Postwork Imaginaries*.

17 See Standing's 2009 book, *Globalization: Building Occupational Citizenship*, and his 2011 book, *The Precariat: The New Dangerous Class*.

18 Two years later, during the COVID-19 pandemic, Dawson restates her position: 'Despite lending my name to a recent [during the pandemic] call for a liveable income guarantee to see people through this crisis, I don't agree that a permanent UBI is the answer to long-term inequality and economic insecurity' (Dawson, *Australian Financial Review*, 9 April, 2020.

19 A conversation on The Recovery in the Bin website, is headed 'Universal Basic Income, a neoliberal scam': https://recoveryinthebin.org/2018/05/15/universal-basic-income-a-neoliberal-scam-discussion/. All participants agree with the statement in the heading. Their arguments are well worth reading.

20 This shall have to be legislated, because neither market forces nor trade unions could bring about such cuts across the board.

21 The Director of the Centre for Equitable Growth at the University of California at Berkeley, Professor Emanuel Saez and Gabriel Zucman told us in their 2014 study, that during the 65 years between 1913 and 1978, the concentration of wealth in the US had declined steadily, but that it has been rising quite rapidly ever since. Also, in 2012 the share of the top 0.1 per cent wealth owners was as large as the combined wealth of the bottom 90 per cent of the US population (Saez and Zucman, 2014: 47, Table 1).

[22] For more information, see: https://www.oxfam.org/sites/www.oxfam.org/files/file_atta chments/bp210-economy-one-percent-tax-havens-180116-en_0.pdf

[23] For more information, see: https://www.icij.org/investigations/panama-papers/

[24] See Cardwell (2017) and Rathi (2017).

[25] See article by Deb Erdley (2016).

[26] See article by Monica Humphries (2019).

[27] See the story of the Australian company Smart Steel Solutions in a recent report of the economic and business advising business, AlphaBeta Advisors and the story of Smart Solutions: http://www.abc.net.au/news/2017-07-06/what-jobs-will-survive-as-rob ots-move-into-the-workplace/8685894

[28] See Borland and Coheli (2017).

[29] Source: USAToday, 24 March 2014. See: http://www.usatoday.com/story/news/nat ion-now/2014/03/24/Minimum wage-rent-affordable-housing/6817639/

References

Abraham, J. (2017) 'Fossil fuels subsidies are staggering $5 tn a year', *The Guardian* [online] 7 August, Available from: https://www.theguardian.com/environment/climate-consensus-97-per-cent/2017/aug/07/fossil-fuel-subsidies-are-a-staggering-5-tn-per-year

Abram, N. J., McGregor, H. V., Tierney, J. E., Evans, M. N., McKay, N. P., Kaufman, D. S. (2016) 'Early onset of industrial-era warming across the oceans and continents', *Nature*, Aug 25; 536(7617): 411–418. doi:10.1038/nature19082.

Acemoglu, D. (2019) 'Why a universal basic income is a bad idea', *Project Syndicate* [online] Available from: http://tankona.free.fr/acemoglu619b.pdf

Akerlof, G. A. (1982) 'Labour contracts as partial gift exchange', *Quarterly Journal of Economics*, 97(4): 543–569. Also republished in G. A. Akerlof and J. L. Yellen (eds) (1986) *Efficiency Wage Models of the Labour Market*, Ambridge: Cambridge University Press, pp. 66–92.

Akerlof, G. A. and Shiller, R. J. (2015) *Phishing for Phools: The Economics of Manipulation and Deception*, Princeton: Princeton University Press.

Allard, T. and Patty, A. (2014) 'Tony Abbott's Work for the Dole scheme doesn't add up', *Sydney Morning Herald* [online] 1 August, Available from: https://www.smh.com.au/national/tony-abbotts-work-for-the-dole-scheme-doesnt-add-up-20140801-zzc8u.html

Alleyne, A. (2004) 'Black identity and workplace oppression', *Counselling and Psychology Research*, 4(1): 4–8.

AlphaBeta (2017) 'The automation advantage', *AlphaBeta* [online], Available from: http://www.alphabeta.com/wp-content/uploads/2017/08/The-Automation-Advantage.pdf

Alt, J. and Iversen, T. (2017) 'Labor market segmentation, and preferences for redistribution', *American Journal of Political Science*, 61(1): 1–36.

Altman, J. C. (2007) *The Howard Government's Northern Territory Intervention: Are Neo-Paternalism and Indigenous Development Compatible?*, Australian National University, Centre for Aboriginal Economic Policy Research, Topical Issue 16/2007.

Alvaredo, F., Atkinson, A. B., Piketty, T. and Saez, E. (2013) 'The top 1 percent in international and historical perspective', *Journal of Economic Perspectives*, 27(3): 3–20.

Amo-Agyei, S. (2020) 'The migrant pay gap: understanding wage differences between migrants and Nationals', International Labour Office (ILO) [online], Available from: https://www.ilo.org/wcmsp5/groups/public/---ed_protect/---protrav/---migrant/documents/briefingnote/wcms_763796.pdf

Anderson, K. T. (1982) 'Last hired, first fired: black women workers during World War II', *Journal of American History*, 69(1): 82–97.

Arrow, K. J. (1972) 'Models of job discrimination', in A. H. Pascal *Racial Discrimination in Economic Life*, Lexington: D.C. Health, pp. 83–102.

Arrow, K. J. (1963) 'Uncertainty and the welfare economics of medical care', *American Economic Review*, 53(5): 941–973.

Arrow, K. J. (1973) 'The theory of discrimination', in O. Ashenfelter and A. Rees (eds) *Discrimination in Labour Markets*, Princeton: Princeton University Press.

Arrow, K. J. (2011) 'Economics and inequality', *Boston Review* [online] 2 December, Available from: https://bostonreview.net/forum/occupy-fut ure/economics-and-inequality

Arrow, K. J. and Debreu, G. (1954) 'Existence of equilibrium for a competitive economy', *Econometrica*, 22(3): 265–290.

Arthur, P. (2009) 'How transitions reshaped human rights: a conceptual history of human rights', *Human Rights Quarterly*, 31(2): 321–363.

Atkinson, A. B. (1970) 'On the measurement of inequality', *Journal of Economic Theory*, 2(3): 244–263.

Atkinson, A.B. and Piketty, T. (eds) (2007) *Top Incomes over the Twentieth Century: A Contrast Between Continental European and English-Speaking Countries*, Oxford: Oxford University Press.

ATSDR (US Department of Health and Social Services: Agency for Toxic Substances and Disease Registry) (2021) 'Toxicological profile for perfluoroalkyls' [online], Available from: https://www.atsdr.cdc.gov/toxp rofiles/tp200.pdf

Aubusson, K. (2017a) 'One third of ICU doctors bullied, survey finds, prompting crackdown by College of Intensive Care Medicine', *Sydney Morning Herald* [online] 27 January, Available from: https://www.smh.com. au/healthcare/one-third-of-icu-doctors-bullied-survey-finds-prompting-crackdown-by-college-of-intensive-care-medicine-20170126-gtz362.html

Aubusson, K. (2017b) 'She was eaten alive: Chloe Abbot's sister Micaela's message for the next generation of doctors', *Sydney Morning Herald* [online] 5 July, Available from: https://www.smh.com.au/healthcare/ she-was-eaten-alive-dr-chloe-abbotts-sister-micaelas-message-for-the-next-generation-of-doctors-20170704-gx4jt3.html

Aubusson, K. (2018a) 'Westmead Hospital ICU stripped of training accreditation over alleged bullying', *Sydney Morning Herald* [online] 26 October, Available from: https://www.smh.com.au/national/nsw/ westmead-hospital-icu-stripped-of-training-accreditation-over-alleged-bullying-20181026-p50c8j.html

Aubusson, K. (2018b) 'Sydney hospital's cardiothoracic surgery unit trainee ban over bullying', *Sydney Morning Herald* [online] 2 November, Available from: https://www.smh.com.au/national/nsw/sydney-hospital-s-cardiothoracic-surgery-unit-trainee-ban-over-bullying-20181101-p50de3.html

Auter, D. H. (2015) 'Why are there still so many jobs? The history and future of workplace automation', *Journal of Economic Perspectives*, 29(3): 3–30.

Bachrach, P. and Baratz, M. S. (1970) *Power and Poverty: Theory and Practice*, Oxford: Oxford University Press.

Baird, M., Ford, M. and Hill, E. (2017) *Women, Work and Care in the Asia-Pacific*, Abingdon: Routledge.

Baird, M., Hamilton, M. and Constantin, A. (2021) 'Gender equality and parental leave in Australia: a decade of giant leap or baby steps?' *Journal of Industrial Relations*, 63(4): 546–567.

Barnay, T. (2016) 'Health, work and working conditions: a review of the European economic literature', *The European Journal of Health Economics*, 17(16): 693–709.

Bartley, M. (1994) 'Unemployment and ill health: understanding the relationship', *Journal of Epidemiology and Community Health*, 48(4): 333–337.

Battilana, J., Yen, J., Ferreras, I. and Ramarajan, L. (2022) 'Democratizing work: redistributing power in organizations for a democratic and sustainable future', *Organization Theory*, 3(1): 1–21.

Becker, G. S. (1964) *Human Capital: A Theoretical and Empirical Analysis with Special Reference to Education*, Chicago: The University of Chicago Press.

Benns, W. (2015) 'American slavery reinvented: The Fourteenth Amendment forbade slavery and servitude, "except for whereof the party shall be convicted"', *The Atlantic* [online] 2 September, Available from: https://www.theatlantic.com/business/archive/2015/09/prison-labor-in-america/406177/

Bertrand, M. and Mullainathan, S. (2004) 'Are Emily and Greg more employable than Lakisha and Jamal? A field experiment on labour market discrimination', *American Economic Review*, 94(4): 991–1013.

Bestelmeyer, P. E. G., Rouger, J., DeBruine, L. M. and Belin, P. (2010) 'Auditory adaptation in vocal effect perception', *Cognition*, 117(2): 217–223.

Beveridge, W. (1942) *Social Insurance and Allied Services* (Cmd. 6404), London: H.M.S.O.

Bhabha, J. (2009) 'Arendt's children', *Human Rights Quarterly*, 31(2): 410–451.

Biaggio, M. (1997) 'Sexual harassment of lesbian at the workplace', *Journal of Lesbian Studies*, 1(3–4): 89–98.

Bibby, A. (2012) 'Co-operatives in Spain – Mondragon leads the way: co-operatives round the world could learn a lot from Spanish co-op giant Mondragon', *The Guardian* [online] 12 March, Available from: https://www.theguardian.com/social-enterprise-network/2012/mar/12/cooperatives-spain-mondragon

Biddle, N. (2013a) 'Education Part 2: School education', CAEPR Indigenous Population Project; 2011 Census Papers, Paper 8. Centre for Aboriginal Economic Research Policy, ANU.

Biddle, N. (2013b) 'Income', CAEPR Indigenous Population Project; 2011 Census Papers, Paper 11. Centre for Aboriginal Economic Research Policy, ANU.

Billinger, S. and Workiewicz, M. (2019) 'Fading hierarchies and the emergence of new forms of organization', *Journal of Organization Design*, 8(17): 1–6.

Binsted, T. (2014) 'James Hardie asbestos compensation scheme millions short after big dividends', *Sydney Morning Herald* [online] 9 September, Available from: https://www.smh.com.au/business/james-hardie-asbes tos-compensation-scheme-millions-short-after-big-dividends-20140908-10duod.html

Black, C. (1907) *Sweated Industries and the Minimum Wage*, London: Duckworth.

Blank, R. M. (1991) 'The effects of double-blind versus single-blind reviewing: experimental evidence from The American Economic Review', *The American Economic Review*, 81(5): 1041–1067.

Blau, F. D. and Kahn, L. M. (2000) 'Gender differences in pay', *The Journal of Economic Perspectives*, 14(4): 75–99.

Borland, J. and Tseng, Y.-P. (2004) 'Does "Work for the Dole" work?' Melbourne: Melbourne University Library [online], Available from: https://minerva-access.unimelb.edu.au/handle/11343/33797

Borland, J. and Coheli, M. (2017) 'Are robots taking our jobs?', *Australian Economic Review*, 50(4): 377–397.

Boulding, K. E. (1980) *Illustrating Economics: Beasts, Ballads and Aphorisms*, Abington on Thames: Routledge.

Broderick, E. (2009) 'The gender gap in retirements savings and unlawful age discrimination against older workers', Australian Human Rights Commission [online], Available from: https://humanrights.gov.au/our-work/sex-discrimination/publications/accumulating-poverty-womens-experiences-inequality-over

Brynin, M. and Güveli, A. (2012) 'Understanding the ethnic gap in Britain', *Work Employment and Society*, 26(4): 574–587.

Bump, P. (2015) 'The disproportional prison population in the United States, visualized', *The Washington Post* [online] 18 December, Available from: https://www.washingtonpost.com/news/the-fix/wp/2015/12/18/the-disproportionate-prison-population-of-the-united-states-visualized/?variant=116ae929826d1fd3

Bump, P. (2016) 'The top 25 hedge fund managers earn more than all the kindergarten teachers in the US combined', *The Washington Post* [online] 10 May, Available from: https://www.washingtonpost.com/news/the-fix/wp/2015/05/12/the-top-25-hedge-fund-managers-earn-more-than-all-kindergarten-teachers-combined/

Bury, J. P. T. (ed.) (1964) *The New Cambridge Modern History*, Volume X, Cambridge: Cambridge University Press.

Butterworth, P., Leach, L., Strazdins, L. et al (2011) 'The psychological quality of work determines whether employment has benefits for mental health: results from a longitudinal national household panel survey', *Occupational and Environmental Medicine*, 68(11): 806–812.

Cadwalladr, C. (2013) 'My week as an Amazon insider', *The Guardian* [online] 1 December, Available from: https://www.theguardian.com/technology/2013/dec/01/week-amazon-insider-feature-treatment-employees-work

Callus, R. (2005) 'The re-regulation of Australian industrial relations: the role of the Hancock Inquiry', in J. Isaac and R. Lansbury (eds) *Labour Market Deregulation: Rewriting the Rules*, Sydney: Federation Press, pp. 11–121.

Caponecchia, C. (2008) 'Cultural change part of stopping the bullies', *Sydney Morning Herald*, 15 July, Available from: https://www.smh.com.au/national/cultural-change-part-of-stopping-the-bullies-20080715-gdsm5h.html

Caporaso, J. A. and Levine, D. P. (1992) *Theories of Political Economy*, Cambridge: Cambridge University Press.

Card, D. (1992a) 'Do minimum wages reduce employment? A case study of California, 1987–89', *Industrial and Labor Relations Review*, 46(1): 38–54.

Card, D. (1992b) 'Using regional variation in wages to measure the effects of the federal minimum wage', *Industrial and Labor Relations Review*, 46(1): 22–37.

Card, D. and Krueger, A. (1994) 'Minimum wages and employment: a case study of the fast-food industry in New Jersey and Pennsylvania', *American Economic Review*, 48: 772–793.

Card, D. and Krueger, A. (1995) *Myth and Measurement: The New Economics of the Minimum Wage*, Princeton: Princeton University Press.

Cardwell, D. (2017) 'Coal country's power plants are turning away from coal', *The New York Times* [online] 21 May, Available from: https://www.nytimes.com/2017/05/26/business/energy-environment/coal-power-renewable-energy.html

Carr, E. W., Reece, A., Kellerman, G. R. and Robichaux, A. (2019) 'The value of belonging at work', *Harvard Business Review* [online] 16 December, Available from: https://hbr.org/2019/12/the-value-of-belonging-at-work

Castilla, E. J. (2008) 'Gender, race, and meritocracy in organizational careers', *American Journal of Sociology*, 113(6): 1479–1526.

Catalyst (2022) 'Women in management: quick take', Catalyst: Workplaces that Work for Women [online] 1 March, Available from: https://www.catalyst.org/research/women-in-management/

Chan, G. (2014) 'Tony Abbott says "coal is good for humanity" while opening a coal mine', *Guardian Australia*, 13 October, Available from: https://www.theguardian.com/world/2014/oct/13/tony-abbott-says-coal-is-good-for-humanity-while-opening-mine.

Chandler, M. J. and Lalonde, C. (1998) 'Cultural continuity as a hedge against suicide in Canada's First Nations', *Transcultural Psychiatry*, 35(2): 191–219.

Chapman, A. (2006) 'Unfair dismissal law and work choices: from safety net standard to legal privilege', *The Economic and Labour Relations Review*, 16(2): 237–264.

Christodoulou, M. (2017) '"This house killed me": DIY home renovators the third wave of asbestos victims', *Sydney Morning Herald*, June 1.

Clément, A. (2005) 'Changing perceptions of the poor in classical economic thought', *Chaiers d'économie Politique/Papers of Political Economy*, 49: 65–86.

Coady, D., Parry, I., Sears, L. and Shand, B. (2017) 'How large are global fuel subsidies?', *World Development*, 91(C): 11–27.

Coady, D., Parry, I., Nghia-Piotr, L. and Shang, B. (2019) 'Global fossil subsidies remain large: an update based on country level estimates', IMF Working Paper, WP 19/89 [online] 2 May, Available from: https://www.imf.org/en/Publications/WP/Issues/2019/05/02/Global-Fossil-Fuel-Subsidies-Remain-Large-An-Update-Based-on-Country-Level-Estimates-46509

Collins, H. (2003) *Employment Law*, Oxford: Oxford University Press.

Conyon, M. J. and Freeman, R. (2001) 'Shared modes of compensation and firm performance: UK evidence', NBER Working Paper, No. 8448.

Cooligan, T. W. and Higgins, E. M. (2005) 'Workplace stress aetiology and consequences', *Journal of Workplace Behavioural Health*, 21(2): 89–97.

Cooper, C. L., Hoel, H. and Faragher, B. (2004) 'Bullying is detrimental to health, but all bullying behaviours are not necessarily equally damaging', *British Journal of Guidance and Counselling*, 32(3): 367–338.

Cooper, D. (2019) 'Raising the federal minimum wage to $15 by 2024 would lift pay for nearly 40 million workers', Economic Policy Institute [online] 5 February, Available from: https://www.epi.org/publication/raising-the-federal-minimum-wage-to-15-by-2024-would-lift-pay-for-nearly-40-million-workers/

Coote, A. (2019) 'Universal basic income doesn't work. Let's boost the public realm instead', *The Guardian* [online] 6 May, Available from: https://www.theguardian.com/commentisfree/2019/may/06/universal-basic-income-public-realm-poverty-inequality

Coote, A. and Yazici, E. (2019) *Universal Basic Income: A Trade Union Perspective*, Public Services International [online], Available from: https://www.world-psi.org/sites/default/files/documents/research/en_ubi_full_report_2019.pdf

Corderoy, A. (2014) 'Indigenous gap is not closing, getting worse in some cases', *Sydney Morning Herald*, [online] 10 September, Available from: https://www.smh.com.au/national/nsw/indigenous-gap-is-not-closing-getting-worse-in-some-cases-20140910-10extj.html

Cowling, S., LaJeneusse, R., Mitchell, W. and Watts, M. (2006) 'The low productivity road to underclass'. *Australian Journal of Social Issues*, 41(2): 221–232.

Cowlishaw, G. (1999) *Rednecks, Headeggs, and Blackfellas: A Study of Racial Power and Intimacy in Australia*, St Leonard, NSW: Allen and Unwin.

Crenshaw, K. W. (1989) 'Demarginalising the intersection of race and sex: a black feminist critique of antidiscrimination doctrine, feminist theory and antiracist politics', *University of Chicago Legal Forum*, 1(1): 139–167.

Critical Theorist and Activist Collective (2015) 'Universal Basic Income, a neoliberal scam: discussion', Recovery in the Bin [online] 15 May, Available from: https://recoveryinthebin.org/2018/05/15/universal-basic-income-a-neoliberal-scam-discussion/

Crothers, L. M., Lipinski, J. and Minutolo, M. C. (2009) 'Cliques, rumors, and gossip by the water cooler: female bullying in the workplace', *The Psychologist-Manager Journal*, 12(2): 97–110.

Cutcher-Gershenfeld, J., Brooks, D. and Mulloy, M. (2015) *Inside the Ford UAW Transformation: Pivotal Events in Valuing Work and Delivering Results*, Boston: MIT Press.

Dabscheck, B. (1987) 'New right or old wrong? Ideology and industrial relations', *Journal of Industrial Relations*, 29(4): 425–449.

Dabscheck, B. (1998) 'The waterfront dispute: vendetta and the Australian way', *Economic and Labour Relations Review*, 9(2): 155–187.

Dahl, R. (1961) *Who Governs: Democracy in an American City*, New Haven: Yale University Press.

Darity, W. Jr (2003) 'Employment discrimination, segregation, and health', *American Journal of Public Health*, 93(2): 226–231.

Darity, W. Jr and Membhard, J. G. (2000) 'Cross-national comparisons of racial and ethnic economic inequality', *American Economic Review*, 90(2): 308–311.

Dave, M. (2021) 'Retracted: resilient to crises: how cooperatives are adapting sustainably to overcome Covid 19-induced challenges', *International Journal of Rural Management*, 17(1): 1–27.

Davis, G. (2021) *On Life's Lottery*, Melbourne: Hachette.

Dawson, E. (2018) 'Plan for universal basic income ignores the value of work', *Sydney Morning Herald* [online] 5 April, Available from: https://www.smh.com.au/politics/federal/plan-for-universal-basic-income-igno res-the-value-of-work-20180405-p4z7vo.html

De Beauvoir, S. (1949) *The Second Sex*, translated into English by C. Borde and S. Maluvany-Chevalier (2011), New York: Vintage Books.

Denniss, R. (2018) 'Why Adani won't die', *The Monthly* [online] May, Available from: https://www.themonthly.com.au/issue/2018/may/152 5096800/richard-denniss/why-adani-won-t-die#mtr

Dervis, K. (2016) 'Brief: income distribution within countries – rising inequality', August, Global Economy and Development Series, Brookings.

Dirks, N. B. (2001) *Castes of Mind: Colonialism and the Making of Modern India*, Princeton: Princeton University Press.

Doeringer, P. B. and Piore, M. J. (1970) *Internal Labour Market Analysis and Market Power*, Westport: Praeger Publishers.

Dominelli, L. (1999) 'Community, citizenship and empowerment', *Sociology*, 33(2): 441–446.

Dorey, P. (2010) 'A poverty of imagination: blaming the poor for inequality', *The Political Quarterly*, 81(3): 333–343.

Duda, J. (2016a) 'Learning from Emilia Romagna's cooperative economy: an interview with Vera Negri Zamagni', TheNextSystemProject [online] 18 February, Available from: https://thenextsystem.org/learning-from-emilia-romagna

Duda, J. (2016b) 'The Italian region where co-ops produce a third of its GDP' *Yes!* [online], Available from: https://www.yesmagazine.org/economy/2016/07/05/the-italian-place-where-co-ops-drive-the-economy-and-most-people-are-members

Edward, C. (2019) 'Green New Deal would crush our liberal values', Cato at Liberty [Blog] 9 February, Available from: https://www.cato.org/blog/green-new-deal-would-crush-liberal-values

Elliot, L. (2016) 'Richest 62 people as wealthy as half of the world poorest', *The Guardian* [online] 18 January, Available from: https://www.theguardian.com/business/2016/jan/18/richest-62-billionaires-wealthy-half-world-population-combined

Elliot, L. (2019) 'World's 26 richest people own as much as poorest 50%, says Oxfam', *The Guardian* [online] 21 January, Available from: https://www.theguardian.com/business/2019/jan/21/world-26-richest-people-own-as-much-as-poorest-50-per-cent-oxfam-report

Erdley, D. (2016) 'Couple turns former miners into workers in region's growing tech sector', *Trib Live* [online] 6 August, Available from: https://archive.triblive.com/news/pennsylvania/couple-turns-former-miners-into-workers-in-regions-growing-tech-sector/

Ewing, K. D. and Hendy, J. (2015) 'Kill the Bill', European Lawyers for Workers Network [online], Available from: http://elw-network.eu/wp-content/uploads/2015/09/Keith-Ewing-and-John-Hendy-Kill-the-Bill.pdf

Fan, J. K., Amik III, B. C., Richardson, L., Scott-Marshall, H. and McLeod, C. B. (2018) 'Labor market and health trajectories during periods of economic recession and expansion in the United States, 1988-2011', *Scandinavian Journal of Work Environment and Health*, 44(6): 639–646.

Feather, N. T. (1990) *The Psychological Impact of Unemployment*, New York City: Springer-Verlag.

Fellner, C. (2018) 'Toxic secrets: The town that 3M built – where kids are dying of cancer', *Sydney Morning Herald* [online] 15 June, Available from: https://www.smh.com.au/world/north-america/toxic-secrets-the-town-that-3m-built-where-kids-are-dying-of-cancer-20180613-p4zl83.html

Ferber, M. and Blau, F. (1987) 'Discrimination: empirical evidence from the United States', *American Economic Review*, 77(2): 316–320.

Ferber, M. and Nelson, J. (eds) (1993) *Beyond Economic Man: Feminist Theory of Economics*, Chicago: The University of Chicago Press.

Ferguson, A. (2020) 'Scourge of wage fraud demands action', *Sydney Morning Herald* [online] 22 February, Available from: https://www.smh.com.au/business/workplace/scourge-of-wage-fraud-demands-action-20200220-p542wc.html

Ferguson, A., Danckert, S. and Toft, K. (2015) '7-Eleven: Investigation exposes shocking exploitation of convenience store workers', *Sydney Morning Herald* [online] 29 August, Available from: https://www.smh.com.au/business/workplace/7eleven-investigation-exposes-shocking-exploitation-of-convenience-store-workers-20150828-gja276.html

Ferreras, I., Battilana, J. and Meda, D. (eds) (2022) *Democratizing Work: The Case for Reorganising the Economy*, Chicago: Chicago University Press.

Ferris, P. (2004) 'A preliminary typology of organizational response to allegations of workplace bullying: see no evil, hear no evil, speak no evil', *British Journal of Guidance and Counselling*, 32(3): 389–395.

Fleming, S. (2019) 'These countries have the most expensive childcare', World Economic Forum [online] 23 April, Available from: https://www.weforum.org/agenda/2019/04/these-countries-have-the-most-expensive-childcare/

Folbre, N. (1991) 'Unproductive housewife: her evolution in nineteenth-century economic thought', *Signs: Journal of Women in Culture and Society*, 16(3): 463–484.

Folbre, N. and Himmelweit, S. (2000) 'Introduction – children and family policy: a feminist issue', *Feminist Economics*, 6(1): 1–3.

Frayne, D. (2015) *The Refusal of Work: The Theory and the Practical Refusal of Work*, London: Bloomsbury Publishing.

Freeman, R. B. and Medoff, J. L. (1979) 'The two faces of unionism', *Public Interest*, 57(Fall): 69–93.

Freeman, R. B. and Medoff, J. L. (1984) *What Do Unions Do?* New York: Basic Books.

Friedman, M. (1962) *Capitalism and Freedom*, Chicago: Chicago University Press.

Friedman, M. (2009) 'On the FDA and its successful banning of the Thalidomide drug' [Video], Available from: https://www.youtube.com/watch?v=dZL25NSLhEA

Friedman, T. L. (2007) 'The Power of Green', *The New York Times* [online] 15 April, Available from: https://www.nytimes.com/2007/04/15/opinion/15iht-web-0415edgreen-full.5291830.html

Fryer, D. M. (1986) 'Employment derivation and personal agency during unemployment: a critical discussion of jahoda's explanation of the psychological effects of unemployment', *Social Behavior*, 1: 3–23.

Fujimura, S. (2018) 'Nassau William Senior and the poor laws: why workhouses improved the industriousness of the poor', *History of Economic Review*, 70: 49–59.

Galbraith, J. K. (1983) *The Anatomy of Power*, Boston: Houghton Miffin.

Gallagher, S. (2020) 'I lost two stone and developed mild PTSD', *The Independent* [online] 20 November, Available from: https://www.inde pendent.co.uk/life-style/equal-pay-day-women-dealing-with-unequal-pay-a9201481.html

Gammage, S., Joshi, S. and van der Meulen Rodgers, Y. (2020) 'The intersection of women's economic and reproductive empowerment', *Feminist Economics*, 26(1): 1–22.

Giddens, A. (1979) *Central Problems in Social Theory: Action, Structure, and Contradiction in Social Analysis*, Oakland: University of California Press.

Gill, F. (1979) *Economics and the Black Exodus: An Analysis of Negro Emigration from the Southern United States: 1910–1970*, New York: Garland Publishing Inc.

Gill, F. (1980) 'The short and the long in the migration decision: an American case study', *Australian Economic Papers*, 19(December): 278–290.

Gill, F. (1984) 'The costs of adjustment and the invisible hand with special reference to the labour market', *Economie Applique*, XXXVII: 523–541.

Gill, F. (1993) 'Statistics in the social sciences – a mixed blessing?', *Labour Economics and Labour Relations of Australian Workplaces*. ACIRRT. The University of Sydney, Monograph No. 10: 293–306.

Gill, F. (1994a) 'Inequality and the wheel of fortune: systemic causes of economic deprivation', *Australian Economic Papers*, 33(62): 139–154.

Gill, F. (1994b) 'Low pay and gender under wage regulation: the Australian experience', in B. Caine (ed.) *The Women Question in England and Australia*, Sydney: Department of History, The University of Sydney, pp. 110–142.

Gill, F. (1996) 'Comment: On ethics and economic science', in P. Groenewegen (ed.) *Ethics and Economics?* Abingdon: Routledge.

Gill, F. (1999) 'The meaning of work: lessons from sociology, psychology and political theory', *The Journal of Socio-Economics*, 28(6): 725–743.

Goffman, E. (1975) *Frame Analysis*, Harmondsworth: Penguin.

Goldin, C. D. (1992) *Understanding The Gender Gap: An Economic History of American Women*, Oxford: Oxford University Press.

Goldin, C. D. and Rouse, C. (2000) 'Orchestrating impartiality: the impact of blind auditions on female musicians', *American Economic Review*, 90(5): 715–742.

Goldsmith, A. H., Hamilton, D. and Darity, Wi. Jr (2007) 'From dark to light: skin color and wages among African Americans', *Journal of Human Resources*, 42(4): 701–738.

Golshan, T. (2017) 'Study finds 75 percent of workplace harassment victims experienced retaliation when they spoke up: what we know about sexual harassment in America', *Vox* [online] 15 October, Available from: https://www.vox.com/identities/2017/10/15/16438750/weinstein-sexual-harassment-facts

Goodin, R. E. and Pettit, P. (eds) (1997) *Contemporary Political Philosophy: An Anthology*, Hoboken: Wiley-Blackwell.

Goodrick, M. and Searson, J. (2022) 'Life is a daily challenge on jobseeker and a $1.80 a day rise will still leave us well short of enough to survive', *The Guardian* [online] 12 September, Available from: https://www.theguardian.com/commentisfree/2022/sep/12/life-is-a-daily-challenge-on-jobseeker-and-a-180-a-day-rise-will-still-leave-us-well-short-of-enough-to-survive

Gordon, D. M. (1972) *Theories of Poverty and Underemployment: Orthodox, Radical, and Dual Labor Market Perspectives*, Lexington Mass: Lexington Books.

Gracely, N. (2014) 'Being homeless is better than working for Amazon', *The Guardian* [online] 28 November, Available from: https://www.theguardian.com/money/2014/nov/28/being-homeless-is-better-than-working-for-amazon

Granovetter, M. (1973) 'The strength of weak ties', *American Journal of Sociology*, 78(6): 1360–1380.

Greber, J. (2021) 'Tech-driven approach best way to avoid climate talks collapse: Taylor', *Financial Review* [online] 26 July, Available from: https://www.afr.com/policy/energy-and-climate/tech-driven-approach-best-way-to-avoid-climate-talks-collapse-taylor-20210726-p58d2p

Greenman, E. and Xie, Y. (2008) 'Double jeopardy? The intersection of gender and race on earnings in the United States', *Social Forces*, 86(3): 1217–1244.

Greenwald, B. and Stiglitz, J. E. (1986) 'Externalities in economies with imperfect information and incomplete markets', *Quarterly Journal of Economics*, 101(2): 229–264.

Grieve, C. (2020) 'Only one woman was promoted to the role of chief executive out of 25 appointments at Australia's large companies over last year, in sign of gender equality in the professional world is going backwards', *Sydney Morning Herald* [online] 17 September, Available from: https://www.smh.com.au/business/companies/absolutely-no-progress-number-of-female-ceos-in-australia-is-declining-20200916-p55w5m.html

Grimshaw, D., Fagan, C., Hebson, G. and Tavora, I. (eds) (2017) *Making Work More Equal: A New Labour Market Segmentation Approach*, Manchester: Manchester University Press.

Grose, T. K. (2018) 'The worker retraining challenge: Sweden and a few other countries are exceptions, a report says, to a world needing to prepare for automation', *US News* [online] 6 February, Available from: https://www.usnews.com/news/best-countries/articles/2018-02-06/what-sweden-can-teach-the-world-about-worker-retraining

Haddad, L. (2005) *Towards a Well-Functioning Economy: The Evolution of Economic-Systems and Decision-Making*, Cheltenham and Camberley: Edward Elgar Publishing.

Hallett, N. (2018) 'The problem of wage theft', *Yale Law and Policy Review*, 37(1): 93–152.

Hamermesh, D. (2011) *Beauty Pays*, Princeton: Princeton University Press.

Hardoon, D., Ayele, S. and Fuentes-Nieva, R. (2016) 'An economy for the 1%: how privilege and power in the economy drive extreme inequality and how this can be stopped', Briefing Paper, Oxfam [online] 18 January, Available from: https://oi-files-d8-prod.s3.eu-west-2.amazonaws.com/s3fs-public/file_attachments/bp210-economy-one-percent-tax-havens-180116-summ-en_0.pdf

Hatch, P. (2018) 'In Amazon's "hellscape", workers face insecurity and crushing targets', *Sydney Morning Herald* [online] 7 September, Available from: https://www.smh.com.au/business/workplace/in-amazon-s-hellscape-workers-face-insecurity-and-crushing-targets-20180907-p502ao.html

Hauge, L. J., Skogstad, A. and Enarsen, S. (2007) 'Relationship between stressful work environment and bullying results of large representative study', *Work and Stress*, 21(3): 220–242.

Hausman, D. M. (1989) 'Economic methodology in a nutshell', *Journal of Economic Perspectives*, 3: 115–127.

Hausman, D. M. (1992) *The Inexact and Separate Science of Economics*, Cambridge: Cambridge University Press.

Hausman, D. M. and McPherson, M. S. (1993) 'Taking ethics seriously: economics and contemporary moral philosophy', *Journal of Economic Literature*, XXXI(June): 671–731.

Hekman, D. R., Aquino, K., Owens, B. P., Mitchel, T. R., Schilpard, P. and Levitt, K. (2010) 'An examination of whether and how racial and gender bias influence customer satisfaction', *Academy of Management Journal*, 53(2): 238–264.

Helmore, E. (2018) 'Over 400,000 people living in "modern slavery" in the US, Report finds', *The Guardian* [online] 19 July, Available from: https://www.theguardian.com/world/2018/jul/19/us-modern-slavery-report-global-slavery-index

Hey, J. D. (1979) *Uncertainty in Microeconomics*, Oxford: Martin Robertson.

Hicks, J. R. (1963) *The Theory of Wages* (2nd edn), London: Macmillan.

Higgins, W. (1985) 'Unemployment and the labour movement's breakthrough in Sweden', in J. Roe (ed.) *Unemployment: Are There Lessons From History?* Sydney: Hale and Ironmonger.

Higgins, W. with Dow, G. (2013) *Politics Against Pessimism*, New York: Peter Lang.

Hildebrand, J. and MacDonald, R. (2007) 'Hardie's final insult to Bernie Wanton over compensation: Shamed company James Hardie made one last effort to rob asbestos victim Bernie Wanton over compensation', *Courier Mail* [online] 27 November, Available from: https://www.couriermail.com.au/news/national/hardies-final-insult-to-bernie/news-story/44ba89044cf2164a4a7c6e61ed623dea

Hirschman, A. O. (1970) *Exit, Voice and Loyalty: Responses to Decline in Firms, Organisations and States*, Cambridge Mass: Harvard University Press.

Hirschman, A. O. (1984) 'Against parsimony: three ways of complicating some categories in academic discourse in papers and proceedings', *American Economic Review*, 74(2): 89–96.

Hodgson, C. (2017) 'Workers in Britain are being underpaid by £2.7 billion each year – but most don't know it', *Business Insider Australia* [online] 11 July, Available from: https://www.businessinsider.com.au/unpaid-britain-report-uk-workers-cheated-out-of-pay-2017-7?r=US&IR=T

Hoel, H. and Einarsen, S. (2010) 'Shortcomings of anti-bullying regulation: the case of Sweden', *European Journal of Work and Organisational Psychology*, 19(1): 30–50.

Hoff, K. and Stiglitz, J. E. (2010) 'Equilibrium fictions: a cognitive approach to societal rigidity', *American Economic Review Papers and Proceedings*, 100(May): 141–146.

Hogh, A. and Dofradottir, A. (2001) 'Coping with bullying in the workplace', *European Journal of Work and Organisational Psychology*, 10(4): 485–495.

Humphries, M. (2019) 'A movement to transform coal miners into beekeeprs is great news for the planet', *Nation Swell* [online] 19 March, Available from: https://nationswell.com/west-virginia-coal-alternative-beefarming/

Hunter, T. W. (1997) *To 'joy My Freedom: Southern Black Women's Lives and Labours After the Civil War*, Cambridge: Harvard University Press.

Hurley, L. and Volcovici, V. (2022) 'U.S. Supreme Court limits federal power to curb carbon emissions', *Reuters* [online] 1 July, Available from: https://www.reuters.com/legal/government/us-supreme-court-limits-federal-power-curb-carbon-emissions-2022-06-30/

ILO (2017) '40 million in modern slavery and 152 million in child labour around the world', *ILO News* [online] 19 September, Available from: https://www.ilo.org/global/about-the-ilo/newsroom/news/WCMS_574717/lang--en/index.htm

ILO (2020) 'Most of world lacks unemployment insurance' [Press release] 21 June 2000, Project code ILO 00/29 [online], Available from: https://www.ilo.org/global/about-the-ilo/newsroom/news/WCMS_007901/lang--en/index.htm

Inman, P. (2014) 'Economics students call for shakeup of the way their subject is taught', *The Guardian* [online] 4 May, Available from: https://www.theguardian.com/education/2014/may/04/economics-students-overhaul-subject-teaching

International Labour Office (2000) World Labour Report 2000: Income Security and Social Protection in a Changing World, Geneva, International Labour Office [online], Available from https://www.ilo.org/public/libdoc/ilo/P/09530/09530(2000).pdf

Isaac, J. and Lansbury, R. (eds) (2005) *Labour Market Deregulation: Rewriting the Rules*, Alexandria, NSW: Federation Press.

Islam, A. and Parasnis, J. (2014) 'Native-immigrant wage gap across occupations: evidence from Australia', Department of Economics Discussion Paper 14/14, Monash University.

Jahoda, M. (1981) 'Work, employment and unemployment: values, theories and approaches in social research', *American Psychologist*, 36(2): 184–191.

Jahoda, M. (1982) *Employment and Unemployment: A Social-Psychological Analysis*, Cambridge: University of Cambridge Press.

Jahoda, M., Lazarszfeld, P. and Zeisler, H. (1971) *The Sociography of an Unemployed Community*, New York: Routledge (first published in German in 1932).

Jerbi, S. (2009) 'Business and human rights at the UN: what might happen next?', *Human Rights Quarterly*, 31(2): 299–320.

Jericho, G. (2016) '10 years on the spirit of WorkChoices still lives', *ABC News* [online] 16 March, Available from: https://www.abc.net.au/news/2016-03-16/jericho-10-years-on,-the-spirit-of-workchoices-still-lives/7248368

Johnson, G. E. (1985) 'Comment on A. Oswald, "The economic theory of trade unions – an introductory survey"', *Scandinavian Journal of Economics*, 87(2): 194–196.

Kall, K. (2017) 'Protection of posted workers in the European Union: findings and policy recommendations based on existing research', Jyvaskylan Yliopisto, University Of Jyvaskya (Finland), September. DOI:10.13140/RG.2.2.32748.26248

Kaufman, B. E. (1986) *The Economics of Labour Markets*, San Diego: The Dryden Press, Harcourt Brace College Publishers.

Kaufman, B. E. (2003) 'John R. Commons and the Wisconsin School on industrial relations strategy and policy', *Industrial and Labor Relations Review*, 57(1): 3–30.

Keynes, J. M. (1933) *Essays in Biography*, New York: Harcourt Brace and Company.

Keynes, J. M. (1936) *The General Theory of Employment, Interest and Money*, New York: Harcourt Brace.

Khambay, A. and Narayanasamy, T. (2021) 'Wage theft and pandemic profit: the right to living wage for garment workers', Business and Human Rights Resource Centre [online] March, Available from: https://media.business-humanrights.org/media/documents/Unpaid_wages_v6.pdf

Knaus, C. (2017) 'US warned Australia over toxic material 17 years ago: Environmental Authorities cited "severe long-term consequences" to human health over chemicals used at defence bases, fire stations and airports', *The Guardian* [online] 2 August, Available from: https://www.theguardian.com/australia-news/2017/aug/03/us-warned-australia-over-toxic-firefighting-chemical-17-years-ago

Korkki, P. (2011) 'For women, parity is still a subtly steep climb', *The New York Times* [online] 10 October, Available from: https://www.cnbc.com/2011/10/10/for-women-parity-is-still-a-subtly-steep-climb.html

Krugman, P. (2009) 'How did economics get it so wrong?', *New York Times Magazine*, 2 September.

Krugman, P. (2014) 'Why we're in a new gilded age', *The New York Review of Books* [online] 8 May, Available from: https://www.nybooks.com/articles/2014/05/08/thomas-piketty-new-gilded-age/

Kurtz, A. and Yellin T. (2015) 'Minimum Wage Since 1938', *CNN Business* [online], Available from: https://money.cnn.com/interactive/economy/minimum-wage-since-1938/

Lacroix, J. and Pranchére, J.-Y. (2012) 'Was Karl Marx truly against human rights? Individual participation and human rights theory', translated by S.-L. Raillard, *Revue Française de Science Politique*, 62(3): 433–451.

Laliberté, P. (2013) 'Editorial section of trade unions and worker cooperatives: where are we at?', *International Journal of Labour Research*, 5(2) [online], Available from: https://www.ilo.org/wcmsp5/groups/public/---dialogue/---actrav/documents/publication/wcms_240534.pdf

Landreth, H. (1976) *History of Economic Theory*, Boston: Houghton Mifflin Company.

Lansbury, R. (2009) 'Workplace democracy and the global financial crisis', The Kingsley Memorial Lecture, University of Sydney, 19 March.

Laski, H. J. (1925) *The Grammar of Politics*, London: Allen and Unwin.

Lee, J. and Smith, A. (2019) 'Regulating wage theft', *Washington Law Review*, 94(2): 758–822.

Lerner, S. (2018) '3M knew about the dangers of PFOA and PFOS decades ago', *The Intercept* [online] 2 August, Available from: https://theintercept.com/2018/07/31/3m-pfas-minnesota-pfoa-pfos/

Lev-Ari, S. and Keysar, B. (2010) 'Why don't we believe non-native speakers? The influence of accent on credibility', *Journal of Experimental Social Psychology*, 46(6): 1093–1096.

Lewis, A. (2009) 'Life without lawyers', *New York Review of Books*, 9–29 April: 56–58.

Liota, M. (2018) 'Overcrowding leads to poorer health outcomes for Aboriginal and Torres Strait Islander people', *newsGP*, [online] February 19, Available from: https://www1.racgp.org.au/newsgp/racgp/overcrowding-a-key-determinant-of-poor-health-outc

Llamas, M. (2021) 'AFFF firefighting foam lawsuits filed over cancer', S. Clifton (ed.) *DrugWatch* [online] 22 February, Available from: https://www.drugwatch.com/news/2021/02/22/firefighters-file-cancer-lawsuits-against-afff-foam-manufacturers/

Longhi, S. and Brynin, M. (2017) 'The ethnicity pay gap', in *Research Report 108: Pay Gap Research*, Equality and Human Rights Commission [online], Available from: https://www.equalityhumanrights.com/sites/default/files/research-report-108-the-ethnicity-pay-gap-executive-summary.pdf

Longo, W. E., Rigler, M. W. and Slade, J. (1995) 'Crocidolite asbestos filters in smoke from original Kent cigarettes', *Cancer Research*, 55(11): 2223–2235.

Lucas, E. R. Jr (2004) *The Industrial Revolution: Past and Future*, Annual Report, 1 May, Minneapolis: The Reserve Bank of Minneapolis.

Lukes, S. (1974) *Power: A Radical View*, London: Macmillan.

Lukes, S. (1996) *Power: A Radical View* (2nd edn), London: Palgrave.

Lukes, S. (2005) *Power: A Radical View* (3rd edn), London: Macmillan.

Macdonald, F., Bentham, E. and Malone, J. (2018) 'Wage theft and unpaid work in social care', *The Economic and Labour Relation Review*, 29(1): 80–96.

Marglin, S. (1974) 'What do bosses do?', *Review of Radical Political Economy*, 6(2): 60–112.

Marmot, M. (2004) *The Status Syndrome: How Social Standing Affects Our Health and Longevity*, London: Macmillan.

Marmot, M. (2015) *The Health Gap: The Challenge of an Unequal World*, London: Bloomsbury Publishing.

Marmot, M. and Brunner, E. (2005) 'Cohort profile: the Whitehall II study', *International Journal of Epistemology*, 3(2): 251–256.

Marmot, N.G., Shipley, M. J., Rose, G. (1984) 'Inequalities in death – specific explanations of a general pattern?' *The Lancet*, 323(8384): 977–1032.

Marmot, M. and Wilkinson, R. G. (eds) (2006) *Social Determinants of Health* (2nd edn), Oxford: Oxford University Press.

Marmot, M. G., Shipley, R. M. and Hamilton, P. J. (1978) 'Employment grade and coronary heart disease in British civil servants', *Journal of Epidemiology and Community Health*, 32(4): 244–249.

Marquand, D. (1997) *The New Reckoning: Capitalism, States and Citizens*, Cambridge: Polity Press.

Marshall, A. (1890) 'Some aspects of competition'. The address of the president of section F – Economic Science and Statistics – of the British Association, at the Sixtieth Meeting, held at Leeds, in September, 1890. *Journal of the Royal Statistical Society*, 53(4), 612–643.

Marshall, T. H (1950) *Citizenship and Social Class: And Other Essays*, Cambridge: Cambridge University Press.

McCallum, R. C. (2007) 'Australian labour law after the work choices avalanche: developing an employment law for our children', *Journal of Industrial Relations*, 49(3): 436–454.

McCartin, J. (2011) 'The Strike That Busted Unions', *The New York Times* [online] 2 August, Available from: https://www.nytimes.com/2011/08/03/opinion/reagan-vs-patco-the-strike-that-busted-unions.html

McKinsey & Company (2020) 'Diversity wins: how inclusion matters', McKinsey [online] 19 May, Available from: https://www.mckinsey.com/featured-insights/diversity-and-inclusion/diversity-wins-how-inclusion-matters#:~:text=Our%202019%20analysis%20finds%20that,in%202014%20(Exhibit%201)

Meikle, J. (2016) 'Thalidomide caused up to 10,000 miscarriages and infant deaths in the UK', *The Guardian* [online] 6 March, Available from: https://www.theguardian.com/society/2016/mar/06/thalidomide-caused-up-to-10000-miscarriages-infant-deaths-uk

Menesini, E. and Salmivalli, C. (2017) 'Bullying in schools: the state of knowledge and effective interventions', *Psychological Health Medicine*, 22(Supp. 1): 240–253.

Mill, J. S. (1844) 'Essay V: On the definition of political economy; and on the method of investigation proper to it', in *Essays on Some Unsettled Questions in Political Economy*, London: John W. Parker.

Mill, J. S. (1869) *The Subjugation of Women*, London: Longman, Green and Dyer.

Mills, C. W. (1956) *The Power Elite*, Oxford: Oxford University Press.

Milmo, C. (2016) 'Margaret Thatcher was urged to make homeless people pay poll tax by senior cabinet minister', *The Independent* [online] 19 February, Available from: https://www.independent.co.uk/news/uk/politics/margaret-thatcher-was-urged-make-homeless-people-pay-poll-tax-senior-cabinet-minister-a6882736.html

Mirkinson, J. (2011) 'Mika Brzezinski on her salary fight, "knowing your value," and those CBS rumors', *Huffpost* [online] 12 July, Available from: https://www.huffingtonpost.co.uk/entry/mika-brzezinski-on-her-sa_n_861139

Mishel, L. and Wolfe, J. (2019) 'CEO compensation has grown 940% since 1978: typical worker compensation has risen only 12% during that time', Economic Policy Institute [online] 14 August, Available from: https://files.epi.org/pdf/171191.pdf

Montgomery, D. (1993) *Citizen Worker: The Experience of Workers in the United States with Democracy and Free Market During the Nineteenth Century*, Cambridge: Cambridge University Press.

Moran, A. (2022) '10 companies that use prison labor to rake in profits', *Career Addict* [online] 15 February, Available from: shttps://www.careeradd ict.com/prison-labour-companies

Morgan, E. S. (1972) 'Slavery and freedom: the American paradox', *American History*, 59(1): 5–29.

Mowat, C. L. (ed.) (1964) *The New Cambridge Modern History*, volume XII, Cambridge: Cambridge University Press.

Moynihan, D. (1965) *The Moynihan Report*, Washington DC: US Department of Labor.

Murdoch, L. (2006) 'Stockmen mark long walk to freedom and land rights', *Sydney Morning Herald*, 17 July, Available from: https://www.smh.com. au/national/stockmen-mark-long-walk-to-freedom-and-land-rights-20060717-gdnz6t.html

Neumark, D. and Wascher, W. (2007) 'Minimum wages and employment', IZA DP No. 2570, Bonn: Institute for the Study of Labor.

Neumark, D., Bank, R. J. and Van Nort, K. D. (1996) 'Sex discrimination in restaurant hiring: an audit study', *Quarterly Journal of Economics*, 111(3): 915–1041.

Nielsen, M. B. and Einarsen, S. V. (2018) 'What we know, what we do not know, and what we should and could have known about workplace bullying: an overview of the literature and agenda for future research', *Aggression and Violent Behavior*, 42: 71–93.

Noonan, M. C., Corcoran, M. E., Ford, G. R. and Courant, P. N. (2003) 'Pay differences among the highly trained: cohort differences in the male-female earnings gap in lawyers' salaries', National Poverty Working Paper Series, #03–1, May, Michigan: National Poverty Center (NPC).

North, D. (1990) *Institutions and Economic Growth: An Historical Introduction*, Cambridge: Cambridge University Press.

O'Brien, G. E. (1986) *Psychology of Work and Unemployment*, Hoboken, NJ: John Wiley and Sons.

OECD (2011) 'Divided we stand: why inequality keeps rising', OECD [online], Available from: https://www.oecd.org/els/soc/49170768.pdf

O'Hara, M. (2020) *The Shame Game: Overturning the Toxic Poverty Narrative*, Bristol: Policy Press.

Okun, A. M. (1975) *Equality and Efficiency: The Big Tradeoff*, Washington, DC: The Brookings Institution Press.

Parsons, T. (1951) *The Social System*, New York: Free Press.

Pateman, C. (1990) *The Disorder of Women: Democracy, Feminism, and Political Theory*, Redwood City: Stanford University Press.

Pateman, C. (1997) 'The fraternal social contract', in R. E. Goodin and P. Pettit (eds) *Contemporary Political Philosophy: An Anthology*, Hoboken: Wiley-Blackwell, pp. 45–59.

Pavalko, E. K., Mossakowski, K. N. and Hamilton, V. J. (2003) 'Does perceived discrimination affect health? Longitudinal relationships between work discrimination and women's physical and emotional health', *Journal of Health and Social Behavior*, 44(1): 18–33.

Peacock, M. (2009) *Killer Company*, Sydney: HarperCollins.

Pencavel, J. (1991) *Labor Markets under Trade Unionism: Employment, Wages, and Hours*, Hoboken: Blackwell.

Pérotin, V. (2012) 'The performance of worker cooperatives', in P. Battilani and H.G. Schröder (eds) *Cooperative Business Movement, 1950 to the Present*, Cambridge: Cambridge University Press, pp. 195–211.

Philip, T. and Mallan, K. (2015) 'A new start: implications of Work For The Dole on mental health of young Australians', Children and Youth Research Centre [online] 26 February, Available from: https://eprints.qut.edu.au/82161/1/Philip%26Mallan_A-New-Start_Implications-of-Work-for-the-Dole.pdf

Phillips, A. (1999) *Which Equalities Matter?* Malden: Polity Press.

Picchio, A. (1992) *Social Reproduction: The Political Economy of the Labour Market*, Cambridge: Cambridge University Press.

Pikulina, E. (2020) 'The power game: people want power over others, even if there's nothing to gain', Inside at UBC Sauders [online], Available from: https://www.sauder.ubc.ca/news/insights/power-game-people-want-power-over-others-even-if-theres-nothing-gain

Pikulina, E. and Tergiman, C. (2019) 'Preference for power', 20 August, SSRN, University of British Colombia, Canada [online], Available from: https://ssrn.com/abstract=3025621 or http://dx.doi.org/10.2139/ssrn.3025621

Pilkington, E. (2018a) 'Fears grow as right-wing billionaires battle to erode US union rights', *The Guardian* [online] 24 February, Available from: https://www.theguardian.com/us-news/2018/feb/24/rightwing-billionaires-union-rights

Pilkington, E. (2018b) 'US's inmates stage nationwide prison labor strike over 'modern slavery', *The Guardian* [online] 21 August, Available from: https://www.theguardian.com/us-news/2018/aug/20/prison-labor-protest-america-jailhouse-lawyers-speak

Plumb, J. H. (1953) *England in the Eighteenth Century (1714–1815)*, London: Penguin.

Polanyi, K. (1944) *The Great Transformation*, New York: Farrar and Rinehart.

Quiggin, J. (2012) *Zombie Economics: How Dead Ideas Still Walk Among Us*, Princeton: Princeton University Press.

Rathi, A. (2016) 'A 1912 news article ominously forecasted the catastrophic effects of fossil fuels on climate change', *Quartz* [online] 25 October, Available from: https://qz.com/817354/scientists-have-been-forecasting-that-burning-fossil-fuels-will-cause-climate-change-as-early-as-1882/

Rathi, A. (2017) 'A Chinese company is offering free training for US coal miners to become wind farmers', *Quartz* [online] 24 May, Available from: https://qz.com/990192/a-chinese-company-wants-to-retrain-wyoming-coal-miners-to-become-wind-farmers/

Razor, H. (2017) 'UBI is just a bedtime story Elon Musk tells himself to help the super wealthy sleep', *Quartz* [online] 13 July, Available from: https://qz.com/1024938/ubi-is-just-a-bedtime-story-elon-musk-tells-himself-to-help-the-super-wealthy-sleep/

Reber, S. (2014) 'A book review of "Sharing the Prize: The Economics of the Civil Rights Revolution in the American South" by Gavin Wright', *Journal of Interdisciplinary History*, 44(3): 414–415.

Rees, A. (1966) 'Information networks in labor markets', *American Economic Review, Papers and Proceedings*, 56(1–2): 559–566.

Rees, A. (1973) *The Economics of Work and Pay*, New York: Joanna Cotler Books.

Reich, M., Gordon, D.M. and Edwards, R.C. (1973) 'A theory of labor market segmentation', *The American Economic Review, Papers and Proceedings*, 63(2): 359–365.

Ridgeway, C. L. (2013) 'Why status matters for inequality', Presidential Address, *American Sociological Review*, 79(1): 1–6.

Robinson, J. (1933) *The Economics of Imperfect Competition*, London: MacMillan.

Rodrigues-Oramas, A., Burgues-Freitas, A., Joanpere, M. and Flecha, R. (2022) 'Participation and organizational commitment in the Mondragon Group', *Frontiers Psychology* [online] 15 March, Available from: https://www.frontiersin.org/articles/10.3389/fpsyg.2022.806442/full

Roe, J. (ed) (1985) *Unemployment: Are There Lessons From History?* Sydney: Hale and Ironmonger.

Ross, R. T. (1985) 'Measuring underutilisation of labour: beyond unemployment statistics', Working Papers in Economics, No. 81, Sydney: Department of Economics, University of Sydney.

Ross, R. T. (2006) 'Recent evidence on health and employment status for indigenous Australia', *Australian Journal of Labour Economics*, 91(1): 65–68.

Ruggie, J. G. (2007) 'Business and human rights: the evolving international agenda. corporate social responsibility initiative', Working Paper No. 31, Cambridge: John F. Kennedy School of Government, Harvard University.

Saez, E. and Piketty, T. (2003) 'Income inequality in the United States, 1913–1998', *Quarterly Journal of Economics*, 118(1): 1–39.

Saez, E. and Zucman, G. (2014) 'Wealth inequality in the United States since 1913: evidence from Capitalizes income tax data', Working Paper 20625, NBER [online], Available from: https://gabriel-zucman.eu/files/SaezZucman2014.pdf

Sainato, M. (2018) 'Exploited Amazon workers need a union', *The Guardian* [online] 8 July, Available from: https://www.theguardian.com/commentisfree/2018/jul/08/amazon-jeff-bezos-unionize-working-conditions

Samsone, R. A. and Samsone, L. A. (2015) 'Workplace bullying: a tale of adverse consequences', *Innovations in Clinical Neuroscience*, 12(1–2): 32–37.

Sandel, M. (2012) *What Money Cannot Buy: The Moral Limits of Markets*, London: Allen Lane.

Savage, M. (2019) 'The Nordic way: the paradox of working in the world's most equal countries', *BBC* [online], Available from: https://www.bbc.com/worklife/article/20190831-the-paradox-of-working-in-the-worlds-most-equal-countries#:~:text=When%20it%20comes%20to%20pay,the%20EU%20average%20of%2016%25.

Saxena, A. (2014) 'Workplace diversity: a key to improve productivity', *Pocedia, Economics and Finance*, 11: 76–85.

Schiek, D. (2018) 'On uses, mis-uses and non-uses of intersectionality before the Court of Justice (EU)', *International Journal of Justice and Law*, 18(2–3) [online], Available from: https://doi.org/10.1177/1358229118799232

Schmitt, J. (2013) *Why Does the Minimum Wage[s] Have No Discernible Effect on Employment*, Washington, DC: CEPR (Centre for Economic and Policy Research).

Schulz, K. and Chamseddine, N. (2020) 'Beyond equal pay' World Bank [Blog] 10 February, Available from: https://blogs.worldbank.org/developmenttalk/beyond-equal-pay

Schumpeter, J. A. (1966) *Ten Great Economists* (4th edn), London: George Allen and Unwin.

Schwartz, B. (2015) *Why We Work*, New York City: Simon and Schuster.

Selgin, G. (2019) 'The modern New Deal that's too good to be true', Cato at Liberty [Blog] 8 February, Available from: https://www.cato.org/blog/modern-new-deal-thats-too-good-be-true

Seppälä, E. and Cameron, K. (2015) 'Proof that positive work cultures are more productive', *Harvard Business Review*, 1 December.

Smith, A. (1759 [2011]) *The Theory of Moral Sentiments*, Chapel Hill, NC: Gutenberg Publishing.

Smith, A. (1776) *An Inquiry into the Nature and Causes of the Wealth of Nations*, Volume 1, Oxford: Clarendon Press.

Smith, W. (2017) 'Unemployment policy in Australia: a brief history', *Per Capita* [online], Available from: https://percapita.org.au/wp-content/uploads/2018/05/Unemployment-Report_Final-1.pdf

Sodha, S. (2017) 'Universal basic income is no panacea for us – and Labour shouldn't back it', *The Guardian* [online] 18 December, Available from: https://www.theguardian.com/commentisfree/2017/dec/18/universal-income-no-panacea-labour

Solow, R. M. (1980) 'On theories of unemployment', *American Economic Review*, 70(1): 1–11.

Spence, M. (1973) 'Job market signalling', *Quarterly Journal of Economics*, 87(2): 355–374.

Spence, M. (1974) *Market Signalling: Informational Transfer in Hiring and Related Screening*, Cambridge: Harvard University Press.

Standing, G. (2009) *Globalization: Building Occupational Citizenship*, Cheltenham: Edward Elgar.

Standing, G. (2011) *The Precariat: The New Dangerous Class*, Camden: Bloomsbury Academic.

Standing, G. (2017) 'The Precariat: why basic income is vital', *Working Class Studies* [online], Available from: https://workingclassstudies.wordpress.com/2017/10/23/the-precariat-why-a-basic-income-is-vital/

https://www.futurework.org.au/self_defeating_economics_of_the_penalty_rate_cut

Stempel, J. (2018) 'NY sue 3M, and five others, over toxic chemical contamination', *Reuters* [online] 21 June, Available from: https://www.reuters.com/article/us-3m-new-york/new-york-sues-3m-five-others-for-cleanup-costs-of-toxic-chemicals-idUSKBN1JG31K

Stern, A. (2011) 'Analysis: Koch brothers a force in anti-union effort', *Reuters*, 11 February, Available from: https://www.reuters.com/article/us-usa-wisconsin-koch-idUSTRE71P28W20110226

Stewart, A., Stanford, J. and Hardy, T. (eds) (2018) *The Wage Crisis in Australia: And What to Do About It*, Adelaide: Adelaide University Press.

Stiglitz, J. E. (2012) *The Price of Inequality*, New York: W. W. Norton.

Stiglitz, J. E. (2016) *Inequality and Economic Growth*, Academic Commons [online], Available from: https://academiccommons.columbia.edu/doi/10.7916/d8-gjpw-1v31

Stiglitz, J. E. (2018) 'The American economy is rigged and what we can do about it', *Scientific American* [online], Available from: https://www.scientificamerican.com/video/a-nobel-laureate-explains-than-economy/e-rigged-americ

Sydney Morning Herald (2009) 'Obituary for Doug Jukes', 11 March.

Tehrani, N. (2004) 'Bullying: a source of chronic post-traumatic stress?' *British Journal of Guidance and Counselling*, 32(3): 357–366.

Terkel, S. (1974) *Working: People Talk about What They Do All Day and How They Feel about What They Do*, New York City: Pantheon Books: Division of Random House.

Theriault, R. (1997) *How to Tell When You Are Tired: A Brief Examination of Work*, New York: Norton and Company.

Thornton, M. and Luker, T. (2009) 'The wages of sin: compensation for indigenous workers', *UNSW Law Journal*, 32(3): 647–673.

Tilly, C. (1998) *Durable Inequality*, Berkeley: University of California Press.

Ting, I. (2015) 'The Sydney suburbs where minimum wage workers can afford to live', *Sydney Morning Herald* [online] 9 June, Available from: https://www.smh.com.au/national/nsw/the-sydney-suburbs-where-minimum-wage-workers-can-afford-to-rent-20150608-ghjc6v.html

Tomlins, C. L. (1989) 'The ties that bind: master and servant in Massachusetts 1800–1850', *Labour History*, 30(2): 193–227.

Travis, A. (2013) 'National archives: Margaret Thatcher wanted to crush power of trade unions', *The Guardian* [online] 1 August, Available from: https://www.theguardian.com/uk-news/2013/aug/01/margaret-thatcher-trade-union-reform-national-archives.

Turnbull, J. (2010) 'Calls to jail workplace bullies', *The Australian* [online] 8 February, Available from: https://amp.theaustralian.com.au/business/latest/calls-to-jail-workplace-bullies/news-story/2cfa0797c7f6dcc2cdd37ec7f056758b

Turner, M. (1983) *Stuck! Unemployed People Talk to Michele Turner: Living Without Work – the Stories that Statistics Cannot Tell*, Ringwood: Penguin Australia.

Tversky, A. and Kahneman, D. (1974) 'Judgement under uncertainty: heuristics and biases', *Science*, 185(4157): 1124–1131.

Tversky, A. and Kahneman, D. (1981) 'The framing of decisions and the psychology of choice', *Science*, 211(4481): 453–458.

United Nations General Assembly (1948) The Universal Declaration of Human Rights (UDHR). New York: United Nations General Assembly.

United Nations Human Rights: Office of the High Commissioner (2011) *Guiding Principles on Businesses and Human Rights: Implementing the United Nations' 'Protect, Respect and Remedy' Framework*, New York, Geneva: UN [online], Available from: https://www.ohchr.org/sites/default/files/documents/publications/guidingprinciplesbusinesshr_en.pdf

van Barneveld, K. (2006) 'Australia workplace agreements under work choices', *Economic and Labour Relations Review*, 16(2): 165–192.

Verrender, I. (2009) 'Cavalier attitude leaves lives and reputations in tatters', *Sydney Morning Herald* [online] 2 May, Available from: https://www.smh.com.au/business/cavalier-attitude-leaves-lives-and-reputations-in-tatters-20090501-aq7q.html

Verrender, I. (2021) 'Expecting a fair tax cut in 2024? Don't count on it, Fair is fair but not when it comes to tax', *ABCNews* [online] 17 May, Available from: https://www.abc.net.au/news/2021-05-17/tax-cuts-in-2014-unlikely-to-be-fair-ian-verrender/100143052

Wallace, N. (2008) 'Bullying caused woman's suicide, inquiry told', *Sydney Morning Herald* [online] 9 July, Available from: https://www.smh.com.au/national/bullying-caused-womans-suicide-inquiry-told-20080709-gds ldf.html

Walshe, S. (2012) 'How US prison labour pads corporate profits at taxpayers' expense', *The Guardian* [online] 7 July, Available from: https://www.theg uardian.com/commentisfree/2012/jul/06/prison-labor-pads-corporate-profits-taxpayers-expense

Waring, S. P. (1991) *Taylorism Transformed: Scientific Management Theory Since 1945*, Chapel Hill: The University of North Carolina Press.

Waring, M. (1999) *Counting for Nothing: What Men Value and What Women are Worth*, Toronto: University of Toronto Press.

Warr, P. B. (1987) *Work, Unemployment and Mental Health*, Oxford: Clarendon Press.

Wearden, G. (2014) 'Oxfam: 85 richest people as wealthy as poorest half of the world', *The Guardian* [online] 20 January, Available from: https://www.theguardian.com/business/2014/jan/20/oxfam-85-richest-peo ple-half-of-the-world

Webb, B. (1926 [1979]) *My Apprenticeship*, Cambridge: Cambridge University Press.

Webb, S. and Webb, B. (1897) *Industrial Democracy*, London: Longman.

Weeks, K. (2011) *The Problem with Work: Feminism, Marxism, Antiwork Politics, And Postwork Imaginaries*, Durham, NC: Duke University Press.

Weller C. E. (2017) 'Supply-side follies: wasteful tax cuts would not boost economy', Center for Economic Progress [online] 26 October, Available from: https://www.americanprogress.org/article/supply-side-follies-waste ful-tax-cuts-will-not-boost-the-economy/

Williams, R. M. and Peterson, C. L. (1998) 'The color of memory: interpreting twentieth-century U.S. social policy from a nineteenth century perspective', *Feminist Studies*, 24(1): 7–25.

Williamson, O. (1975) *Markets and Hierarchies: Analysis and Antitrust Implications: A Study in the Economics of Internal Organization*, New York: Free Press.

Williamson, O. E., Wachter, M. L. and Harris, J. E. (1975) 'Understanding the employment relationship: the analysis of idiosyncratic exchange', *Bell Journal of Economics*, 6(1): 250–278.

Wilson, D. and Macdonald, D. (2010) *The Income Gap Between Aboriginal People and the Rest of Canada: Growing Gap*, Ottawa: Canadian Centre for Policy Alternatives [online], Available from: https://policyalternatives.ca/sites/default/files/uploads/publications/reports/docs/Aboriginal%20Inc ome%20Gap.pdf

Wintour, P. (2015) 'Biggest crack down on unions in 30 years', *The Guardian* [online] 15 July, Available from: https://www.theguardian.com/politics/2015/jul/15/trade-unions-conservative-offensive-decades-strikes-labour

Wright, C. F. and Clibborn, S. (2018) 'Employer theft of temporary migrant workers' wages in Australia: why has the state failed to act?' *The Economic and Labour Relations*, 26: 465–473.

Wright, G. (2013) *Sharing the Prize: The Economics of the Civil Rights Revolution in the American South*, Cambridge: Harvard University Press.

Xie, Y. and Goyette, K. (2003) 'Social mobility and the educational choices of Asian Americans', *Social Studies Research*, 32(3): 467–498.

Young, I. M. (1989) 'Polity and group difference: a critique of the idea of universal citizenship', *Ethics*, 99(2): 250–274.

Young, M. (1979) *I Want to Work*, Stanmore, NSW: Cassell Australia Ltd.

Zhang, X. and Yu, J. (2022) 'Impact of abusive supervision on psychological engagement and absorptive capacity among students: mediating role of knowledge hiding', *Frontiers Psychology* [online] 11 February, Available from: https://doi.org/10.3389/fpsyg.2021.818197

Zimbardo, P. G. (2011) 'The prison experiment', *Stanford*, July/August.

Index

Printed in the USA
CPSIA information can be obtained
at www.ICGtesting.com
JSHW010844251023
50683JS00017B/41

9 781447 369936